A SPY'S JOURNEY

A CIA MEMOIR

FLOYD L. PASEMAN

ZENITH
PRESS

"What does he next prepare?
When will he move to attack?—
By water, earth, or air?
How can we head him back?
Shall we starve him out if we burn
Or bury his food supply?
Slip through his lines and learn—
That is work for a spy!
(Drums)—*Get to your business, spy!*

—*from* "The Spies' March," Rudyard Kipling

To my family, Jill, Ashley, Adam, my grandson Brett, and to Dulcinea, Hamlet, Elliot, and Cleopatra.

First published in 2004 by Zenith Press, an imprint of MBI Publishing
Company, Galtier Plaza, Suite 200, 380 Jackson Street, St. Paul, MN
55101-3885 USA

© Floyd L. Paseman, 2004

All rights reserved. With the exception of quoting brief passages for the
purposes of review, no part of this publication may be reproduced without
prior written permission from the Publisher.

The information in this book is true and complete to the best of our
knowledge. All recommendations are made without any guarantee on the
part of the author or Publisher, who also disclaim any liability incurred in
connection with the use of this data or specific details.

This material has been reviewed by the CIA. That review neither
constitutes CIA authentication of information nor implies CIA
endorsement of the author's views.

Zenith Press titles are also available at discounts in bulk quantity for
industrial or sales-promotional use. For details write to Special Sales
Manager at Motorbooks International Wholesalers & Distributors,
Galtier Plaza, Suite 200, 380 Jackson Street, St. Paul, MN 55101-3885 USA.

ISBN 0-7603-2066-7

Edited by Steve Gansen
Layout by Lynn Dragonette and LeAnn Kuhlmann
Cover by Tom Heffron

Front cover photo by Lee Klancher
Back cover photo by Peter Gallante, courtesy Cardinal Stritch University
Author photo (inside back flap) by Adam Paseman

Printed in United States of America

CONTENTS

PREFACE

Why this book at this time? I felt that my reflections after one of the longest careers in U.S. intelligence history—and after more than a decade at the tops ranks of the Central Intelligence Agency—would be of general interest and would help shed some much-needed light on what intelligence really does do, really does not do, and how fragile the whole process of human intelligence really is. I decided to proceed with a memoir with the encouragement of one of the best intelligence historians in the United States, Dr. Ralph Weber, who repeatedly reminded me, "You are the only one who can tell your story." This, and a belief that the readers of history deserve a recounting of history as it really was, led me to this work.

ACKNOWLEDGMENTS

I would like to acknowledge the significant help from several sources: First, Dr. Ralph Weber of Marquette University, who was responsible not only for my entry into academia, but who also urged me to do my memoirs while my memory was still fresh; second, Dr. John Krugler, also of Marquette University, who was one of the first professors to recognize what we as CIA officers had to offer, and whose critical look at intelligence issues contributed greatly to my doing the same thing; and Dr. Terry Roehrig, of Cardinal Stritch University, who also saw the value of a practitioner's point of view to his political science and history department and whose counsel was also of great assistance.

I also wish to thank the Center for the Study of Intelligence, whose director at the time, Dr. Brian Latell, was very enthusiastic about my participating in the Officer in Residence program and without whose support I could not have participated in this most important program. I also wish to thank the Center's History Department, in particular Dr. Michael Warner and Dr. Kevin Ruffner, both of whom took extra time to provide me with valuable materials for my teaching.

I could not have maneuvered through the book publishing process without MBI Publishing Company. Working with Steve Gansen, one of their premier editors, was a pleasure. Richard Kane's encouragement kept me going as well. Richard was patient with all my status notes and worked hard to bring this book to publication. These gentlemen made the process easy and enjoyable. They are true professionals.

Lastly, I would like to thank Dr. Scott Koch and Mr. Bruce Wells of the CIA Publication Review Board, without whose help I would have been unable to navigate the incredibly arcane twists laid out by my own Directorate of Operations.

In the end, any errors are of my own making. However, as they used to say in the television drama *Dragnet,* "The story you are about to hear is true." All of it.

INTRODUCTION

I t is important to state at the outset that, in the tradition of intelligence memoirs, the names, places, dates, and targets in this book have been changed to protect the identities of agents and the operations in which I participated. There are two exceptions, in which times and events were in the public record: my time as chief of the East Asia division, and my time as Chief of the CIA, Germany. Even in these cases, out of necessity, I have altered an occasional name or place to protect agents and operations. And, of course, there are many more stories of success that I cannot go into, since many of the players in these successful operations are still alive and thus, at risk. Nonetheless, all the accounts are real and the events took place exactly as described. Events occurring during and after my overt assignment as an Officer in Residence in 1998 are accurate as written.

PROLOGUE

In 1994, the U.S. media reported on the difficulties of being the Central Intelligence Agency Chief in Germany. They noted that CIA chiefs there usually had a difficult time carrying out their tasks and that there was unanimous agreement within the CIA Directorate of Operations (DO) that Bonn was a damn hard posting. They had that right!

My selection as CIA Chief, Germany, had progressed in fits and starts—an indication, perhaps, that few in the clandestine service are inclined to deal with the headaches and challenges of the German job. I guess I should have been forewarned. When I took the personal phone call from the Deputy Director for Operations (DDO) congratulating me on my new assignment as CIA Chief, Germany, I might have dickered in advance for a promotion that never came, even though I served longer in this thankless job than any chief in memory. The irony is that I took that call as two other senior posts in Europe were offered to me at the same time—neither of them Bonn. However, I am getting ahead of myself.

ONE

IN THE BEGINNING

1963–1967

It was a sorority woman who first drew my attention to the CIA. Early in the spring of 1963, a high-achieving fellow student at the University of Oregon and member of the Alpha Gamma Delta sorority approached me and told me that she had applied for, and been accepted by, the Central Intelligence Agency. She suggested that I should apply, considering I had garnered academic honors. She provided me with the sterile address the CIA used for applicants, and, curious more than anything else, I sent a short note off asking about the possibilities of employment. Several weeks later, I received an envelope addressed to me with no return address. I opened it, and the letter inside was folded so the CIA emblem was not visible until the letter was unfolded. "We are pleased to hear of your interest in the CIA. Someone will be contacting you." So much for that, I thought.

I had missed the normal summer ROTC camp to work on a National Science Foundation grant I had earned, and thus had to wait until December, 1963, to graduate and be commissioned a second lieutenant in the U.S. Army. Then, one day at my apartment I received a telephone call from a man who identified himself only as a CIA recruiter. He told me he would be in town one week hence and set up an appointment for me to come to his motel room for an interview and formal application. He gave me the number of the room where I was to meet him and admonished me not to tell anyone I was applying to the Agency. He did not give me his name.

That was secret enough to ensure I showed up at the prescribed time and place. At the appointed hour, I timidly knocked on the door of the designated room. A tall, balding middle-aged man opened the door, confirmed I was who I said I was, and said to me, "Can you wait just a minute—I am on the phone to Washington." I certainly was not going to interrupt his call, so I waited nervously outside for about five minutes before he again opened the door, invited me in, and introduced himself. I had just been lured into the shadowy world of espionage by one of the great CIA recruiters, Tom Culhane.

Tom Culhane, as I would learn, was legendary as a recruiter for the CIA in the Pacific Northwest. He was a handsome man, urbane, eloquent, and friendly, with an easy manner to him. He also, I was to learn, had a flair for theatrics; he drew all those he interviewed into wanting to join the ranks of the clandestine service even though we had scant idea of what that really meant.

Culhane had done his homework on both my academic and work past. He knew I had come from a working-class family with little income. He knew what honors I had collected in high school and college, and had a familiarity with the fact I had worked my entire time in college just to get though financially. He administered a standard Agency aptitude test, which took several hours. In the end, he told me I was attractive as an applicant, but that the Agency would want me to go ahead and spend my time first in the military and then confirm my continuing interest. He asked me a host of questions ("What would your reaction to danger be?" "Would gunfire scare you?" "Can you keep a secret?" "Can you live and work without recognition?"). In the end, I assured him none of the above would be a problem, and he told me, "Someone will contact you in two years as you end your military service." He also told me to keep our meeting secret, noting that the CIA did not want its applicants to reveal their employment in case they went into the clandestine arm of the Agency. I assured him I would keep his confidence and departed. I was later to learn that Culhane was considered among the best, if not *the* best, recruiter for the CIA. He had been a case officer himself, and had served in the troublesome Mideast where he distinguished himself. I was also to learn that he had recruited probably one-third of my classmates when I entered the CIA. Over the years, he became so good and well known as a recruiter that the *Washington Post* ran an article about him.

I thought little or nothing about this for the next two-plus years. I enjoyed the Army immensely and extended my time. I got a good amount of intelligence-related work in the Army. I went first to Armored Basic Training at Fort Knox, Kentucky; then I was selected for Communications School at Fort Sill, Oklahoma, where I spent a good deal of time working with cryptographic and classified coding systems. I finally wound up in Bad Hertzfeld, Germany, where I was immediately assigned as squadron (battalion) communications officer. I was responsible for the secure communications systems and equipment for the Fourteenth Armored Cavalry Squadron. It was terrific experience that was to be useful in my later CIA career.

As part of my duties, I was also assigned to be in charge of our Radar Platoon, which did the outpost work on the East German border and was very much a reconnaissance operation. During this time, I learned why we were there. The East Germans, under the direction of the Soviet Union, had a nasty habit of coming across the border and actually kidnapping West German citizens. They would use them for propaganda purposes and later release them. Our mission was to prevent this. We would ride the border area in a jeep, with a West German military officer and usually with a trained German shepherd dog. It was great, rewarding duty, and it was fascinating to watch the dogs work. I learned the value of these fine animals, trained to go through gunfire, fire, and to climb obstacles 10 feet high to get to their prey. And, I also learned how much the Germans really like and admire Americans. When we would go into a local *gasthaus* (tavern) to warm up, it would be impossible for us to pay for our meals. They wanted us on the border so badly they simply would not accept our payment, no matter how hard we would try. In the evenings, if we were staying overnight, we would enjoy the Germans' company over a brew or two as well.

Later, I was sent to a school for reconnaissance platoon leaders, and learned more yet about intelligence, particularly about debriefing the sources that came across the border. I worked with the local military intelligence personnel, most of whom were undercover, and learned a good deal from them as well. This school also continued to feed my interest in intelligence in general. I acquired a number of skills there, such as escape and evasion, demolitions, advanced map work, and foreign-made arms and weapons that proved useful in the future.

It is easy to understand why the CIA wanted us to have military experience before hiring us. First, it gave us good working experience, responsibility, and a chance to mature a little before taking on the awesome responsibilities given to officers at a relatively young age in the CIA. And some decided not to enter the Agency after military service. The Agency, likewise, got a chance to decide if they were interested in the individual before making a commitment of substantial time and money. Military service worked to everyone's benefit.

Finally, however, I decided to leave the military in the fall of 1966, though I had considered a military career. Things had gone very well for me, and in early 1966 I was rewarded with the command of a tank company, even though I was only a first lieutenant at the time and there were other officers in Europe senior to me waiting for just such an opportunity. I ended my service there by being awarded the Army Commendation Medal for my work. It was indeed hard to leave, but I had decided I simply could not make a career of the Army, as much as I liked it. I simply have always had trouble taking orders without knowing why. I knew that sooner or later that would be a stumbling block to further advancement in the Army. But I made great friends there. I decided to continue my time in the U.S. Army Reserve, which would prove valuable in my CIA career by keeping me in touch with the U.S. Military and up to date on their needs, and gave me the credentials to deal with the military in a closer relationship than I would otherwise have had.

I returned to Oregon and began the process of seeking employment. I didn't try to contact the CIA and just assumed that, since they had not contacted me in the Army, they had no further interest in recruiting me. It turns out that nothing could have been further from the truth.

I finally landed a terrific and well-paying job with a marketing research company in the Midwest. I went through their training school and graduated at the top of the class of new marketing-research employees. The company rewarded me by sending me to work in the San Fernando Valley—one of its largest markets—with my headquarters in Los Angeles. My job was to travel the length of the valley and stop in at food stores and pharmacies and do audits on merchandise sales. It was traditional marketing research. I worked hard there and got to be very close friends with one of the top officers, who took me under his wing. Ultimately, however, this fine officer lost out in gaining a top position in the region to one of the company founder's nephews. This was my first lesson in the politics of private industry. Shortly afterward, the father of one of my college roommates who lived in Los Angeles—a very well known and respected hydraulic engineer for a major aircraft manufacturer—was summarily fired from his job due to the fact that his salary had gotten too large.

Having witnessed private industry firsthand, I received a phone call from Washington, D.C., asking me if I could fly there for three days of further interviews with the CIA, and I was inclined to do so. I did tell the person on the other end of the telephone that I would have to let someone in my company know what I was doing since I would miss several days of work. They agreed to tell my colleague what was going on and to ask him to keep it to himself.

I was very pleasantly surprised that my friend was enthusiastic and agreed to take my route over himself for three days so I could fly back for the interviews. He told me that, if he were younger and had the same opportunity, he would take the offer and give up his current career. Armed with this, I flew back to Washington.

The interviews went very well, with the exception of a long and grueling time on the polygraph. The operator was thrilled to discover that I was a twin. "I've never done a twin before," he exclaimed gleefully. Everything was going OK on that damned instrument until the operator asked me if my twin brother and I had ever engaged in any homosexual activity. I told him no, and the instrument, according to him, confirmed this. He, however, postulated that the machine doesn't catch everything and went through the lame drill of leaving the room and returning to ask me if I had reconsidered my answer to that question. I told him the only thing I was reconsidering was why the hell I was putting up with this nonsense. After a few more attempts, he lamely told me that everything looked OK but that we might have to revisit the issue. I left and flew back to Los Angeles later that week. Shortly thereafter, I received another telephone call telling me I would be hired if I agreed to accept the salary of a GS-07 ($7,000 in those days). I accepted. This was a major mistake. I could have asked for—and received—a lot more.

TWO

TRAINING TO BE A SPY

1967–1969

I n March 1967, I entered the Central Intelligence Agency with a large group of classmates—over 100 new career trainees (CTs) as we were called. The CIA was in its biggest buildup since the Korean War. The class was one of three that were being assembled that year. The increase in number and size of classes had to do with the expansion of the Agency as well as the other U.S. Government agencies that needed to deal with the Vietnam War. It did make for a most interesting class. I was one of the few who did not have an advanced degree (thus, the Agency's belief that they could hire me cheaper, although I had military experience many of my classmates were missing). We had a former marine embassy guard, a former city policeman, and lawyers by the dozen, including practicing lawyers from around the country, and a woman who had been a judge. Also in my class were an executive from a major automobile manufacturer, a golf pro, five former Special Forces non-commissioned officers, and three women who had just graduated and were starting their first job. One of the other more interesting classmates had been channeled into the career program after nearly four years working in the "secret war" in Laos. He had been a "kicker"—one of the incredibly brave individuals who dropped supplies out of the back of the Agency C-47s to the Laotian Montagnards who were our surrogates in the war.

I worked in a transit job for three months until the training started in earnest. I was sent to work in the Central Cover Staff

(CCS), which turned out to have been a most interesting and useful pre-training assignment. I was allowed to actually take over several accounts and learned a great deal about the basics of setting up "cover," the identity and occupation used by an agent or case officer to conceal his espionage or clandestine operational activities.[1] I also acquired a lasting knowledge of the importance of individual cover in protecting both our officers and our operations. It was knowledge that was to serve me well throughout my career. It was also the assignment that brought me into direct contact with a man whom I and hundreds of other Agency employees regard as one of the true heroes of our generation, Richard L. Holm. He met disaster when he was involved in attempts to rescue hostages in the Congo.[2] I was later given the task of helping set up the cover for one of his overseas assignments. Through this experience, I also discovered the lengths to which the Agency would go to assist its people and its families—one of the Agency's great qualities. I then knew that should any of us have to risk our lives, the Agency and my colleagues would move heaven and earth to take care of our families and us.

But, one of the more interesting CIA flaps occurred immediately upon my entry to the Agency. I had been through all of the processing when the *Ramparts* magazine flap occurred. This episode involved the disclosure on February 14, 1967 of the secret link between the CIA and the National Student Association (NSA). NSA was a democratic counterpart to the many Soviet-inspired student groups operating worldwide at that time. The CIA had funneled a subsidy of at least $3 million dollars to the NSA since 1952. By this time, NSA had chapters at over 300 U.S. universities. There was a huge uproar, and I got caught in the middle. There were two reasons for this: one, I had known the fellow who blew the news of the operation, because he was at the University of Oregon when I was there. Within days of my coming on board, I was called in

1. Leo D. Carl, *The CIA Insider's Dictionary of U.S. and Foreign Intelligence, Counterintelligence, and Tradecraft* (Washington, D.C.: NIBC Press, 1996), p. 127.
2. Richard L. Holm, *Studies in Intelligence, Winter 1999–2000. A Close Call in Africa: Plane Crash, Rescue and Recovery,* pp. 17–28.

repeatedly to tell what I knew about the person, whether I had any influence over him (no), and so on. But there was another reason. As the story unfolded, a young reporter at the *Eugene Register-Guard* broke a number of new revelations. His name was Lloyd Paseman—my twin brother! And, our office of security wanted to know if I knew what my brother knew. Of course I was not going to admit that I knew anything, and they finally gave up. But it was an eventful beginning.

I also discovered early that working for the CIA has many strange aspects, many of which I'll mention later in the book. Two of the early ones, however, involve contradictions between the CIA's penchant for secrecy and some of the things they do. For example, the CIA runs a regular bus on many routes around Washington to get people where they need to go without the hassle of parking. However, they used Blue Bird buses—actually painted bright blue—to do this. Obviously, these buses stood out as CIA buses, and everyone around town knew what the buses were. However, when you got on the bus, you had to show a badge before the operator would tell you which bus covered which route. I never understood why they didn't use a military-colored bus—and there were many around Washington—instead of the Blue Birds. They might as well have put a sign on them.

The second thing I learned is that Agency folks stick together. There was a famous bar in downtown McLean called O'Toole's that was the watering hole for the well initiated. If you went to O'Toole's, you were immediately identified as being CIA. Half of the members who went there simply took their Agency badges and stuck them in their pockets. So you could tell all the CIA people by the chains around their necks leading to their shirt pockets.

I then was given an operational assignment before beginning formal training. I consider myself fortunate to have been assigned to work in the Directorate of Operations, East Asia Division, where I became intimately familiar with the business of intelligence reporting. I worked for one of the sternest taskmasters in the business, but I acquired a knowledge of how requirements are generated, how to determine the value of intelligence, and how it gets to the consumer. For an entry-level officer, this was basic hard work without the thrills of the operational side. However, it left me with a lasting skill and appreciation for this side of the business. It also served me exceptionally well; from my first assignment on, I took exceptional pride in writing and composing all of my own intelligence reports into as close to a final product as possible. Consequently, I found that more of my intelligence was disseminated than that of my colleagues.

Finally, my 100-plus classmates and I were drawn together and began our introductory training. It was a fun, fruitful time, and friends I made then are still colleagues and friends 30 years later. During these years, it was also Agency policy that incoming officers from the four Agency Directorates—Operations (the DO); Intelligence/Analysis (the DI); Administration (the DA); and Science and Technology (the DS&T)—enter into introductory training together. In that way, all would learn at least the basics of all four Directorates. It was excellent training, and included everything from basic intelligence writing and how aerial photography is done, to clandestine tradecraft (techniques of spying), logistics, and communications. Many of the officers who went into the non-operational directorates have remained my friends through the years and have provided me with great advice in their fields throughout my career.

We also had outstanding instruction about our primary enemy —communism. We were instructed in communist theory—both Soviet and the Maoist. And we spent a lot of productive time studying and understanding covert action, which has been defined as "a clandestine operation designed to influence foreign governments, events, organizations, or persons in support of United States foreign policy; it may include political, economic, propaganda, or paramilitary activities."[3] We studied the history of the Agency, including lessons

3. Carl, *CIA Insider's Dictionary*, p. 129.

learned from both its successes and its failures.

I finished in the top of my class in the operations portion of introductory training, confirming what I believed from the beginning, that I was best suited for clandestine activities and the Directorate of Operations—the DO or clandestine service, as it is also known. Before individual directorate training began, we were asked to state our preferences, which would then be used to find the perfect match with an advisor.

A few words about my advisor are in order. He came from the administrative end of the house and appeared disinterested and lazy. Throughout the entire introductory training period, which lasted nearly three months, he talked to me personally only once, on the first day advisors were assigned. I put in to become a member of the DO. Given my performance in the introductory phase, I thought all was in order. To my horror, when assignments were announced I was informed that I was to go to the Directorate of Administration. I made an urgent appointment to see my advisor. I told him, quite honestly, that I did not intend to join the CIA to do administrative work. He said that he had decided that I would best fit in a support role. I pointed out that he had not discussed this with me, and told him frankly that I would fly back to California the next day rather than continue. So he took me to see his superior, and after a short session I was asked to wait outside. When they emerged after a few minutes, I was congratulated on my appointment to the Directorate of Operations (DO). I had learned a lesson that day—you must be your own personnel officer, and if you believe you are right, stick to your position.

In September of that same year, operations training began in earnest at the legendary Camp Swampy secret training facility in the Virginia Tidewater region. My group was again over 100 strong, scheduled for traditional clandestine spy training and then paramilitary training. There was little doubt that the majority of the class was headed for Vietnam. Every one of my colleagues had been hired at a full grade higher than me—as GS-08s. I was more than a little aggravated and went to see my new advisor who told me that had I held out for a higher grade, they would have given it to me. Despite my protests they refused to increase my grade to that of most of my colleagues. In fact, it took me nearly four years to catch up to the grades of my classmates. Again, you have to be your own personnel officer in the DO.

I will not dwell on clandestine training here. Simply put, it was outstanding in comparison to any training I had received in the military or in private business. It was indeed Espionage 101, but it was intensive, and instruction came from people who were real experts in the craft. Long days and nights were the norm—just as in real life, where the preponderance of your duties takes place in the evenings or on weekends.

I also learned in my early training the essentials of cover—that is, keeping the nature of your true affiliation secret. It works well—outside of Washington where anyone with a little knowledge of the CIA quickly sees through the flimsy cover mechanisms that have been set up for officially covered CIA officers entering duty.

We also learned the tradecraft—secret writing, clandestine photography, how to select and use dead-drop sites, and how to recruit individuals for espionage against their own governments. In clandestine photo training, we learned to fashion and use concealment devices for cameras and how to take photos even while under observation. Several more enterprising individuals adapted their techniques by taking photos of their girlfriends in various stages of undress and making prints in the darkroom.

And we got our first dose of the real characters that seem to gravitate to the clandestine service. One of my primary advisors was an old Near East hand—that is, an acknowledged expert in language, culture, and customs of the Near East. He had served under fire on occasion, and had seen the Agency pull out all the stops to bring proper medical care to his ailing wife. As a result, he was a dedicated, firm devotee of the CIA. He was also wilder than the proverbial March hare. One Thursday evening after we had been out late at night on a surveillance exercise, he suggested a late-night dinner at a restaurant 30 miles away. Several of us took him up on it, and he proceeded to consume a substantial number of martinis— and we did, too. Nonetheless, he drove us back. After we somehow made it back onto post, he told us he would show us some driving tips—and proceeded to drive up onto the lawn of the dormitory where we were staying, and did a number of large donuts on the lawn. We were mortified to be reprimanded the next day by the administrative officer of the base.

We also spent a lot of time in the student recreation room— described well also in *The Masters of Disguise*.[4] We liked to relax, and relax hard. We conducted "carrier landings," where we took a running dive at full speed along the length of a table, clearing all objects in our path. Also popular during paramilitary training were PLFs, "parachute landing falls," where we leapt from a high object— normally the bar—and landed as if we had parachuted. Despite—or perhaps because of the amount of lubricants normally consumed in advance—no one was ever injured during my stay there. In short, it was a wild and woolly place at times, even though we all took our training very seriously.

Although I had plenty of action-oriented training in the military, including substantial weapons work, the Agency's paramilitary training was outstanding. Two great benefits of the paramilitary training are the camaraderie and learning who you can and cannot rely on in the group. Additionally, the stress of paramilitary training weeded out a number of people who simply were not cut out for the clandestine life. One such individual does bear mentioning, and to protect this officer's identity, I'll use one of his nicknames as a pseudonym. Due to his frequent ineptness, he was called "Gomer" after the lead character in the hit 1960s television comedy *Gomer Pyle*, starring Jim Nabors as the inept Marine

4. Antonio J. Mendez, with Malcolm McConnell, *The Master of Disguise: My Secret Life in the CIA* (New York: William Morrow, 1999).

25

recruit. Our Gomer carried impressive academic credentials—Phi Beta Kappa and a law degree. But he had no common sense. During our training, Gomer managed to alienate almost every instructor by picking up whatever weapon lay in front of him and attempting to disassemble it before class started. In one particular episode, Gomer was fiddling around with a Belgian FAL 7.62mm rifle, which was a favorite of our staff due to its near indestructibility and precision craftsmanship. Our instructors were fond of saying that the weapon was idiot-proof. However, Gomer managed to prove them wrong by launching the gas propellant spring clear across the room, to land neatly on the instructor's desk at the beginning of class. The instructor, a retired master sergeant with multiple jumps in combat, asked Gomer about his parentage in no uncertain language. Later, as we began jungle training, we were taught the basics of rappelling with nothing but rope—no seats or attachments. At first, we worked from a high tower—probably 25 feet up in the air. Just as Gomer was straddling the rope to take his turn rappelling, I noticed that he was doing it in such a way that, when he took his first step off the tower, he would go down head-first. I leaped to Gomer's assistance, much to the disappointment of my classmates, who suggested that I had prevented true justice from being done.

Imagine then my disgruntlement to find that Gomer would be right behind me in the "sticks" jumping out of the C-47 aircraft during parachute training. Nervous? You bet I was, especially since it was Gomer's duty to hook me up before I jumped out of the aircraft. With what I knew about Gomer, I approached the jumpmaster and asked him to please check my connections after Gomer did and then right before I jumped out of the aircraft. Sure enough, Gomer had not fastened my connections correctly, and my chute would not have deployed properly without the intervention of the jumpmaster. After that, Gomer's days were numbered, and he departed shortly thereafter without much fanfare.

But romance was also on my mind during and after training. In the early part of training, I had met and courted a beautiful and vivacious young woman who was the sister of the woman one of my colleagues was dating. After my training was complete and I returned to the Washington, D.C., area, I proposed to her. To my great fortune, she accepted, and we were married on July 6, 1967. She has been by my side ever since and was a source of great strength during many harrowing moments over the next 35 years.

After training, which took nearly one-and-a-half years, we were assigned out to area components. Given that the Vietnam War was underway, we knew that most of us would be assigned to Far East Division (FE)—at the time, along with Soviet European Division, the flagships of the Agency. Despite having been to Europe with the Army, I was pleased to be assigned to FE Division. It was indeed a large crowd, however. During an early session to discuss assignments, a man from Far East Division came in, talked a little about China, and noted that they were looking for people to study Chinese full-time for two years to become China specialists. When he asked for a show of hands of those interested, I noted no one raising their hand—most wanted to get right out to Vietnam where the action was. Frankly, I had no interest in serving in Vietnam. So I raised my hand and was selected for Chinese language training. I would spend the next two years fully engaged in learning that magnificent language, and become a China hand—an occupation that would consume my next 30 years.

THREE

*JUNGGWO HWA**—
LEARNING CHINESE

1969–1971

I loved studying Chinese from the start. I was somewhat of a musician anyway, and I found a close tie between music and the tonal qualities of Chinese. As with espionage and paramilitary training, Agency language training was second to none. I began my study with only three students in the class, allowing for a great deal of individual attention and permitting no room for the unprepared to hide. The teaching staff of two females and one male was tremendous. Their primary role was to teach us the things, not from a textbook, that anyone who wished to be fluent should know. For instance, we learned the Chinese equivalent to, "It's better to fart and bear the shame than keep it in and bear the pain." I also learned the real Chinese words for the various body parts—information of great importance when traveling in Asia.

The fellow who ran the Chinese department was considerably interesting. Like many colleagues I would meet over the years, he was something else. He had a beard that looked like pork chops and a mustache—which led to the nickname "Weird Beard" in Chinese. (The Chinese are very fond of nicknames, normally calling attention to some defect or odd part of someone's character—all done without conscious intent to harm.)

*The phonetic spelling for Chinese characters that translate to "Chinese language."

One of the great ceremonies and important steps in starting out as a Chinese expert is acquiring a Chinese name—in Chinese, of course. Our male instructor was always assigned this task, and he would put great thought and effort into the process. In my case, he came up with *"Pei Fulai"* which means "Overflowing Happiness"— a great name, and one that all agreed fit my temperament. It also has a very rare Chinese character for the surname—also a plus when dealing with the Chinese.

However, just as in our other training, the impulse to have fun was simply too much to avoid. I recall vividly one of my two class- mates coming into Beginning Chinese class carrying a whoopee cushion and placing it on the chair of our best—and most gor- geous—female Chinese instructor. The inevitable happened. She came in for class, greeted us, wrote a few Chinese characters on the board, and then sat down and "Pfffffffffft!" She turned 30 shades of red, and ran from the room. We did not see her for a week and got a lecture about Chinese customs from Weird Beard.

Following one year of this intensive training, we were dispatched overseas to Taiwan. There, at a facility utilized by all elements of the U.S. government, we finished our training with a second year of advanced study living in a Chinese-speaking community. It's also noteworthy that in this early period my wife presented me with our first child—a beautiful baby girl. She was to spend nine of the next ten years of her life living overseas with us.

The school was superb training at the highest level, yet it also had its moments of fun. The superintendent of the school was a pseudo-intellectual who had adopted the title "Dr.," although he had not gotten his doctorate degree. It was the subject of repeated struggles—he would insist we call him Doctor, and we would call him by his first name. He almost came to tears over it on a number of occasions. It was further complicated by the fact that he was a practicing missionary, and illegally used the U.S. Government mail system to acquire things for his local church. He had been warned numerous times that this was illegal but continued to use it throughout his stay there. In short, he was considered fair game for a bunch as cruel as any classroom of practical jokers.

I recall three of the most devilish events that took place during the Doctor's reign. In the first instance, we learned that the good Doctor was using the school facilities (illegally) to bring his flock in to hear his lectures on his missionary work. It was not long until we also found a slide carousel that he used as a visual aid. Needless to say, some enterprising lad (OK, it was me) suggested that it would be interesting if we removed one slide in the middle and replace it with a copy of the most recent bare-ass-naked Playmate centerfold. Having been trained as clandestine photographers, this was a cinch. In any event, the good Doctor had one of his monthly sessions with his flock, put the carousel into motion, and halfway through his session came to the *pièce de résistance*. It emptied the room, and the Doctor subjected us to yet another crying session the next morning.

He did recover in time for the great gin-and-tonic caper. We were going through a hell of a summer, with temperatures in the hundreds and no fans or air conditioning. Despite repeated pleas to cancel classes under these unbearable circumstances, the Doctor refused, so what follows was inevitable. One of the greatest practical jokers I have known—a non-CIA officer—got together with several colleagues and decided to make life more bearable by filling our classroom water cooler with gin and tonic. By the end of the day, all the students were well aware of the ruse and class decorum degenerated accordingly. Additionally, several of the instructors made one trip too many to the cooler, and by the end of the day the good Doctor was again moved to tears. It was clear that his days as director of the school were numbered. After the Doctor departed, we were blessed with the arrival of a new director who had both a great sense of humor and had mastered the Chinese language. I have never found another linguist his equal in writing Chinese characters. It earned him the immediate respect of both students and instructors.

We did, however, play a great practical joke on him during a trip to climb the highest peak in Taiwan, Yu Shan (Mount Yu). Nearly 13,000 feet at its summit, it was a difficult climb. Our group totaled 12 people, and we made the journey from a scenic resort area at Sun Moon Lake by old steam locomotive—a trip of over four hours to the base camp. It was a beautiful trip, with all of us riding on flat-cars, that took us through the highest reaches of the beautiful island. From the base camp, we went by foot—a hike that took more than two 12-hour days. We camped that night at a youth hostel. It was there that the idea struck me to suggest that a few of the large rocks outside would fit nicely into the director's bag. We loaded his bag with about 25 pounds of rocks and covered it with his material. The next day, he huffed and puffed for hours, noting that he felt like he was carrying a ton of rocks. Finally a few giggles turned him on to the joke, and he emptied his bag—at us. He took it well, and we all enjoyed the climb.

I was present during one of the great scandals at the language school. One of the elderly instructors, a large, portly man with a limp (nicknamed "Limpy Lo") frequently gave lectures on esoteric subjects such as, where the best clay for making pots for brewing tea comes from. These were also known as "Lo's Lectures." We all attended, and we did indeed learn a lot about Chinese culture from this elderly gentleman. However, late one afternoon I stumbled on a group of female instructors tittering away in hushed tones about what to do, what to do. I fetched the director, and without too much prodding we learned that Limpy Lo had expired in distinguished fashion that afternoon—at a local "no-hands bar." Turns out some-one had to go retrieve the unclad body, make arrangements, and, of course, avoid sullying the reputation of the teaching staff in the process. The director handled it admirably, but of course by this time the entire student body and faculty knew the truth—Limpy

Lo had died with his boots—and everything else—off. Some felt he grew in esteem.

Toward the end of the time at language school, I also had the occasion to take my family on an orientation trip to several Asian nations, including Hong Kong. While there, I acquired a number of Chinese language materials—including some newspapers that had major articles about the People's Republic of China (PRC) with front page photographs of the Chinese Foreign Minister, Zhou Enlai. No problem with that, except that I forgot that communist materials were forbidden in my host country. I had also purchased a tricycle for my then-two-year-old daughter. When I returned from my trip and went through customs and immigration, I had a rude awakening, indeed. The customs official opened my bag, only to come face to face with the PRC's Zhou Enlai. Senior officials were called; my family and I were taken into a side room for questioning. No matter what I said, the officials maintained that I had committed a serious crime—attempting to bring subversive materials into the country. On top of that, the inspectors completely unpacked and disassembled my daughter's tricycle, leaving her sobbing at the customs desk. Finally, they let us go, but they handed back the tricycle, missing many bolts and nuts, in pieces.

I learned my Chinese thoroughly, and it stood up well over my career. I can still speak it reasonably well now 36 years later. The fact that the school was located in a small village really helped me to learn everything about how to get by and live with the language. I still, for example, remember the Chinese words for flush toilet, having had to repair several during my time at the language school. We learned excellent, colloquial Chinese, and learned a great deal about the culture as well. I was ready for assignment.

FOUR

AN APPRENTICE SPY

1971–1974

"Now it is not good for the Christian's health
to hustle the Aryan brown,
For the Christian riles and the Aryan smiles
and he weareth the Christian down;
And the end of the fight is a tombstone
white with the name of the late deceased,
And the epitaph drear:
'A fool lies here who tried to hustle the East.'"

—*from* "The Naulakha," Rudyard Kipling

A fter graduating from language school, I was assigned my first job, as an undercover translator/protocol officer for a military unit in an East Asian country. As was the case with many of our officers, my cover job was full-time, leaving me to do my espionage work at night, on the weekends, and on holidays. The job did give me two things: good access to targets (those we could potentially recruit as spies) and a great deal of independence. At the same time, I was going through a period in which I was exerting my own independence from things in general. I was opposed to the Vietnam War, having lost two of my roommates to the conflict. It did not make it any easier that I was one of only two civilian employees in an office of all military personnel. I did have, however, the complete support of the commanding general of the unit—a two-star general whose main interest was in providing me the cover and capability to do my intelligence work. He was also pleased to have someone with my language expertise on board.

I did continue to demonstrate my independence in a number of ways. Once, I grew a huge Afro. I could not get a hat over it by the time I finished letting it grow. I also worked on a goatee. Complemented by my suits—ultra-modern with wide ties and wide cuffs, I was definitely not to be mistaken for a military person. It drove the executive officer, a lieutenant colonel, absolutely nuts.

I worked outside the normal facility in my first assignment. I also acquired my first agent to run. He was an agent normally used to train the new case officer—that is, one who has only marginal access to intelligence. So, if he is compromised there is no great loss of intelligence. Secondly, he is an experienced agent who won't mind the mistakes made by the new case officer and may help the officer plan better surveillance detection routes, emergency signals, and more. Lastly, he has been "turned over" to a number of case officers over the years.

He was to be a perfect match for me. I was eager and ready to roll. My first comeuppance came during our first meeting. All of it had to be held in Chinese since the agent spoke no English. I met him in a park at night. When we sat down to begin the meeting, I asked him several polite things that a younger person normally asks a Chinese elder.

"Where is your home province?" I inquired.

"Funan," he responded.

"Funan?" I said. "Where in the world is Funan?"

"Funan, Funan," he repeated, and then drew a map.

He was from Hunan—one of China's most famous provinces. He had a terrible Hunan accent. I could barely understand a word he said—and after the U.S. government had sent me to Chinese language school for two long years. I was devastated. We managed to communicate by writing, and I ran him for my entire tour with pad and pencil. It turns out I was not the only case officer who could not talk to this man. Working with him did make me appreciate the difficulties involved in running foreign agents in foreign languages.

He was a good, dedicated agent—motivated in his case by money. But he was diligent beyond belief. Shortly after I began to run him, we experienced our first crisis. The People's Republic of China was holding military exercises in the Taiwan Straits, and Taiwan went on alert. The agent made an emergency signal—by leaving a chalk mark on a certain telephone pole at a certain time—meaning he needed to meet with me. I reviewed the previous officer's emergency meeting plan instructions, only to find out that the emergency meeting site and time was in an open park near midnight. To compound a developing problem, a major typhoon had just made its way to the island, and all vehicles and personnel were ordered off the streets. I pondered the situation and decided that I had to live up to my end of the bargain and make the meeting. About 10:00 that night, I donned heavy rainwear, rolled my bicycle out, and to the horror of my spouse, rode off in the dark with 100-mile-per-hour winds scattering debris all over the place and rain coming down in sheets. I rode through back streets because I had seen several police cruisers out stopping those few souls who were out and sending them home. I rode about five miles to the park, chained my bike, and went into the park. It was not hard to recognize the agent; he and I were the only people out for miles. He was standing exactly where the emergency plan called for, covered by a heavy military slicker. We met for about 15 minutes, he passed me some significant information about the crisis, and we departed. At our next regular meeting, we selected an emergency site indoors. However, I learned how dedicated most agents are, and was inwardly pleased that I had made the meeting despite the circumstances.

I gained a tremendous amount of experience during my first tour. One incident taught me not to depend too heavily on the famous polygraph. Due to my fluency in Chinese, I was called upon to translate often during the polygraphing of Chinese-speaking agents. So, it was not unusual that I was asked to join the polygraph operator, the case officer, and the agent in a designated locale where I would be the translator.

The technique of the polygraph was already well known—rehearsal, questioning, re-questioning, and determination of whether or not the machine indicated the agent was lying or hiding anything. We were doing the exam at an unoccupied safehouse (a location unknown to the local counterintelligence service to be used in meeting an agent). The case officer went into another room so as not to be involved or responsible for the experience the agent was about to have. The examiner went over the ground rules, did the procedures, and administered a test examination. By the time we finished and proceeded through the real examination, the agent had been hooked up to the machine for around two hours—an uncomfortable experience, as I can testify from personal experience. Then disaster struck. The examiner and I went outside the building, where the case officer was given the good news—the agent was clean. We all congratulated each other, had a smoke, and went to go back into the house. I grasped the door handle, and it came off in my hand. We were locked out with the agent still inside hooked up to the machine. For the next hour, we searched around the house trying to find an open window or one I at least could break. I finally broke a basement window, and went and let the other two officers in. Imagine our surprise when we walked into the room to apologize to the agent—only to find him drenched in sweat. "OK, I confess—I have been lying and passing you false information for years," he said to me in Chinese. He further noted that he knew we had caught him when we went outside and did not come right back in. He was terminated within the next several meetings.

Early in my first assignment, I chanced to make the acquaintance of a very interesting Special Forces master sergeant. My wife and I became bridge-playing friends with him and his wife. He of course knew where I worked, and had a great respect for the CIA. I assumed of course that he had some experience or contact with us professionally. Gradually, I found out where and why. He had been seconded to the CIA in 1967 and sent to Bolivia. There, he worked with the Bolivian military on the operation to root out the legendary Ché Guevara. He was an advisor to the unit that actually captured Guevara on October 9, 1967. He had several photos confirming his presence at the capture. He never talked much about the episode, and, being new in the business, I never asked. I regret to this day that I did not ask more questions about the execution of Guevara. I recall still the great fuss about Guevara's diaries, and recall that this master sergeant, who spoke fluent Spanish, actually read the diaries. Over the next two years, he was of tremendous help to me professionally, introducing me to a host of interesting people in the local military. He was the first of many people I knew who had such fascinating experiences.

Working outside the office in my first assignment was at times difficult. I had only occasional meetings with an inside officer, so when we did meet a lot of time was needed to train me as an inside officer. I had good contacts, and the office was very concerned about my cover and my security. They gave me good guidance on my cases and on my developmental work. But, for about one-and-a-half years, one of our senior officers kept sending critical notes to me. "Do this, do that." It really began to eat at me, and I finally asked for a personal meeting to get my concerns off my chest. I made my one and only trip inside the office to do so. As soon as we entered, the senior officer asked to see me. Here we go, I thought. However, he immediately congratulated me on a well-deserved promotion. I was stunned—both at the promotion, but also at how pleased he seemed to be. Later, one of the other officers told me that this senior officer had made a personal appeal to ensure my promotion, and that he considered me his finest young officer. I learned an important lesson, and one that I never forgot over my entire career—things are not always as they seem, and in espionage you never know who your friends and enemies really are. This same officer became one of my mentors later in my career. He also distinguished himself in Vietnam and later during the Marcos crisis in the Philippines. I learned a lot from him over the years.

I was not quite so lucky with one of the chiefs who came in later in my first tour. Bald as a billiard ball, he was one of the old aristocrats, wealthy, and of European background and experience. By this time my rebellious days were in full flow (see photo, page 162). I had a huge Afro, and my ties were so wide they covered my whole shirt. Flared trousers and boots completed my ensemble. This chief would send me notes, typically with one message: "Get your hair cut!" On top of that, he wrote in green ink, and all other personnel were forbidden to use green ink. Naturally, I wrote single-word notes back to him each time—"No," also in green ink. He was furious, but my work was first class, I was one of the best linguists around, and my cover boss, an Army general, was very pleased with my work for him and his office, and he praised me to the chief at every opportunity. So I made it through the series of orders to get my hair cut. But, more was to come.

Things were going very well, indeed. Then, at a large formal reception, one of our senior military officers in country inadvertently disclosed some top-secret sensitive information we had acquired from one of my agents. That information suggested that the host country government had embarked on a serious weapons acquisition program, in secret, despite direct assurances to our government. Our military officer, to his everlasting credit, demonstrated great integrity and turned himself in the following day. The officer said that he realized from the host government officials' reaction that they were unaware that we had acquired this intelligence.

Given the military officer's acknowledgment of his error, we now had to effect a major damage-control effort, since my agent was one of only a handful of people who could have been the source of the information. Fortunately, I had rehearsed this type of scenario and immediately put emergency meeting plans into effect. However, our meeting site was a long distance away in an isolated locale.

I made my way to the meeting site, but the agent failed to show up the first two days. By now, I was seriously concerned about his fate, and whether or not I would be wrapped up as well. Finally, the agent showed on the third day. He was greatly alarmed at what I had to tell him—that there had been a serious compromise of the information he had provided to me, and that there was a greater than average chance that he would be pulled in for questioning. We rehearsed for this eventuality, and it paid off. He was pulled in, inter- rogated, but never admitted to his work on our behalf. The host counterintelligence service was never able to pinpoint the source of the intelligence. Nonetheless, we lost the valuable services of this brave agent, as he remained under suspicion for the rest of his career. It was of small benefit, but he was honored for his service to us.

I felt I understood how things were done when I was called into the office of the senior U.S. military commander in the country. He handed me an eyes-only message to him from a senior ranking member of a congressional committee. The note was short: "I am arriving to visit. Make sure I get to play Sangran." The general and I both knew that Sangran was the real hot spot for ladies of the night, and the spot to which most visitors went. I looked at the general, and he told me, "You meet him at the military airport when he comes in and take care of his request discreetly."

"OK," I said—the epitome of discretion.

I made several calls, had things lined up for the congressman, and was very pleased with myself. I stood at the door when his plane landed, and, to my horror, he emerged from the aircraft carrying his golf clubs. I immediately remembered that Sangran had also recently opened a new world-class golf course. It took all I could do to control myself and welcome the congressman ("We'll be on our way, Sir; I just need to make one call.") and make a pleading phone call to the manager of the Sangran Golf Course. He was most gracious and in fact pleased to set up the congressman and the local club champion for a match. It all turned out terrifically, including the evening when I was present as the general hosted a dinner for the congressman. On passing by, the general looked at me and said, "Say, you're pretty good!" I did learn another valuable lesson that helped me throughout my career—never assume anything.

As I neared the end of my tour, I ignored three separate suggestions that I volunteer for duty in Vietnam. The Agency presence there was enormous, and it was consuming all of our case officers. As the saying went, "There are three types of case officers: those who have been to Vietnam; those who are in Vietnam; and those who are going to Vietnam." Nonetheless, I had no desire to go to Vietnam. I did not go while in the Army, and I had no idea of what we were really trying to do there. And the death of two close friends in Vietnam while we were all in the Army also furthered my belief that we had no real idea of what we were doing there. I got a final note that the deputy from Vietnam was coming to our area and wanted to interview me, and, further, that if he agreed, I was going to be assigned there or else I should, as he said, consider my career options. That was plain enough, so I accepted an appointment to see him. I went to his luxurious temporary duty (TDY) quarters and rang the bell. He appeared at the gate, looked at me, and said, "Get your hair cut before you come to Vietnam!" It was the same officer who had previously been my chief.

I looked at him and said no. He thanked me for coming, closed the gate, and went back inside. Two days later, I received a cable from headquarters saying I had been rejected for duty in Vietnam. I had no assignment, and my career seemed in shatters.

As my family and I were packing to return to headquarters, I got a cable that offered me a lateral assignment to another Asian station that was desperate for a Chinese linguist. I accepted on the spot. There was more than a little irony in the ensuing events. During the first three months of my new assignment, first Hue, then Danang, then Saigon itself fell to the onrushing tide of the North Vietnamese Army, and we suffered our worst military and political defeat in history. The upshot was that hundreds upon hundreds of our case officers were rushed out and back home, where they wandered the halls trying to find assignments. While they were now searching for jobs, I proceeded to have one of the finest and most productive assignments of my entire career. I went to bed for many years thanking my hair.

CIA officers do a lot of funny things to maintain and enhance their cover. In one unique experience, two factors were at play: one, the army unit I was assigned to was doing a lot of charity work, both out of conviction and out of the desire to enhance the public-relations image of the military in this country. The second factor was my fluency in Chinese. As the two factors worked together, I found myself assigned to temporary duty as a translator for two Special Forces personnel who were up in the highest mountain area in the country. They had promised to build a suspension bridge across a mountainous ravine to enable the indigenous inhabitants to move their products to market without traveling nearly 27 miles out of the way—all on foot. They had gathered a work force of 100-plus natives to do the work (a major engineering accomplishment) under their guidance, but they could not communicate with the workers. Several of the natives spoke Chinese, so I was assigned to the camp to be the interpreter.

I was up in the mountains for nearly three months at a time in two intervals, during which the skills of the two Special Forces personnel impressed me greatly. One had an engineering degree, and the other had the normal Special Forces skills, including demolitions. We worked very hard during the non-rainy season to get things ready. There were, of course, unexpected incidents, and work was slow and laborious. The Special Forces man would give instructions in English, I would translate them into Chinese, and one of the workers would translate them into the native dialect. The natives were bright and hard working, and they learned a lot of English during the construction. One of the first terms they learned by experience was, "Fire in the hole!"—the term yelled out just prior to detonating explosives. In fact, most of them learned it the first time. As we lay behind a big boulder to set off the first charge, the Special Forces fellow yelled, "Fire in the hole!" I translated it into Chinese, and while the worker was in the midst of translating it to the crew, the charge blew and scared the heck out of them. So the next time we yelled "Fire in the Hole!" no translation was needed and everyone ran for cover.

Special Forces had arranged to have a huge cement mixer ferried in by a "Jolly Green Giant" crane helicopter. Used for transporting huge equipment over long distances, the Jolly Green Giant is one of the largest heavy-lift helicopters in the U.S. military.

It was quite an event—the entire village came out, and we had a devil of a time keeping everyone from going underneath the crane as it tried to lower the mixer down into the ravine where we were working. While we escaped tragedy that time, we weren't always so lucky. In another instance, one of our trucks had wandered too close to the edge of the mountain path, and a worker was trying to push up against the truck to keep it from tipping over. It fell over and crushed the poor fellow to death. Due to local custom, we stopped work to observe three days of mourning. A second worker was bitten by one of the many poisonous snakes that inhabited the country. He died a terrible death, trembling with fever, blinded by the venom as it attacked his nervous system.

That also led to an unusual situation: a village council demanded money for the family of the deceased worker. We informed them that this was not possible, since the U.S. government had no liability in this matter, and further, that we were doing work for their benefit. The council powwowed for a while, and then sent two armed natives to take one of the Special Forces fellows and myself back to their village as hostages. Both Special Forces fellows asked what we should do. I suggested simply, nothing. The villagers would not be able to extort money from the U.S. government, and they couldn't complete the bridge without us. They took the two of us and held us in a small room while they decided what to do. I was moderately concerned—particularly since this tribe was only recently reported to have given up headhunting. After six uncomfortable hours, the tribal council decided to release us, and we went on from there to build one of the most magnificent suspension bridges in Asia—the bridge at Hao Cha. It provided significant economic benefit to the tribe, and I am still proud to have played a role in its construction. A footnote to this story, however, tells you something about the U.S. government's way of operating. After I submitted my expenses, I found that the allowance for my temporary duty had been reduced because government quarters had been provided. Well, they had—I spent nearly six months sleeping in one of their tents.

FIVE

STILL LEARNING THE CRAFT

1974–1977

My second assignment, which would again utilize my language skills, came while I was working directly inside a CIA facility for the first time. This job proved to be a real benefit to my career.

While on this assignment, my wife blessed me with a healthy baby boy, and my job blessed me with one of the best supervisors I would ever have. He welcomed me, told me he knew all about my resistance to going to Vietnam, and that he was only concerned with how well I worked in this assignment. That part settled me down. The boss took me around and introduced me to everyone who was anyone. As we stopped at the desk of one officer—I knew him in passing, as he was also a Chinese linguist—the boss said to me in front of this officer, "Whatever you do, stay away from this jackass. He is a worthless officer who won't be around long." Wow, I didn't know whether to run and hide or what. As it turns out, the boss was right on both counts.

I was working with, in all, a great group of middle-grade officers who ensured that I got off to a good start. And being one of the first summer rotating officers to arrive proved to be quite beneficial. As such, I was given a large group of agents to run and handhold until more help arrived. I had nine agents to deal with (a good load is normally three to five max). I worked really hard that summer until help came. And the hard work helped me greatly, because I was then given the choice of which agents to keep for myself, and which to pass on to other officers. Naturally, I kept a couple of the best and produced some first-class intelligence from several terrific operations.

I also had early in this tour two other excellent superiors. One was my direct branch chief, a man who had been awarded the Intelligence Star for valor behind enemy lines. The second was the deputy—considered a legend in the business of technical operations.

Technical operations include the use of technology or equipment as a key element in the effort to collect secrets and intelligence. For instance, implanting a secret listening device into a room, briefcase, or piece of furniture to record someone's conversations is considered a technical operation. An operation to illegally and secretly enter the premises of another country's mission or facility to make copies of their codebooks is a technical operation. And operations in which we have intelligence transmitted either by short-wave radio, by secret writing, or by microdots, are also technical operations.

And we did technical operations. After I had been in country only two weeks, I was part of a team to make an entry into the mission of a hostile country to install a listening device. This was tense but exciting stuff. While I can't go into details here, I learned that good officers take the initiative. Our agreement with our headquarters was that we would do an initial survey from outside and then regroup and get headquarters' permission to go inside the walled compound and make another survey before doing the entry for real. We had set up an observation post (OP) in a nearby apartment, and I was assigned two tasks. One was to bring in my dog so one of the surveillance teams could walk her around the neighborhood to provide cover for their evening activity. Second, I was to walk around the neighborhood with the tech that was going to install the device, and take notes of his observations. So far, so good. But as we rounded one of the darker corners of the compound, the tech said to me, "Hey, lift me up so I can look over the wall."

"OK," I said. After I raised him up, he quickly put one foot on my shoulder and went over the wall into the compound. I almost had a stroke. I wandered around the area for a while, waiting to see if he would need help getting back out. In about five minutes, all hell broke loose. I heard someone running inside the compound, a dog snarling, and over the wall unassisted came the technician. We ran a little ways, and then assumed a walk back to our OP. The deputy asked us what had happened.

"I saw a chance to get a good look at the locks on the building and decided to make an imprint," the tech replied, and he produced a sample of the lock. He also noted, "And, we learned they keep patrol dogs around." The deputy praised him for both his courage and his seizing the opportunity, and I learned another lesson—you must take the opportunity when you have it.

The operation went successfully forward several nights later—but again, not without incident. Involved in this operation was one of our officers, who would later haunt me in a second assignment. Let's call him "Dufus" to save him embarrassment. We had surveillance patrols out, our observation post was in place, and all parties were ready to go as darkness approached. We had gone over the ground rules, including what to do if apprehended—basically, ask to see someone at the American embassy. When caught *in flagrante* with audio bugs and such inside a foreign mission, there is no cover story. We had three surveillance teams deployed complete with radios. We had stakeouts in several cars in the event police entered the area. As we were ready to go over the wall, we threw meatballs with mild tranquilizers over the wall for the dog. Just as I was to hoist our audio specialist over the wall, we heard our radio broadcast the prescribed message telling us to stop and return with all haste to the observation post. We stopped our activities and returned as calmly as possible to see what had gone wrong. Dufus had called the emergency when he had noticed that one of our surveillants had a U.S. government

49

pen in his pocket. Dead silence. Finally, the deputy looked at him and said, "So what?"

Dufus replied, "If the police or someone else see him, they would know he is with the U.S. government."

"He's with the U.S. government, you moron," shouted the deputy. "He is not the one we worry about; he has a real and legitimate cover story." The deputy was livid that in addition to calling off the operation with this call, Dufus had heated up the area with all the unnecessary running around that would likely draw the attention of neighbors or local security officers. After calm returned, we persuaded the deputy that, if we waited several hours, we felt we could re-deploy and still carry out the operation. Although he didn't like it, he reluctantly agreed. First, however, he ordered Dufus to go home, and to have nothing further to do with this operation. We finished the operation with no difficulty. Dufus went home after only two years on his assignment.

My second assignment continued my education in Asian culture. I was meeting one of our sensitive assets out of town to ensure that we avoided surveillance or an encounter with anyone familiar with the asset. He was a senior distinguished member of the host government, and it would have been difficult to explain his being with me. So, we traditionally met out of town in a variety of places, taking great care to ensure we did not meet twice in the same location. In this instance, we had planned to meet way out of town, at a locally famous hot springs hotel. I spoke enough of the local dialect to make it easy to get a hotel reservation, done only after arrival to ensure no one knew in advance where I was staying. I arrived the day before to scout the area and do a normal surveillance detection run (SDR), and to also be in position to watch my agent arrive so I could make sure he didn't bring anyone with him.

After checking in, I saw that the hotel had a traditional family hot springs sauna pool. I decided to take advantage of it, so I put on my robe and slippers and went down to the bathhouse. As I got near, I could hear the sound of what sounded like young women giggling. No matter, I thought, as I saw there were separate men's and women's changing rooms. So I went into the men's room, disrobed, and walked out the door to the pool stark naked. All the giggling stopped as I saw six or eight elderly women swimming around the pool in the nude. As I stepped down the steps and into the boiling water, they all shrieked and ran for the steps. They dashed out of the pool, scaring the hell out of me, shouting "foreigner, foreigner!" They dashed for the women's dressing room, and I saw the obvious—there were two areas for disrobing, and one pool for everyone. In the meantime, the manager of the hotel ran into the pool area, where I was now the only one present. Highly excited, he first made all sorts of gestures, and then told me in halting English, "You can't soap up in here," indicating that he feared that I was going to use the pool as we foreigners use our bathtubs. I told him I understood the local custom of washing outside the tub, and using the tub only for relaxing. He walked away, but later I learned that he drained the pool and refilled it just in case. So much for keeping a low profile. I used many local facilities in the time I was in Asia after that, but I always assured the managers that I knew how it was done. And, to this day, I am also puzzled about the same thing that puzzles Asians: why do we sit in a tub, scrub ourselves down, and then lie in the same dirty water?

I learned a lot about recruiting and motivating agents during this tour. In one case, I made a significant recruitment based on ideological motivation. I had made the acquaintance of a well-known and respected foreign journalist who had written extensively about events in East Asia, and who had obvious contacts of importance. We started meeting quite discreetly for drinks in the evening to talk about Asia. Finally, over drinks late one evening he asked me pointedly, "Do you work for the CIA?" I hesitated only a moment and told him that I did. Slightly taken aback, he suggested that meeting in the open as we were was probably not a good idea. I agreed and set up our next meeting at a local hotel with a room I had rented with an alias.

I didn't know what to expect at this meeting. I believed then, as I still do today, that good officers never lie to their agents or their developmentals, that is, the people a case officer has deliberately developed a relationship with to assess their access to secrets and the possibility that they would agree to work as a spy for the U.S. government. There were only two questions: would he show up and would he accept recruitment to work as an agent for the U.S. government? He did show up, but he then went into a long rambling monologue about how he simply could not accept working as a secret agent for the U.S. government. After a while, I looked him in the eye and simply said, "I am sorry to hear that—and I think our National Security Advisor will be disappointed."

"You mean the National Security Advisor knows who I am?" he asked.

I told him that no, he didn't know his identity—only a handful in my agency did—but that the National Security Advisor had received some of the reports I had prepared from our meetings and commented very favorably on them.

"OK," he said, "in that case, I accept." He became one of our best reporting assets, motivated ideologically to help the United States, whose presence in Asia he considered essential in keeping peace in the region.

I made a second recruitment that was, frankly, easier. This involved a well-known author who traveled frequently to denied areas of Asia. Again, we had been meeting for some time when I proposed to him that I would like to hire him to gather information that I could not gather myself, since I could not travel to denied areas as an American. He gave me a funny look and said, "I suspect you are CIA, but don't tell me. The answer is, yes, I will service your request for one thousand dollars per report. I need the money to buy myself a fancy car that I cannot afford. You also need to know, however, that after I earn enough to pay for the car, I will want to stop working for you, and want your agreement to that." I was pleased, and I did agree to his terms. Interestingly, when I reported all of this back to my headquarters, everyone kept sending me messages that he would obviously continue to work past his stipulated time, for the money involved. I responded many times that no, I believed he meant exactly what he said. He worked for me very successfully for several years. Then his company assigned him to a job in New York City, where he would cover events around the United Nations. According to our agreement, we terminated our relationship as he was leaving the country; he had earned just enough, and he had in fact purchased the car he so desired. The postscript came two years later, when I returned home for a visit and was asked to go contact him in New York, and renew our relationship. I argued strenuously that it was not a good idea—that the man meant what he had said, and that we should honor our agreement. Nonetheless, I was ordered to go make contact. I did, and he was delighted to see me until I asked him if there were any chance he would assist us again. He told me he enjoyed meeting and working with me personally, but that he meant what he said and asked that I honor our agreement. Chastened, I told him I understood and would insist that my headquarters not bother him again. To my knowledge, we have honored that agreement, although several snide comments were made when I reported that I did not control this man to the liking of headquarters. True, I did not, nor did I want to. He had fulfilled his promise, and it was our turn to fulfill ours.

Just working in the office was a new experience for me. In my previous tour, I worked under a cover outside of our office. So I was new to working around the talented—and at times quirky—people who do this business. The CIA workforce is the most diverse in the government. Coupled with the CIA-instilled ethic of telling it like it is, this diversity and quirkiness can lead to some funny episodes.

My second chief during this stint was an excellent manager—and ambitious. He was determined to increase the number of intelligence reports we put out, thus quantifying our progress under his leadership. We would get together every week, and the chief would go around the room (we had a lot of officers) and ask, "How many intelligence reports are you putting out this week?" The pressure was designed to keep us meeting our agents and pushing for more and better intelligence, but it didn't always work. I remember one time when the chief insisted that one officer had not produced enough for the week in progress. Finally, the chief asked the officer to try to get something from one of his agents.

The officer sputtered, "OK, I'll write one on [the subject] right away."

"Good," responded the chief. "When did you meet him?"

"Next week," responded the officer to the assembled laughter.

This same chief was aware that I was running an agent who had access to important information about China. Consequently, he was determined to get a scoop when Chairman Mao Zedong died after a long illness. The chief called me at home and ordered me to call my agent and have an emergency meeting to get a report about Mao's death, the aftermath, and other information. First, I told him that this was not a subject for telephone conversation (we always assumed our phones were tapped). Second, I said I didn't want to endanger the agent by doing so under these circumstances since any phone conversation could bring the agent to the attention of the local intelligence service. And third, I believed that the agent would not have access to anything of interest that I could not get later at a meeting I had scheduled in several days. The chief was furious.

"I am *ordering* you to go make that call!"

"OK," I responded, "but this is stupid and inappropriate."

I then went out into the late evening, did a surveillance detection run (SDR), and stopped to call my agent's telephone number. When the agent answered, I hesitated, then hung up without speaking.

There was no way I was going to call this agent out after my chief had discussed things over open telephone lines. Additionally, my agent lived in a compound with colleagues. In short, it was an order that I could not accept at the risk of endangering my agent for information I knew he would not have.

The next morning the chief called me in and asked what I had gotten from the agent. "Nothing," I replied. "He hopes to have something for me when we meet in a few days."

"Dammit! You didn't call him did you?" responded the chief.

"Yup, I called him," I responded truthfully. It was a silly, dangerous game that I refused to play.

While this episode illustrates the chief's belligerent side, he could also be inventive and supportive. We had been struggling for some time to try to penetrate the mission of a denied-area embassy located in the country—all without success. Finally, in a stroke of luck, we learned that one of the embassy's senior officials would go far outside of the city on Sunday mornings to watch model airplanes being flown at a local club. Armed with this information, I went to the area several times hoping for a chance encounter, but to no avail. I saw the official and could confirm that he went there regularly, but I still couldn't meet him. Finally, the idea hit me. Join the club, become a regular member, and make his acquaintance that way. Several of my colleagues pointed out that this would be time consuming, costly, and the weather was freezing. Nonetheless, I approached the chief, who immediately approved all expenses for this operational approach. I learned how to fly as well as build my own remote-controlled aircraft, and I was finally invited to join the club. Sure enough, on my second outing as a club member, another member introduced the target individual to me. Over the next couple of weeks, I persuaded the fellow to have a try at flying my remote aircraft himself under my direction. He was reluctant to do so, given the value of the aircraft. Nevertheless, one freezing-cold Sunday morning he agreed. After I had launched the aircraft, I let him take over the control, and he promptly flew the plane into a dive and into a frozen river. It was a beauty of a crash. The poor fellow was beside himself, and I suggested to him that we could go out for a warming brandy and that this was all a part of the business of learning to fly the aircraft. He accepted my invitation, we began to meet regularly, and he produced some important intelligence for the U.S. government.

We had a senior Asian officer of substantial talent who had served in country for some time. During a weekly meeting debate, the subject came up as to how we could terminate an agent who, we discovered, had been falsifying information. We generally liked to leave all assets feeling decent about themselves and their relationships with us regardless of what ended the relationship. It's just really important to intelligence operatives that there aren't disgruntled former agents running around. In this particular case, we had initial discussions on ending the relationship with the agent, but he demanded absurd amounts of cash. Since we knew he was a fabricator—which he would not admit—we had no inclination to give in to what we viewed as blackmail just to end the relationship peacefully.

We had discussed the issue ad infinitum, when the Asian officer volunteered to try to talk some sense into the agent. We all agreed that we needed someone who was more senior and more persuasive. In the end, the officer came back with the agent's agreement to accept our original proposal. Very impressed, I later went into his office to find out how he did it. I asked him, "How in the world did you get him to accept our proposal where other officers have failed?"

The officer looked at me, leaned back in his chair, reached into his pocket, and extracted a long switchblade stiletto. "I don't know," he responded. "He seemed to change his mind as I was paring my nails."

Good fortune is also essential in good intelligence operations. On one occasion, we had been sitting around brainstorming trying to figure out how to get an officer in touch with a senior KGB counterintelligence officer in hopes of securing an important defensive agent who could report on that service's efforts against us. Finally, one of our officers noted that this target had been invited to a reception at the home of a Third-World diplomat he knew. He suggested that he could get me an invitation, and, with luck, I might be able to find our target in the huge crowd that was sure to be there. As with all operations, you try everything until you find the right solution. And there were two other problems: we didn't have a photo of the target, and the home of the diplomat holding the reception was in a part of town where it was difficult to navigate the streets. So my wife and I set out by car to find the reception. We found the area, but could not find the address. No one we asked could help. Now the reception was in full swing, and I decided we'd be better off on foot. So we parked our car and set out on foot. After several blocks with no luck, a black Mercedes-Benz pulled up next to us. The driver rolled the window down and asked in a heavy Russian accent, "Could you please tell me where [the address of the reception] is located?" I told him no, we were looking for that address ourselves. He suggested we could do better together, and asked us to hop in the car. We did so, and as we introduced ourselves I almost fell over—he was the target we were going to the reception to meet.

We drove around together exchanging chitchat until we finally found the reception. As we got out of the car, the target asked me, "Since you were on foot, could I give you a lift home after the reception?" Although it meant leaving our car overnight in a strange location, of course I agreed. After the reception, he drove us home, and I invited the target and his wife in for a late evening drink. It was the beginning of a long—and successful—effort against the target.

Since he was a senior KGB officer, he was an important target for us to recruit. And I really needed to develop this relationship so we could use him as a source of information inside his own country. But just as important, as a KGB officer he could provide us with information about KGB efforts against CIA operatives both in our country and other places he had served. It would be a counter-intelligence bonanza.

After the earlier meeting, things moved well and rapidly. With many intelligence officers on both sides of the Cold War during this period, liberal use of alcohol was commonplace. In the case of this fellow, it was a daily event for him. He drank like a fish. Given that, and my desire to move the relationship into a private venue, he was most amenable for us to have a series of exchange dinners at his place and mine. The only problem was that when we were at his place the flow of liquor began within minutes of entry and continued in many cases well into the night. He also liked baiting my wife with questions like, "So, you think I am trying to get you drunk?" in an effort to force her to drink more than she wanted. Fortunately, she remained relatively sober on these occasions so we could get home safely. But I awoke many mornings after drinking way too much vodka, vowing, unsuccessfully, that it would never happen again.

But the cultivation and development of this target had other repercussions on my activities. He was responsible for my being wrapped up by the local national police force. It developed after one of our late evening visits to a local nightspot where, this time, we were nearing the final negotiations on whether or not he would become a spy for us. Everything hinged on our guaranteeing that we could get his 16-year-old son out of his country if necessary. We could not make such a guarantee, and that turned out to be the deal breaker. We had most of the final discussions in a bar downtown, and things stretched way past the midnight hour. We were both really tired, and I suggested that we reconvene in several weeks. He agreed, and, as was our custom, one of us would depart 30 minutes ahead of the other. This time, I went first.

After I exited the bar, I immediately looked up to the top floor of the building and noticed a local man in a dark suit with a small red button in his lapel. I was sure he was a local government police-man, since he was glancing into windows of shops that had been closed for hours and wandered away when I appeared. Just to be sure, I took the first elevator, and when I reached the ground floor, I took a stroll around the building. I saw two other people in dark blue suits with red buttons in their lapels, and knew now that I had been identified by the police and picked up as their surveillance target. I also suspected that it was probably surveillance of the KGB officer that then led them to me.

I returned home and first thing the next morning I reported my suspicions to my immediate boss. We set up an elaborate SDR for me, including a place where we had total photographic coverage. Sure enough, a full six-man local surveillance team was on me. Back at the office, we were discussing the fact that my time and usefulness were now severely limited, when my immediate boss was called to the chief's office. When he returned, he was agitated. He immediately informed our personnel in the office that the head of the host country's counterintelligence service had just visited our chief, and had laid out before him photographs and written accounts of my full activities over the past two weeks—including phone calls I had made, the SDRs I had taken, and more. This evidence also indicated that the counterintelligence service police had fielded a full 24-person team to cover me 24 hours a day. It was damaging evidence indeed. He then informed me, in a voice loud enough for everyone to hear, "Fella, it looks like your career is finished. You better pack your bags." I tried to explain to him that I had taken exceptional measures to ensure the security of my operations, and that the surveillance was not directed at me but at the KGB officer. He would have none of it, and I detected more than a little smugness on his part. Shortly thereafter, I was summoned to the chief's office. "Farewell, pal," my boss intoned as I went off for what I dreaded would be orders to go home immediately.

Well, was I surprised. The chief laid out all of the photos, surveillance reports, and other evidence of all of my activities, and I suspected I was in for a stern reprimand—or worse. Before I could defend myself, he remarked, "Damn, I hope all our officers do their work as well as you do. Damn good tradecraft!" Even though I had been "made" by the host country's counterintelligence service, and the evidence was laid out for my own chief to see, he understood that counterintelligence had gotten on my tail because of the KGB agent, and not through any fault of my own. I felt an enormous burden lift. The chief continued, "The chief of counterintelligence asked me how much longer you would be in country. I told him you would be here until your tour ended this summer. He suggested several times that it might be better for you to leave earlier, but I told him you would finish what you came here to do. The only thing he did demand was to meet with you personally to ask you about your operations and work here. I told him he was free to see you at any time, and he asked to make a car pickup of you this evening at the corner of [such and such] street. I told him you would be there. Keep up the good work, and keep your mouth shut when you see him."

I floated back to my office, where my immediate boss, smirk and all, asked, "When do you leave?"

"This summer, as scheduled," I replied. He sat in silence. Immediately thereafter, the chief called all the supervisors to his office, showed them the materials, and instructed them, "Make sure your officers see this and that they do their operational work as well as Mr. Paseman."

That evening I briefed my wife on my close call with career ruination. I told her I was going out that evening on business, not mentioning the upcoming car pickup, since I didn't want to worry her. I went to the designated site, and, right on time, up pulled a black chauffeur-driven Mercedes. The back window came down, and a most impressive man leaned out and said, "Please get in, Mr. Paseman." I got in, and the chief of counterintelligence introduced himself and suggested, "Mr. Paseman, let's go back to your place where we can talk." I did not object, but when the Mercedes pulled into the driveway and the two of us walked inside, my wife was certainly somewhat curious—and concerned. I told her everything was fine, that this fine gentleman and I needed to conduct some business, and she went upstairs. For the next hour, he interrogated me. "Mr. Paseman, are you running any citizens of my country? Are you willing to provide me with a list of your agents?" I assured him that no, I wasn't of course (I was), and no, I wasn't doing anything other than working against the KGB (I was), and no, I could not provide him with any additional information. The gentleman stood up, thanked me for my "helpfulness," and ended a rather strained conversation. As he exited the door he commented, "Mr. Paseman, you are very good. However, I suggest the remainder of your tour should be rather boring." I assured him that was very likely.

I had to avoid crossing paths with another agent since that would have dangerously exposed them. Fortunately, we had planned for all contingencies. Following standard procedure, other officers picked up every one of my agents successfully. A postscript: My wife and I had packed our bags for our final departure and were waiting for transportation to the airport, when a driver and car showed up with the message, "The chief wants to see you immediately." Here we go, I thought—I almost made it out of this intact. My wife anxiously awaited my return, as time was getting short to make it to the airport. I got to the facility and was immediately escorted into the chief's office. He got right to the point. "I know time is short," he commented. "Have you seen your performance report?" I responded that I had. Despite the fact that my immediate supervisor was still smarting over recent developments, he was smart enough to have written me a fabulous fitness report. "I am exercising my prerogatives as chief, so I am rewriting it." With that he handed me a memo that informed the promotion panels that, "This is the finest officer I have seen in 30 years of business. It is incumbent upon the organization to advance officers of this caliber ahead of their peers." I was speechless. He asked if this met with my approval, and, if so, told me to get out of his office and make my flight. I beat a retreat, and we made the flight on time. I was promoted shortly thereafter.

All operations have their lighter moments, as the following four incidents reveal. One evening I was meeting a terrorist suspect in an out-of-the-way hotel. Due to suspicions about the possible terrorist, I was operating in disguise to prevent him from identifying and perhaps targeting me later. As the evening wore on, we had several beers while talking. All of a sudden, as I was putting down my glass of beer to ask some more questions, I noticed that the terrorist suspect had a startled look on his face. When I looked down at my beer, I saw why—my mustache was floating on top of my beer. I paused for a moment, then reached into the beer, picked up my mustache, excused myself, went to the bathroom, glued it back on, and resumed the session. I had not been warned that alcohol would dissolve the mustache glue. For his part, the terrorist suspect never said a word about it.

Dissolvable paper is another trick of the trade—it even comes in flavors so you can enjoy it while eating the evidence. One evening as I went to call an agent, I took along a small pad of the paper, which I normally used to take notes. In an emergency, I knew that I could flush it down a toilet or throw it into a washbasin to destroy evidence of my espionage activity. That night, as rain slashed in sheets from the sky, I went to a public phone booth, made the call, and set up a meeting with my agent later that night. I took numerous notes on the pad, and as I started to leave the phone booth, I decided to call home to let my wife know I'd be late. As I finished the call, I looked down, and there was my entire water-soluble pad with all my notes floating on top of a puddle. With great care, I was able to pick up the pad, which was floating, fortunately, on its thick binding and saved all my notes.

In another incident, I took my wife to the largest sports facility in the country to watch a martial arts demonstration during a rare moment of leisure during this tour. The place was packed, but fortunately we had good seats. During the halftime break, I told my wife I was going to step out for refreshments. As I stood up, however, I noticed across the stadium a young woman—one of my agents—waving to me, indicating that she wanted to see me. I whispered to my wife that, if the woman were to come over, she knew me by an alias. So things were OK, but when I turned to go up the stairs, I saw a second agent making his way toward us. And he knew me by yet another name. As I was deciding my next move, I heard someone call out one of my aliases. It was yet a third agent, and—yes—he knew me by still a third name. I quickly told my wife, "Meet me at the car and don't ask any questions," and left her there while I made for the exits. I did successfully avoid all three agents. Fortunately, my wife was most understanding.

The fourth humorous episode was also a learning experience. I was out on my business, and taking great care to do a good surveillance detection run. I had a small suitcase with me, and I took a taxi to a small subway station on the outskirts of town. I took the subway, and changed trains at three separate stations. By this time, two or three hours had passed. Finally, I went on a walking route and went through a department store. Coming out the other side, I got in line at the taxi stand and got into the same taxi I had taken in the first place. I could barely tell him where to take me. It was all innocent enough, I guess, but I aborted the meeting just in case. Too much coincidence, and I have always been a believer in the line Goldfinger used with James Bond: "Once is coincidence, twice is happenstance, three times is enemy action." So I missed the meeting, just in case.

Sometimes the demands of espionage intrude into your personal life. Once while on this tour I needed some minor surgery, and I selected a U.S. military facility to have it done. Two aspects of this were unfortunate: first, the facility was a five-hour train ride away. Second, the procedure was done on an outpatient basis, meaning I had to return home afterward. Predictably, the train ride home after the surgery was not a pleasant experience. But once I got home, everything was fine until I received an emergency meeting request from one of my agents late in the evening. You do what you have to do in this business, so I loaded up with painkillers and plenty of admonitions from my loving spouse and went out to make the meeting. This was an important debriefing, and we completed it without the agent noticing that I was sweat-soaked from pain throughout.

In intelligence operations you seldom know anyone by their real name. Your fellow officers have aliases and pseudonyms galore. Your agents get cryptonyms to protect their identities. The upshot of this is that soon your circle of friends and acquaintances get nicknames to make things easier. Also, most of the nicknames have something generally to do with either physical features or personality. Some more memorable nicknames are:

- *Nickel Nose*: an agent with a nose that's unusually large for an Asian. Given by an officer who noted, "You could put a roll of nickels in each nostril."
- *Dumbo*: an agent with large ears highlighted by her insistence on wearing a hat for disguises, which pushed them out even further.
- *Sir Oval*: a case officer with a significant paunch.
- *Honda Bob*: a manager who checked up on his officers by motorcycle.
- *Lightbulb*: a chief with no hair.
- *Motor-Mouth*: a very senior officer who simply couldn't let anyone else have a say about anything.
- *Hair-on-Fire*: another very senior officer, most noticeable by the fact that he was always in motion with some new proposal or scheme—running around as if his hair were on fire.
- *Broadway*: another senior officer known for having a slick answer to any problem and whose current job was always the best he ever had.

- *Dufus*: the officer who spotted the U.S. government pen and aborted our technical operation.
- *Moneypenny*: one of the heroines of my career, nicknamed after James Bond's Miss Moneypenny. She was a financial genius who taught me how to get money for operations (see chapter 12).
- *FNU/LNU* [fahnu lahnu]: probably the most famous person in the intelligence world. It stands for first name unknown/last name unknown. Intelligence officers often request traces, or record checks, from headquarters to see if someone we have recently met has anything in their file. Frequently we would get back a response of either first name unknown or last name unknown. So we'd often ask, "Has anyone found FNU/LNU yet?"

SIX

JOURNEYMAN SPY

1977–1979

As I embarked on my third straight overseas assignment I was really on a roll from the previous tour. During a short TDY at headquarters, I was briefed on the state of affairs in my new country. Excited to arrive in country, I was ready to go to work upon arrival. On my first day, the chief called me in and asked me to immediately go to an adjoining country and attempt to recruit a denied-area official who was in touch with one of our officers in that country. I eagerly agreed and flew out that same day.

When I arrived and was briefed by the officer working the case, I discovered that it was not much of a case at all. It was in fact what we call a gangplank recruitment attempt, or simply asking a departing official to work for us without laying any advance groundwork. But I made the attempt and walked up to the official and asked if I could speak to him for a moment. He was naturally wary, but agreed to listen to me. I had a proposal—cash for espionage. He was incredulous and refused outright. I went back and reported this to the officer in country, who said he was not surprised but that it was worth the try. I grumbled that this was a poor way to do business, and headed back to the airport.

After arriving back in country, the chief immediately called me into the office and asked for a report. As I began to explain that the recruitment attempt hadn't worked, he exploded, "What the hell kind of officer have they sent me anyway?"

"One that knows better than to try that half-assed approach and one who doesn't ever let anyone yell at him," I responded. I then turned and walked out the door, slamming it for emphasis. Shortly thereafter, the deputy came to my office and told me it would be best if I apologized to the chief. I told him that it would be a cold day in Asia before I apologized, and called my wife to tell her not to start unpacking too soon, since we might be leaving shortly. I told her I would explain things later. Meanwhile, the chief's secretary called and said he wanted to see me. I told her to relay the message that I would be glad to stop in if he could assure me there would be no more yelling. She called back, telling me that it would be a good idea if I came in. Fearing the worst, I reluctantly went back in and walked into his room, with the secretary closing the door behind us. The chief turned around and said to me, "You know, given your expertise in China, I thought maybe we could sit down and get your input into our programs here to see what we can do better."

That was that. He never raised his voice to me again during the tour. In fact, after our pleasant meeting he invited my wife and me to his home for dinner that evening. When I returned home after the meeting with the chief, my wife was clearly worried.

"You'll never believe this," and I told her what happened as we dressed and went off for a perfectly enjoyable evening with the chief, who was a most gracious host.

I had no idea about the shock that was to come next. A couple of days after arriving in the country, I went to get my mail and returned to my office. For some reason, the door was locked. I beat on the door for minutes, then decided it had been locked accidentally, so I went to the support area to see if there was a spare key. The secretary said to me, "Well, it's just Dufus using your office." I couldn't believe it—he had been transferred here from my previous post. Was I distressed now.

"Why has he locked me out of my own office?" I asked.

"Well," the secretary replied with a grin, "he requires anyone entering the office when he is there to use the secret knock, and then he'll open the door."

"Secret knock? Tell him to open the damned door to my office and let me in or I'll kick it in and him with it," I responded. She dutifully made the telephone call to my office to ask Dufus to let me in as I went back down the hall.

The door was open this time, and Dufus explained to me, "You see, the secret knock is just in case someone who doesn't know I'm an intelligence officer tries to get in, then they won't blow my cover."

"You jackass," I replied. "We're in a secure area." With that, I forbade him from ever entering my office again and he left.

But that wasn't the end of my encounters with Dufus. Late one evening, I was entertaining some local officials at my house. It was a critical evening, because local regulations forbade local officials from being in the homes of U.S. government officials. The people in my home that night were younger local officials, and they had taken a risk just to show up. Things were going quite well, and darkness had just fallen. Suddenly, I looked up and saw Dufus looking in my living-room window. I excused myself, went outside, and asked him what the hell he was doing. I also noticed he had a tennis racket in his hand. He explained to me that he was doing his surveillance detection run (SDR) before he went to meet an agent and noticed I had some local officials in my home.

"Yes," I noted.

"I recognize one of them and would be glad to come in and introduce you to him," he explained.

"You moron," I fairly shouted, "I've already met him. Otherwise, he wouldn't be in my house."

Additionally, I pointed out to him that since he didn't play tennis, any enemy agent performing a good surveillance of him over a period of time would find his carrying a tennis racket strange and unusual. Also, since there were no lighted courts, playing tennis at night would have been impossible. Dufus finally left. He returned to assignment in Washington, and was put into non-operational jobs for the remainder of his career.

This tour was to a smaller facility, and to a country with definite Third-World credentials. We joked that it was a country in the fourteenth century moving rapidly to the twelfth. As with many assignments to such countries, you run across some real characters along the way.

Representatives from almost all of the communist countries were posted here. Generally, the poorer the country, the more representatives from denied-area countries that can be found. (A denied area is a country that's hostile toward the United States and closely monitors the activities of official Americans during their stay.) The senior diplomat in country was an old East German diplomat who had been there for nearly 11 years. He hadn't returned to East Germany for several reasons. If he returned, he was afraid he would be unable to leave again, plus his government didn't want to pay the expense of relocating him. Also, his government benefited from having the senior diplomat in country—an important diplomatic point in the social game.

Along the way, this senior diplomat had acquired quite a taste for distilled barley. He was a drunken sot who typically got blind drunk at diplomatic receptions. One of our senior officers had been assessing him for recruitment as a spy, but headquarters had no interest in him because of his drinking. And, with 11 years away from his own country, headquarters considered him unlikely to have access to any useful information. When we decided to take a fresh look at him, we were introduced at an evening outdoor reception. The diplomat was already looking tipsy, and as we talked he kept spilling brandy down the front of his suit. We were standing just next to a hedge on a small hillside, and I excused myself to get another beer and some napkins to dry him off. "Hurry back," he said, "I won't go away."

When I returned, he was nowhere in sight. Then I heard a yell. "Help me up!" he screamed. He had fallen over the hedge and rolled to the bottom of the hill, a glass of brandy still in his hand. I helped him up, and we finished our conversation. I later reported to headquarters that I didn't think this fellow was good agent material.

It was at this same party that I discovered a KGB agent attempting to target me. A young Russian couple had shown up on the scene during my second year in country. We had done background checks on them and confirmed that both were KGB officers. He was a nice chap, interested in chess and reading while she, quite simply, was a knockout. We knew she was a senior officer due to political connections from her father. My wife and I did enjoy their company during our limited time together. Then, one evening at a social event where there was dancing, the fellow engaged my spouse in a conversation on the other side of the room. The KGB woman asked me to dance and I accepted. She adroitly maneuvered me to a dark corner on the other side of the room, and I looked down and there were only three legs on the dance floor—two of which were mine. She had curled one leg up around my thigh as she tried to whisper in my ear, "Let's go back to my place."

I stopped dancing, looked her in the eye, and said, "I'm gonna do you a *big* favor."

"What's that?" she responded.

"I'm gonna stop this before my wife sees you and kills you." Stunned, she desisted and never made another move in my direction the rest of the tour. It does illustrate, however, that the KGB often employed sex as an operational tool.

The KGB would also do anything to maintain superior standing. After I had been in country for a while, I was regarded as one of the best tennis-playing foreigners there. I had played in [the country's] Open Tennis Tournament, and had won a number of matches throughout the area. It aggravated the KGB, which was no longer targeting me, that I had not taken their earlier bait. So I wasn't surprised when one of Russia's top female tennis players appeared at the Soviet embassy ostensibly as a cultural officer. Nor was I surprised that she sought me out immediately and challenged me to a game of tennis. I accepted, and of course, when I showed up, half of the Russian embassy was on hand to cheer her on. She was a terrific player, and bigger than me. However, I managed to eke out a victory, and did so the next three or four times she challenged me. Interestingly enough, after she lost to me the fourth time, her assignment was cancelled and she returned to Moscow.

A third character of note during this tour was the Israeli ambassador to the country where I was stationed. He was a senior Israeli Ministry of Foreign Affairs official who was on his last assignment and had been rewarded with an ambassadorship for his long and dedicated service. He was also an avid tennis player, and quite good at that, as he had been at one time on the Israeli Davis Cup team. I was not quite up to his caliber, but I was good enough to make our matches challenging for him. The problem was that he cheated. He had, he believed, a responsibility to call all the lines on both sides of the court; these calls were, of course, always in his favor. If I successfully lobbed a ball over him, even if we could find the clay marks where the ball landed, he would inevitably call it out.

After a few months in country, he was virtually isolated and no one wanted to play with him or against him. I also quit playing with him. The diplomatic community, however, arranged a doubles tournament during that spring.

I was on the organizing committee, and we tried to pair up individuals who didn't have a natural partner. More than half of the players were from communist bloc countries, allied with the Arab nations and with no diplomatic relations with Israel. Thus, despite several attempts to line the Israeli ambassador up with a partner, all the candidates refused to play either with him, or even against him. After I threatened to cancel the tournament and withdraw the American contingent from competition, the Soviet Bloc players grudgingly agreed to play against him with me as his partner. When I told the ambassador of this agreement, he was resistant at first. He insisted that he would rather play alone, and if the bloc players refused to play the matches, they would count as forfeits. I argued with the ambassador that this would probably mean he would be champion without a match being played. What meaning would such a championship really have? He finally agreed to the plan with me as his partner, and the tournament got under way.

I still do not recall who won—heavy betting predicted that the ambassador and I would crush all opponents in a shoo-in. But only several games into the match, I ran to the side of the court to return a terrific shot that nose-dived in as it skipped past me. I signaled the ball in, and returned to the baseline for the next serve. The ambassador, however, walked to the net and explained to the opponents that, "Floyd was wrong, the ball was out." An argument of three against one ensued. The ambassador held his ground, embarrassing me greatly. Our opponents offered to replay the point, but the ambassador refused. Our opponents gave in. On the next serve to my side, a looping, blooping easy-to-return ball, I simply stood there and watched it go by. The Israeli ambassador was stunned. We lost the match finally, and the ambassador and I never played together again on either side of the net. Later a representative from the Soviet embassy approached me and asked, " Floyd, are you Jewish?" I responded that I was not, but the Soviet said, "Why else would you play with that man?" I tried to explain that I felt everyone had a right to enter the tournament and was simply trying to expedite things. The Soviet walked away, shaking his head.

It was also during this tour that I really got to know and love Australians. They had a relatively large embassy in country, with wonderful facilities to host community events, including a pool, tennis courts, and a bar. I played a good deal of tennis there, and was initiated into the Limp Fall Society. According to the rules of the Limp Fall Society, whenever someone walks into an Aussie bar and yells "Limp Fall," everyone collapses to the deck. Those left standing then have to buy a round for everyone in the bar. This was explained to me after a round of tennis and an invitation to the Aussie bar to be initiated. Sure enough, we walked in and my partner yelled, "Limp Fall," and all the patrons, about a dozen in total, went limp and hit the deck. "You buy," he explained. I did so, and to this day have taken a couple of spills to the floor when Limp Fall is called out.

I did do one good deed during this assignment. We were operating in a very repressive society. One day the ambassador called me and asked if I could talk to a young woman whom he had just seen and talk some sense into her. I agreed, and shortly thereafter met her in the receiving area. She was from Amnesty International (AI), and was insistent that she was going upcountry to visit some areas where AI suspected political prisoners were being held. The ambassador had told her that there were several small rebellions going on in the region where she wanted to travel and strongly suggested that she not go. She explained to me her doubts about what the ambassador had told her, that she thought he was trying to keep her from discovering the truth. I told her, "Miss, in all likelihood, your assumptions are probably correct. Without a doubt, there are probably some political prisoners in a number of camps upcountry. There are several small wars going on between different ethnic groups, and they do not treat prisoners well in general. However, unless you want to experience firsthand—as a prisoner yourself— the treatment they get, I advise you to cancel your plans and leave the country when your visa expires. Your chances of being captured—and they do ransom prisoners as well—are quite good."

The woman sat there stunned for a couple of moments and asked me directly, "Do you work for the CIA?" I told her that I did, and she remarked, "I trust that you would tell me the truth—I will forgo the experience." She did in fact depart the next day. I felt I had saved her from probable capture and a potentially horrific experience.

It was also in this country that I learned that the acquisition of important intelligence did not necessarily mean that this information would make it to either the analyst or the consumer. I was running an agent with terrific access to information regarding developments inside China. As a result, he was a key asset when Chairman Mao Zedong of the People's Republic of China died just before I arrived at post. Everyone expected some sort of a power struggle to take place, and one of the key intelligence questions was: Who will replace Chairman Mao? Within days of my arrival, my agent signaled that he wanted an emergency meeting. We met late at night in a car pickup meeting, and he informed me that he had learned that Hua Guofeng would replace Chairman Mao as the most powerful man in China. I was a China hand, and I had no idea who Hua Guofeng was.

"Who the heck is he?" I asked my agent.

"Don't know," he replied.

This was some state of affairs. I told my agent to try to find out who Hua was, and that I would do my homework too, but we clearly needed to get this information to Washington immediately. I researched all my reference material and found no listing of Hua anywhere. Nonetheless, I prepared the intelligence report for headquarters. My boss was very uncomfortable. "How can we send this in? How do we know it's true? It doesn't make sense." While I agreed, I also argued that we had the responsibility to send it in, and also noted that my agent had an excellent reputation for providing accurate information. That carried the day, and we submitted the intelligence. It took less than 24 hours for us to receive a blistering admonition from headquarters, which refused to disseminate the intelligence in Washington due to, as they put it, "the extreme impossibility that an unknown by the name of Hua Guofeng would ascend to the leadership of China." My chief sternly lectured me about the need for accurate intelligence from my sources, and I was downtrodden, to say the least.

It didn't help much when, two days later, an official announcement came from the People's Republic of China that "Chairman Hua Guofeng has assumed the mantle of Chairman Mao." So, we missed telling our policymakers in advance about this momentous event because we failed to think the unthinkable—a cardinal sin for any intelligence organization. Of course, we never got anything resembling an apology from headquarters.

We as an organization were also going through some difficult times. We had a new Director of Central Intelligence (DCI), and it was clear early on that he had no particular fondness for the clandestine side of the house. The new DCI brought on a special assistant to take a fresh look at how we conducted our business. It wasn't too long thereafter that all field elements—those located and operating outside Washington, D.C.—received a cable noting that we were to pay particular attention to the moral aspects of our business. Specifically, we were to proceed with instructions that, "the recruitment of individuals for the purpose of espionage should be a morally uplifting experience." *Holy moley*! It wasn't that we disagreed with our agents acting morally, but we were also trying to persuade drug runners and terrorists to work as spies for the U.S. government. The cable drew widespread derision, and even more when we learned that this assistant would personally visit a number of field locations (including ours) to discuss their instructions and review our recruitment processes to ensure adherence. Fortunately for me, my chief decided to send me off on a trip elsewhere at the same time. No doubt my chief suspected, correctly, that I wouldn't just sit and listen to the assistant lecture us on the morality of spying. Avoiding the special assistant's visit probably saved both our careers.

But this did come at a terrible price. It was well known early on that neither our new president nor his Director of Central Intelligence liked human spying—preferring what they saw as the antiseptic approach of intercepting conversations (signals intelligence) or studying satellite photos (imagery). Frankly, I never quite understood why one form of spying was OK but using humans for the same job was considered distasteful.

The upshot of these developments was the "Great Massacre," in which the director decided that it was time to eliminate the bloat left over from the Vietnam War. Overnight, he terminated the careers of over 800 Directorate of Operations case officers. You can imagine the effect on morale, and the director's actions did long-lasting harm to our ability to collect human intelligence. Most of those fired were veterans of substantial fieldwork, most had at least one esoteric language, and many were over 40. Our collection capability was decimated. We regained some of our losses after President Reagan took office. But following the excesses in Nicaragua and the Iran/Contra affair, we reverted to about where we were at the end of the previous administration—with pretty poor human-collection capability left. (This came back to haunt us terribly in September 2001).

During this, my third overseas tour, a vehicle I was driving almost floated out to sea. We were in a tropical rainforest that had frequent monsoons, and flash flooding could occur without warning. Late one evening, after the martial law curfew, I had a meeting with one of my agents just outside of town. I took a sterile vehicle and did my normal countersurveillance run to ensure that I was clean. I then drove without lights to the pickup point, and my agent jumped into the passenger seat. We began to drive around as I debriefed him. About ten minutes into the meeting, the monsoons hit. Still, I drove around trying to complete our meeting. But when I turned and drove down one road, heavy floodwater rushed in from nowhere. All of a sudden, our car started to float. We both remained relatively calm until the waters took us toward the local river that ran into the ocean. As our car floated toward the river, I told my agent to get his ass out of the car. He pushed his door open and abandoned the car. I stayed in the car as it started to enter the river. Fortunately for me, it caught on the edge of a bank, and I could then abandon it. I had to wade 50 yards to high ground, and I made my way on foot back home. All night long, I rehearsed the cable I was going to have to write about how the vehicle went down the river and into the ocean. Fortunately, the next morning I went back to the area, and someone had salvaged the car and had it sitting on high ground. I took my key, started the car, and drove it back. We had to refurbish the interior, but we didn't have to send the humiliating cable telling headquarters that our car just happened to float away.

Over the years, I've dealt with a fair number of unsavory agents, and I've recruited a couple myself. One of them was a narcotics asset. He was as tough a person as I ever dealt with, and had been imprisoned and tortured by the police of two different countries. He earned his living as a smuggler of jade—and heroin. He had pockmarks from smallpox and scars on his face and shoulders from war and fights for survival. He spoke excellent Chinese, and I met him through an introduction from another asset reporting on narcotics for us. I didn't control this agent; he agreed to work for us for the money. He did like me, and he always promised me that he would never betray me to others in the narcotics business. And he lived up to his promise. But he had a habit of showing up unannounced, late at night, at my home. Several times he scared the hell out of my family. Even when I wasn't home, he would simply walk into the house (heavily armed), go over to the bar, pull out a bottle of his favorite (Johnnie Walker Red), and finish off the bottle. If I were home, he still would come in, go over to the bar, pull out the Johnnie Walker Red, and proceed to finish off the bottle as we conducted our business. Strangely, I never feared him. We had an excellent relationship, and he respected my ability to deal with him in his native Chinese tongue. He produced a tremendous amount of good, verifiable intelligence that helped us bust a number of drug operations. Unfortunately, on one of his smuggling trips he got into a gunfight with his traveling companions and was killed.

One of my favorite tales concerns the ingenuity of case officers. One of my friends was running a denied-area asset. As a result, we seldom had the opportunity to meet with him face-to-face, and used a courier system to both give the agent our requirements and to get reporting back from him. The problem was how to pay the agent. He wanted a hedge against inflation and asked to be paid in gold rings. That in itself was not a problem. The question was concealing the rings so the courier could take them across borders safely. Finally, the officer decided to bake the rings into a pie and have them carried across that way. (We amused ourselves by singing "Four and Twenty Blackbirds Baked in a Pie" to his great displeasure.) As we brainstormed the idea, we realized that someone at the border crossings might want to taste the merchandise, and that appeared to be a real problem. Finally, I suggested we simply make the pie taste so awful that, if offered a sample, no one would want seconds. The pies were baked with the greenest, sourest apples we could find. It worked. The pie reached its destination intact.

But, with the arrival of a new chief, the tour wasn't all a bed of roses. A pleasant enough man, and a man of courage who had been in service in the war zones of Asia, he nevertheless was a breed of chief that believed things were owed to him because of his position. Over several months what I was seeing started to bother me. I noted shortly that after we purchased watches as gifts for our local government official friends, my chief and his wife began sporting new watches remarkably similar to the gifts. Ditto when we passed out new tennis rackets to our contacts—suddenly new ones showed up in the hands of our chief and his wife. When new tires showed up for official vehicles, the chief's personal car appeared with new tires.

During this time, I was fortunate to receive perhaps the finest fitness report in my career, which made a decision I needed to make even more difficult. Things came to a head for me when, during a visit to my chief's home, I saw official serial numbers on a number of items in his home, indicating equipment that had been taken from official installations elsewhere.

I knew what I had to do. We were scheduled to have an inspector general (IG) visit in the next few weeks. According to regulations, any officer can request to see an IG, with no questions asked. However, when I signed up for an appointment, the chief came to me and asked, "What are you going to see him about?" I told him that I just wanted to see the IG, and he finally left grumbling. Sure enough, the IG arrived, and during my session with him, I reported my suspicions that our chief was misappropriating U.S. government property for his personal use.

The IG clucked and took everything down, and I thought that would be the end of that. However, minutes after the IG had his farewell session with our chief, and for the first time during the IG's visit, I was called to the front office. The chief told me very sternly that, "I have been watching you for some time now, and it is clear to me that you don't have what it takes to be a supervisor in this organization." I was stunned tremendously, as this was the same officer who had endorsed my previous fitness report. It was not until later that I learned that the IG was a close personal friend of the chief from a previous assignment. What was clear was that nothing was ever done about the chief's allegedly dipping into official property. This experience taught me a lesson about the Agency IG system. IGs, hoping for plum assignments, have a personal stake in not rocking the boat. I never again trusted an IG investigation until the inspector general position became presidentially appointed and congressionally approved, which came much later in my career.

In one humorous episode from an inspector general's visit, a large amount of explosives and thermite grenades from a neighboring country's facility wound up at our facility when a communist takeover closed down their operations. No one knew how the explosives got to our country, but the IG ordered us to dispose of the unauthorized materials. Fine, well, and good. I wrote a cable back to headquarters and asked them how to mail or pouch these materials back to where they came from. A long silence ensued. Finally I received a cable that assured me that we couldn't possibly have these materials on hand, since there was no record of them ever having been sent to us. "OK," I wrote back, "what do you want us to do with them?" I got a one-line response: "Be inventive."

Inventive I was. I lined up one of our communicators, and we decided that we could burn the thermite grenades in a 50-gallon drum that we kept on the roof for emergency destruction purposes. So late one evening, after dark, we took the grenades up to the roof and set the first one off in the drum. Wow! Smoke, fire, and enormous heat encircled us. We put a lid on the drum, but we couldn't put out the grenade. Worse still, we saw parts of the roof begin to smolder and melt. Fortunately, as we began to move the drum toward the edge of the roof (using asbestos gloves) with the intent of pushing it off the roof, it finally burned out. Sweat-soaked and all, we made the obvious decision not to discharge the remaining grenades.

But we still had the remaining grenades, ammunition, and explosives to dispose of. We held an informal meeting with a few of our more ingenious people, and one of them offered to assist. He was a member of a local yacht club and suggested that we simply go out yachting a couple of times late in the evening when no one was around and deposit the material in the lake. So we proceeded. However, only a very small yacht was available, and when we loaded all the material into the boat it took on water. So we had to make several trips out, but we did finally complete our objectives per headquarters' instructions. Since we never heard anyone talk about a geyser erupting on the lake, we assumed that all the explosives sat safely on the bottom of the lake.

Due to our hardship status, we were entitled to receive a monthly pouch of video movies for entertainment. The chief always took the entire shipment home first, and then they would trickle down to the rest of us. But this time the pouch included a video of the first U.S. space shuttle landing in the United States. The chief invited all the chiefs of the local security apparatus to view the landmark film at his house. This was a major event, because the local chiefs were basically forbidden from coming to our homes. But they made an exception for this historic occasion.

We all showed up for the big event at his house, and he offered an eloquent introduction about the U.S. space program, then started the video. Instead of the shuttle gliding across the screen, however, it was Fred Astaire and Ginger Rogers in *Top Hat*. Whoever had taken all the videotapes home to set up for our chief had gotten them mixed up. Our guests, apparently unwilling to trade a shuttle landing for tap-dancing, got up and left shortly afterward. Now that was funny!

In another caper, we were only able to laugh about it after we left post. At most hardship posts, theft is a major problem. So most posts hire local nationals to provide some semblance of security for our families and housing areas. But we had a lazy lout who was paid to come into our housing compound after dark and supposedly guard us until daylight. One evening after midnight, I was restless and heard what I thought were a few sounds in the yard. I got up, went downstairs, and turned on the outside light. I immediately saw our Honda station wagon, which we parked right under the carport, and all the rubber and aluminum trim that holds the windows in place was shredded and lying on the ground. All the windows of the car, front and rear, were gone. Thieves had come into the compound and removed them. I immediately ran around to the back where I found our guard sleeping in the dark. I kicked him as hard as I could, and to his everlasting intelligence, he jumped up and ran before I could beat the daylights out of him.

That was bad enough, but I really lost my cool when two days later I received a reprimand from the post administrative officer alleging that I had threatened a local employee. I grabbed the notice, walked into the admin officer's office, looked him in the eye, tore the reprimand into tiny pieces, and dropped them onto his desk.

Further, I informed him that it would be in his and the post's best interest that I never see or find that guard again. And, on top of everything else, we had lost all our car's windows just as the monsoons began. The car's interior was completely mildewed, and we had to rent a car to make it through monsoon season.

In many of our smaller denied-area hardship posts medical emergencies can strike without warning. A communicator with a family history of heart disease was assigned to one hardship post, even though we had inadequate medical care. We had one physician who drank to excess and a medical technician. Beyond that, we were at the mercy of the local medical system that for 25 years prohibited its doctors from training outside the country. They also prohibited the importation of foreign products, including medicines. Our best hope, in the event of a medical emergency, was to evacuate our employee or family member on U.S. government aircraft to a neighboring country for medical treatment.

But in the communicator's case, proper treatment came too late. One afternoon, the communicator collapsed as he was getting into his car after a game of tennis. An embassy wife, who happened to be a nurse, and I pulled him out of the car and attempted CPR. But it was clear he had died immediately from a massive heart attack. Unfortunately, we had to continue our efforts as someone tried to find a doctor to declare him dead. We struggled over his lifeless body for three hours, alternating CPR, until the doctor arrived, injected adrenaline directly into his heart, and declared him dead. It was my difficult duty to notify the communicator's wife and family of his death.

And I had my own health troubles. Toward the end of my tour, I contracted a serious case of hepatitis from eating uncooked food at a reception. I felt sick within a few hours, but I never counted on being close to death. My case progressed so badly that a doctor from a neighboring country was called in, and he determined that I was too ill to be evacuated by air. In private, the doctor suggested to me that I put my personal affairs in order. As I started about the business of completing wills and other arrangements, I tried to reconcile myself to the possibility that I would not be leaving the country alive. After two months of difficulty, I began to recover with the help of a case of Coca-Cola and a pound of hard candy a day. The Coke and candy replaced sugars that my liver was failing to produce, and the treatment worked well enough to get me back on my feet and to recovery back in the United States. My son, who was then four years old, had watched me consuming these huge amounts of Coke and candy in bed, and commented to my wife, "Boy, I wouldn't mind getting hepatitis myself." We had a good laugh.

When I finally recovered enough to go downstairs for the first time in two months, I went outside and found my son walking around our yard in his bare feet. Since we had a real problem with cobra snakes, we *never* walked around without shoes on. So in my first venture outside in months, I admonished my son, and as he went inside to put on his shoes he said, "I liked it better when you had hepatitis and left me alone." Brash, but still funny. I did not fully recover from the disease for two years.

I finally got back on my feet, and the chief came over and pronounced me fit enough to be his tennis partner in the National Open Tennis Tournament. Despite my wife's pleas, and against my own best judgment, I struggled out of bed and partnered up with my chief for the tournament. He was a good player, and I had won several previous tournaments. But I played terribly this time, and we lost in the first round. The chief was agitated and kept telling me how terribly I had played. "I guess I should have gotten someone else as a partner," he said, and I didn't reply. Later, as my tour was about to end, the chief personally rated me and dropped me a full category in every rating area. He offered no explanation but included a comment in his narrative that I can still remember today: "This officer's performance was hindered by the fact he allowed himself to become sick and unable to do his work." Although this review was a cause for grievance, I decided to cut bait and get out while I could. Upon my return to headquarters, I learned that I had been promoted.

One of the things I have always loved about the Agency is that your reputation—the so-called hallway files—tells more of the story than official records. And I learned that I had an excellent reputation for being good at espionage and that the promotion panel ignored the last fitness report from my chief as out of character.

Game, set, and match to me.

SEVEN

BACK HOME IN EAST ASIA

1979–1980

After I returned home to an assignment at headquarters for the first time in a decade, I was anxious to work on the Asian target. I was more than pleased when the chief of the East Asia division called me in and told me of an assignment overseeing an operational proposal that would be worldwide in scope, and put me into liaison with the FBI as well. I went back to my newly assigned desk and began to set up shop. I was pleased.

I wasn't so pleased when two hours later a colleague who had just returned showed up to take his assignment—the same as mine. I told him not to set up yet, and that I would hold up starting my assignment and would be right back. I went back up to the chief's office, where he sheepishly asked me what was wrong. I asked him about my colleague, and he admitted that he had offered us both the same job. He then went into a spiel that there was room for both of us to be deputy chiefs. I looked him squarely in the eye and told him not to worry, that I had no intention of sharing the job he had promised me, and that I was going to go find work elsewhere. He sputtered and said, "Give me some time to work something out." I went down to the cafeteria to get a cup of coffee, and when I returned to clean out my desk, my colleague had moved on to another job. Here I learned that if I just stood up for myself and my beliefs, the Agency would do the right thing in the end—even if it took some serious convincing.

One thing I did enjoy was visiting a number of our locations that were assisting us with our business in China. One such trip took me to London, which is always a great place to visit. While there, I was able to spend a good deal of productive time working with other China specialists. One evening, I was guest of honor at a dinner hosted by our London chief. He was a bright, effective officer who had adopted something of a British persona, which was not unique. The CIA has a large number of Anglophiles who seem to want to pass themselves off as British. Historians will recall that the legendary CIA chief of counterintelligence, James Jesus Angleton, was an Anglophile as well. As we sat at the dinner table, the subject of briefing our respective senior political leaders came up. The senior British representative present noted that it was difficult to get the Queen to understand our business. Our chief took a moment and said, "My dear fellow, if you can't brief your Queen properly, I would be so very pleased to do so on your behalf." Wow. That ended the evening, as our guests excused themselves and left in a huff. Then the chief turned to me and said, "I say, do you suppose they didn't like my suggestion?" I said nothing.

While assigned to headquarters, I witnessed a remarkable incident that came to be known as the great strawberry theft. The DCI at the time was fond of strawberries and kept a bowl of them in a small refrigerator outside his office. One evening he went to get his strawberries, and they weren't there. He must have been quite upset, because, according to an eyewitness, he exploded and ordered security to investigate the theft of his strawberries. Since this DCI had fired a lot of people who had a lot of friends, the inevitable happened. Instead of just letting it ride, a notice came out of headquarters requesting help in finding the strawberry culprit. The next morning, someone had posted a printed response in every elevator at headquarters claiming responsibility for taking and eating the strawberries. It was signed "The Phantom." Rumor has it that the DCI went ballistic, but someone must have talked him out of a broader investigation, and the incident died out.

It was also during this headquarters stopover that I learned one of the best-kept secrets in Washington (that is, it was until it was blown in a book about Robert Hanssen)—the favorite hangout for FBI and Washington-based CIA operatives (as well as KGB agents) was a place called The Good Guys.[1] The dancing girls couldn't exactly be called strippers, since they began their routines totally nude, except for a garter belt on one leg where adoring patrons would stuff their money. I noticed (from afar) that patrons typically began by stuffing $1 bills into the dancers' garter belts. After a few drinks, they upped the ante to $5. I was there a couple of times, each at the insistence of either an FBI or CIA colleague. It was a dimly lit place, and the food was only average. But what ambiance! CIA business was not discussed there as far as I could tell, and that was a good thing.

I spent barely one year in the desk assignment, but it proved vital to renewing contacts and giving me experience in headquarters' end of espionage. I quickly discovered what most operations people learn—that I much preferred overseas work to headquarters work. I just didn't like the bureaucracy involved in headquarters assignments. But I do have to say that the Agency is streamlined and efficient in comparison with any other branch of government.

1. Adrian Havill, *The Spy Who Stayed Out in the Cold: The Secret Life of FBI Double Agent Robert Hanssen* (New York: St. Martin's Press, 2001), pp. 101–102.

89

EIGHT

A CHANGE OF VENUE

1980–1983

Once word got out that I was available for another field assignment, I didn't have to wait long for an excellent opportunity. I heard that the Agency was encouraging rotational assignments to areas outside of one's area of expertise, so I looked for an assignment that would enable me to broaden my experience. When asked if I would like a European assignment, I discussed it with my wife, and we decided that we liked the idea of going to Europe. It would be a change of pace from the Far East— and I thought of sipping wine along the Via Veneto or eating canapés in a Paris bistro.

Yup, a European assignment sounded great.

I wound up in a European assignment all right, in the southern tier where terrorism was a significant threat, and where Americans were regular targets. But it was a chance to get experience outside my area—and the chief there wanted an Asian specialist to work with the country's growing Asian population. It turned out to be a terrific professional experience in which I earned the first of two rapid promotions.

Little did I know that a few months after I began this assignment I would be spending New Year's Eve under a table with another man. Here's how it happened.

I had formed a good relationship with our technical experts— something that all good case officers learn is of tremendous value early in their careers. These are the guys with the toys that give us tremendous capabilities in running our operational intelligence agents. They provide the basics—secret writing, covert communications, microdot photography, locks and picks, listening devices, and more. Without them, we would be hamstrung in collecting our intelligence.

Upon arrival, I learned that they were planning an operation to retrieve a state-of-the-art listening device that had been planted in a dining-room table of a senior officer of a hostile intelligence service. After some relatively good audio production (known as a "take"), the device had gone dead. Our headquarters understandably wanted to retrieve the device to both analyze why it went off the air, and also to prevent the opposition from retrieving it. As planning progressed, the technicians asked if I'd like to go along. Of course, I wanted to go. My mission would be to act as an additional pair of eyes—and it was unwritten policy that in all entry operations a case officer had to go in with the tech. This was to ensure that case officers planned these operations well, since they had to take the same risk as the techs.

As we planned the operation, we included all the normal activities: ascertaining when the target would be gone, putting countersurveillance out on the street to warn us if trouble was coming, getting two-way radios ready, and assembling the tools we would need. As in all well-run, important operations, we decided to rehearse things to avoid preventable problems. Our headquarters approved the plan, with the caveat that, once we got to the target apartment's door to determine what type of key we needed for an undetected entry, we would return to headquarters to discuss the operation before attempting the actual retrieval.

We decided that the New Year's holiday would provide an excellent opportunity for our rehearsal. We learned that the target and his wife would be out New Year's Eve, so that evening we began our first reconnaissance. We waited until dark, and when our countersurveillance determined that the target and his wife had departed, the tech and I, admittedly nervous, made our entry into the target's apartment house. So far, so good.

We got as far as the door, noted the type of lock, and made a wax impression of the keyhole. Next I saw the tech take a lock pick out of his pocket and open the door. As I protested, he went right into the dark apartment. I couldn't let him go in alone, so I went in, too. We fumbled around looking for the table where the device had been planted. We could use only a small penlight. It wasn't long before my radio squawked, scaring the hell out of us, so I reached over and turned it off. We spent the next three hours under each table in the apartment, lying on our backs, tugging, pulling, and examining.

Finally, with both of us soaking wet with sweat from both the exertion and the tension, we determined that the device was nowhere to be found. We made our way back out, and exited without a trace. By this time, the New Year had come and gone. Our surveillants and our boss were beside themselves with worry that something had happened to us. Like good professionals, however, they stayed off the radios and kept in place in case we needed them. When we got outside, I turned the radio back on and made contact, and we all returned to the rendezvous point. After all the tension, the conversation turned to what the two of us were doing on our backs in the dark on New Year's Eve. I would never live this down.

I also learned from this tech that you have to seize every opportunity, and it makes good sense to go in only once if at all possible. Our headquarters was a little miffed, but I learned that, in operations, the final decision must rest with those taking the risk. As for the listening device, we later found it in a warehouse where the target and his wife had stored the table, which we bought once we had the opportunity.

I also learned from this tour about the value of having good, intelligent children around—and of the necessity to keep them in mind when conducting espionage. Two stories will illustrate this.

Both my daughter and my son knew that I was gone a good bit of the time in the evenings and on weekends, and that I sometimes just plain disappeared for a few days at a time. To date, this had not been a problem. With my five-year-old son, it was simply, "Dad is going to see a man about a horse," and that stopped all the questions. But I'd have to come up with better cover stories after an acquaintance who didn't know what I really did for a living dropped by one evening. My son answered the door.

"Is your dad in?" he inquired.

"Oh no, Dad's out seeing a man about a horse," my son replied, adding, "Dad goes out a lot to see that man about a horse but he hasn't bought one yet." We later laughed it off, but I did begin to explain my frequent absences a little more honestly.

The second story illustrates the value of including your family in your activities whenever you can. On one occasion, headquarters had been interested in establishing contact with a senior intelligence officer from the Eastern Bloc for some time, but no one had yet been able to establish the contact. We finally learned that the target, as a relatively accomplished tennis player, was signed up to play in the International Open Tennis tournament of this country. This was a big event, and despite the odds against my meeting him this way, I, too, entered the tournament. The first problem came up early—the target and I were seeded in different brackets. Consequently, if we both won we wouldn't meet until the championship round. We also discovered that the target, under strict rules from his host government, showed up just in time to play his matches and left immediately afterward.

We both advanced several rounds until I came up against the top seed in the quarterfinal round. I knew I would not beat this excellent player, and I felt discouraged that after all this time we still hadn't accomplished the one thing we wanted—to get an introduction to the target. My wife and son had attended the tournament to give me support, when we noticed that the target had stayed around to scout out his next opponent. But he had moved off all by himself, and an approach directly to him would have alerted him, and others, of our interest. As I mused about how to solve this dilemma, my wife and I noticed that our son was playing in the dirt, enthralled with a handful of old rusty screws he had dug up. Unbeknownst to us, my son had wandered off and had gone up to the target, handed the handful of rusty screws to him with the admonition "Don't lose these," and went off to dig elsewhere. The target was absolutely in stitches and later came up to us after our son had returned and introduced himself. Still laughing, he handed my son back the screws, saying, "You see, I did as you asked—I didn't lose your screws." This started a long and productive friendship between the target, his wife, and my family. It turns out the target and his wife could not have children, and the target loved spending time with my son. In spite of our best-laid plans sometimes things just work out on their own.

This target and I ended up spending a lot of time together. He was disenchanted with his government's repression, and we spent a lot of time talking about the internal affairs in his country. He had no doubt after a while about my true affiliation or the purpose of my in-depth questions. It was clear he was wrestling with the idea of accepting a formal recruitment to work for the United States, but we just couldn't quite make the turn to formalize this. We arranged to meet at an island outside the host country to discuss things further. He wanted a vacation and time to consider what he was doing, and I agreed to meet with him. I took my family along so there would be a reason I was there. I saw him in passing the first day, and he told me he was staying at a beach on the other side of the island. He told me he would contact me when he was ready to get together, but after several days I still hadn't heard from him. I fretted and finally decided to look for him. As I approached the beach, I noticed immediately that everyone was nude. The nude lifeguard came up and told me if I was going to wander on that beach, I would have to take off my suit. My God! I tried to explain to the lifeguard that I was only looking for a friend. "Sure, sure—the suit still has to come off," he said. What to do? I removed the suit, and walked out to where the water was waist high. I walked maybe a half mile, and I heard someone yell, "Floyd, I'm up here." It was the target, lying bare-ass naked next to a stunning big-breasted girl who was also naked. And it wasn't his wife.

I walked up said I was glad to see him. He was more than a little sheepish and said, "You know, I was going to call you but I got distracted," which I understood. He introduced me to the woman, and I carried on a conversation as best as I could. As I backed out into the surf to return to my part of the island, he said he'd contact me that evening. He did, and he asked if I would keep our nude-beach encounter between the two of us. I assured him I would, and we began a formal relationship to everyone's benefit. I reported my success back to headquarters omitting certain details, but I couldn't help reporting that we got the bare facts out.

But, as with all my tours, I continued to learn that spies are a different breed and can only be counted on to do the unexpected. Two examples from this tour illustrate my point.

I had inherited an excellent denied-area agent from an officer who had in fact recruited the agent and turned him over to me to finalize the recruitment, and then to run him to produce intelligence. (A turnover is a change in the officer who deals with the agent.) As with many good agents, this one didn't want to be turned over to another case officer. But the case also demonstrated the importance of listening to the original recruiting case officer's opinions. We had reported the agent's reluctance to headquarters regularly, and we had to finally argue that the recruiting case officer nonetheless believed the agent would take the turnover. "He'll do it, he'll do it," the case officer insisted.

The case officer believed that all we needed was a little drama, so he built the following scenario: he would tell the agent that I, the new case officer, was Mr. Big back in Washington and that I had been sent out especially to work with him. The case officer assured the agent that, although I had been reading the reporting, I had no idea of his identity.

Further, the case officer managed to arrange for the agent to meet me accidentally on several occasions at large diplomatic receptions. So the stage was set: As far as the agent knew, I was there to work with him, but didn't yet know who he actually was. The agent loved the drama even though he still maintained he would not work for another case officer.

Finally one evening the original case officer picked the agent up and told him that tonight was the night he would meet Mr. Big. The agent protested mightily, but agreed, for the sake of the case officer, to meet me. Yet, the agent insisted he was going to tell me that he would not work for another case officer.

So we set up the scenario on the evening in question. I was to open the door to my hotel room, see the agent, and feign absolute astonishment that this man was our agent in place. The knock came, I opened the door, feigned stunned surprise, and yelled, "It's you? It can't be!" The agent loved it. He left the other case officer standing outside, took some sheets of paper out of his coat pocket, and proceeded to give me an important top secret report he had just taken out of his embassy. I had to remind him that we needed to bring the other officer in from the hallway.

In short, the turnover went exceptionally well, just as the recruiting officer had promised. I never forgot the importance of having the original case officer design his agent's turnover—or the importance of adding a touch of drama to keep the agent engaged. Most agents thrive on the thrill of espionage and will agree to be turned over to keep that thrill alive.

This particular agent was outstanding. He was loyal to the United States, and we became very close. As his assignment to this host country wound down, headquarters and I agonized over our ultimate goal—to have the agent back in his home country equipped with communications equipment. We wanted him to report secret information from inside the very government to which our access was denied.

We decided this agent was indeed inside material and began the laborious project: training him to operate the equipment; dead drops, in which an agent drops materials in a predetermined spot for later retrieval by a case officer so the two parties won't be spotted together; and other procedures. We were down to the last stages, and I was ready to pick up a practice dead drop from the agent. All was going well, the "cache is ready" sign was out, and no one was in sight. But just after I retrieved the material, my agent popped out of some bushes and shouted, "You were right, we could do this. You found it and got it." I had to report this, and headquarters was aghast. No amount of explaining by the agent—that he just wanted to watch the pickup in person—would make any difference. Despite his promise that he would never do that kind of thing again, wiser heads prevailed, and we decided we couldn't risk running him inside. (To run an agent is to work with him clandestinely—that is, to meet him and obtain the secrets he has access to—all out of public view.)

I also learned that a good agent, like a good case officer, must be where he is supposed to be. In this case, I had been running an agent for nearly a year, and the two of us had to conduct our meetings very discreetly. I had acquired a safehouse for this operation by getting a local citizen to provide me with a key to his apartment, and then leave the apartment at predetermined times. The safehouse was in a large, tall building in a residential neighborhood. The agent had a key to the apartment, as I did, and we met regularly and successfully in this venue. The outside air was cold and snow was on the ground when one of the largest earthquakes to ever hit the area—over 8 on the Richter scale—hit us. It destroyed many houses, split the major hotel in town up to the sixth floor, and damaged nearly every building in town. Now I had a problem: Our safehouse was on the 33rd floor, we had a regularly scheduled meeting the morning immediately after the quake, and aftershocks were still occurring. My boss argued that we abort the meeting, saying the agent wouldn't show up, but I convinced him that I should go. Something in my gut told me this guy was different.

I went through my normal countersurveillance procedures and left our facility by taxi to go to a busy downtown location. I went shopping for several hours, using the store windows to check for surveillance and looking outside while inside the stores to identify anyone as a possible hostile surveillant. I made a few purchases to appear normal to anyone who might be following me. I next took a subway back to the outskirts of town where I had lunch. From there I took another taxi back to the vicinity of the safehouse and walked the rest of the way.

When I arrived in the courtyard outside the apartment building, the entire neighborhood was milling around. The earthquake had forced them out of their homes. It was bitter cold, and some of them were burning pieces of furniture in the yard just to stay warm. I began to think my boss was right.

Only minutes away from our appointed meeting time, I looked up across the courtyard just in time to see the agent go into the building and start up the stairs. I waited a few minutes and followed him into the building. The elevator was out of service, so I walked up 33 flights of stairs in nearly total darkness because there was no electricity. Wet with sweat, I made the entry and greeted the agent. We congratulated each other on taking our responsibility seriously enough to make the meeting. We then started the debriefing process.

Suddenly the earth began to shake—an aftershock! We lost our footing and both of us fell to the floor. But we kept our wits about us. Without a word, we got up, moved expeditiously—ran!—down the 33 flights of stairs. At the bottom we made arrangements to meet elsewhere, and I stayed in the building for another 15 minutes after his departure for security reasons. We both received commendations from headquarters for our dedication. Like any good agents and case officers, we were where we were supposed to be when we were supposed to be there—earthquake be damned!

Never forget that the vast majority of CIA spies are loyal and dedicated, and believe in the ultimate good of our work. In one case, one of my agents gave his all and died on the job. He wasn't one of our top agents, but he was the kind of steady reporter our business is built on. He came from a region where we had little coverage so his opinions and comments were of some interest. He was a scholarly fellow who was well known in literary circles. I took him over from another officer, and we developed a good bond. As with many good agents, he continually looked for an opportunity to do more. Almost every meeting with him ended with the comment, "We gotta keep the communist bastards at bay, don't we?" Since I often had to travel to meet him, we had several designated sites where we would both show up if either instituted the emergency-meeting signal. Late in my tour I got an urgent signal that he desired a meeting. I made my normal trip to the site, taking a considerable amount of time to ensure I was clean before making the meeting.

When I arrived at the site, an elderly distinguished-looking woman was waiting. It was our agent's wife. She emotionally thanked me for coming, and told me that our agent, her husband, was dead. He had suffered a heart attack several days before and died on the street. She was aware of his work on our behalf, and of the emergency meeting arrangements. I spent a long time with this elegant and graceful woman. I asked her what we could do to help, and she replied, "Nothing, I just wanted you to know that he's dead—and that he was proud of what you were all doing together." It choked me up, and I managed to make arrangements to see her in several weeks after the funeral. With the concurrence of headquarters,

I saw her one more time and read to her a letter from the director thanking her husband for his service. I did explain to her that she would be unable to keep the letter for security reasons, and she understood. I was also able to get her to accept, reluctantly, a small stipend as a gesture of our appreciation.

In another case, a good case officer's judgment came to naught. Elections were coming up in our host country, and it appeared to most of us that the vote would go against the government that had been friendly to U.S. policy for over a decade. Our agents were reporting that a revolution was in the air, which would likely result in a decidedly anti-American administration. Unfortunately, both our ambassador and our chief failed to see the writing on the wall, and they were adamant that the current administration would be victorious. We held several meetings on the subject, and our chief would finish each meeting by arguing, "You people don't really see the bigger picture. You don't have the contacts that the ambassador and I do." True, we didn't have the contacts the chief and the ambassador had—contacts with a huge vested interest in the status quo. Finally, we received a request from our headquarters to predict the election results as best we could so they could send a report to policymakers in Washington.

So we made one last check two days before the election by dividing up areas of the city and suburbs and visiting political rallies of both the incumbent and the leftist parties. I went to a suburb that typically voted for the incumbent party, and I was stunned to find that the incumbent rally was sparsely attended and without enthusiasm. Conversely, the leftist party rally was crammed with emotionally charged people from the neighborhood who were enthusiastically chanting slogans.

We held a big meeting the next morning and asked for everyone's thoughts. Those who had gone to the rallies found the same thing I found. The chief was getting aggravated, so he called for a show of hands to predict who would win the election, and this would determine the report we would send to headquarters. The vote was unanimous that we were going to see a change of government. That did it for the chief. After a severe tongue lashing, he again told us that we didn't see the big picture. With that, he drafted our "official" position—that the election might be close, but that the incumbent party would win.

On election day, the incumbent party took their worst beating ever, and a government hostile to the United States took power. Headquarters chastised us several days later for missing the call so badly. I vowed that if I were ever in a senior management position, I would listen to the officers who make their living on the streets.

After the election, everything changed for the worse. The new leftist government immediately pulled police support from our building, and this was during a large anti-American demonstration. A number of us were inside our building on Friday night when the protests began. Thousands of people marched and demonstrated right outside, throwing bottles and eggs, and blaring hate propaganda from megaphones. It was scary: we were really trapped inside. Given the way things were going, we were preparing to burn and destroy our documents. While we had started planning for trouble after the election, we now found ourselves stuffing documents into bags, into shredders, and generally hunkering down. Meanwhile, the new prime minister and his wife led the march and taunted us by megaphone. Both, by the way, had been educated in the United States, and both of their children had recently been to the U.S. Embassy to have their U.S. passports renewed. We made it through the night, but this marked the beginning of many difficult years with the new regime, a time when the specter of terrorism was raised throughout the region. Over the next six months, our cars were firebombed, two policemen guarding our building were shot, and several U.S. military personnel were killed in a bombing. And, shortly after my departure, our defense attaché at the embassy was assassinated.

A CHANGE OF VENUE

Shortly after the election, my wife experienced a terrible incident. Our car had diplomatic license plates that easily identified us as Americans. One evening as we entertained guests, my wife decided to drive up the hill to buy some things for dinner. It was dusk, and visibility was poor. As she returned home, a motorcyclist tried to pass her on the right, and he hit her a glancing blow. What should have been a minor incident escalated. Fortunately, my wife called to tell me she was in trouble. By now a crowd surrounded the car and was rocking it back and forth. I called the police station nearby, and they promised to send a car out immediately. A friend then drove me to my wife—and of course, the police never showed up. After we skidded right up to the car, I got out, pushed my wife to the passenger side, and accelerated into the crowd, scattering them out of the way. We made it out, but we avoided that area afterward. If you've ever been surrounded by an angry crowd that was trying to overturn your car, you'll know the terror my wife and I felt. Unfortunately, things would only get worse.

I was assisting an agent working inside the communist bloc who had escaped hot pursuit by his own intelligence service. The agent came out several times to meet a headquarters officer, and I was the support officer on the ground. Part of my duty was to help plan an escape route if the agent ever had to flee his own country. In this assignment, I traveled to the agent's country, learned the trains and roads, and devised an escape plan. I opted for a route with several checkpoints that would allow us to intercept the agent at a specific point, whisk him out of the country, and get him to safety in the United States. I didn't think we'd actually use this particular route, but I devised the best plan I could.

And it was a good thing I did. Several years later, we received an emergency message from headquarters that our agent was in flight, so we activated the plan. This was exciting. We had a good lock on both the agent's travel and on the pursuit team, we made the pickup at the designated spot, and got the agent to safety.

Under the new leftist government, local intelligence and police would no longer help us in our struggle against regional terrorist organizations. In one instance, we acquired some excellent and disturbing intelligence indicating that a Libyan hit team—a group of thugs who engaged in officially sanctioned murder—had entered the country to assassinate the U.S. Ambassador. We had acquired a photo of one of the reputed team members from the reporting agent, and we learned that the hit team would operate out of a bar downtown, the Red Lion. We also knew approximately when the team planned to assemble in the bar. Our deputy—an officer who had earned the Intelligence Star, the Agency's highest decoration for valor, for his work behind enemy lines in Laos—was a good friend of mine. He went to the local police and reported the information. They worked out an agreement—if our deputy would go to the Red Lion at 8:00 that evening, the police would arrive shortly thereafter. The deputy would finger the terrorists for the police, who would then arrest them.

The deputy asked if I would help him with the identification and arrest. Understanding his request for backup, I agreed. As we prepared to leave the office, he called me in, opened his safe drawer, and asked me, "Which piece would you like to pack?" I chose a Smith and Wesson 6-inch stainless-steel revolver. He picked up a 14-shot 9-mm Browning automatic. We stuck the pieces in our waistbands and headed for the bar. We arrived about half an hour early, as planned, to get the lay of the land before any action started.

The bar was almost empty, just a few patrons and a couple of hookers. We sat down, ordered a couple of beers, and sat back. After a couple of sips, I noticed that we'd sat near a corner of the bar, which was quite a distance from the door. It seemed like a safe place to wait for the Libyans (and, we hoped, police) to arrive. Right on schedule, four gangly Libyans entered the bar. Two carried heavy duffel bags, which possibly contained weapons.

The Libyans sat on stools at the bar, between us and the door. Suddenly feeling uncomfortable, I whispered to the deputy that things just didn't look right. He agreed, but suggested that we hang tight and wait for the police. By 8:30, it was obvious that the police weren't coming. Meanwhile, the Libyans kept looking at us, and I told the deputy that I thought we should get out of the bar. He agreed, and then motioned to two of the prostitutes to join us for a beer. They sat down with us, I ordered four beers, and after a few swigs, I invited them back to our room for a little fun. They agreed, and we escorted the women to the door, keeping them between us and the four Libyans, two of whom were now within arm's reach of their duffel bags. After we exited the bar, the deputy gave the hookers a couple of big bills, bid them goodnight, and we proceeded to vacate the area with all due haste. We had been set up, and the local police had no intention of helping us.

The good news that we later learned from our agent is that the four Libyans aborted their mission because they knew we were onto them. I never felt heroic about the incident, but I felt pretty good that we thwarted the Libyan's plot to assassinate our ambassador. I felt pretty good about making it out of that bar alive, too.

In another story of courage in the line of duty, one officer got a lead to meet a lieutenant colonel in Libya, one of our priority terrorist target countries. The officer found the home where this colonel was to stay for the next two or three days. Our officer had secured headquarters' permission to determine by reconnaissance if we could provide enough security to send our officer into the home to attempt to recruit the colonel to work against his own government. We knew we could get close, and we did our homework and set up several radio surveillance points to alert us to any signs of unfriendly cohorts in the area. The officer asked if I would drive him up to look around the area, and I agreed. Our instructions from headquarters were very specific: "Under no circumstances attempt the recruitment without prior additional headquarters approval."

I was not surprised when I picked up our officer and he laid two loaded 9-mm automatics on the seat between us. We drove up into the area, confirmed via radio that our trial surveillants were in place, and drove up to the house in question. The officer turned to me and asked, "We've come this far—why don't I just go up, knock on the door, ask if the colonel is there, and if so, set up a follow-up meeting?"

While his proposal made me nervous, I understood his reasoning. Someone was eventually going to have to take the risk, so I agreed and made him assure me that he would remain in my immediate sight. Sticking the 9-mm pistol into his waistband, he went right up to the front door.

I could see everything. He rang the bell, a young lady appeared, he said a few words, and a man, obviously our target colonel, came to the door. I could see them exchange a few words, and then our officer nodded his head and went into the house. I immediately called our surveillance team on the radio and told them to stand by, that we had launched and that we needed to maintain radio silence at all costs. I then chambered a round into my automatic, laid it on my lap, glued my eyes to the door, and dripped huge beads of sweat.

Half an hour later, our man was still in the house. Just as I radioed surveillance to proceed to the area, telling them I was going in, the door opened and our man came out. He shook the colonel's hand and came back to the car. I could only ask him, "What the hell did you go into the house for?" "I thought I might only have one chance to make our pitch—so I took it," he replied. The colonel turned down our recruitment pitch, and headquarters was most displeased with both of us.

The most difficult and potentially fatal incident of my entire career followed shortly thereafter. It occurred during the ill-fated hostage rescue attempt at Desert One in 1980, during the Iranian hostage crisis. I had been working very hard—as had many of our officers in many locations—and our primary intelligence mission was to locate where the hostages taken from the U.S. Embassy in

Tehran were being held, so they could be rescued. I was interviewing a hundred people a day from those who were streaming out of Iran seeking safety—all with the goals of getting information about the hostages and putting an agent back into the country to report on the crisis in real time. It wasn't unlikely that the high profile I would acquire from this would lead to the Iranian Intelligence Service—the Ministry of State Security—identifying me as a CIA officer.

I managed to recruit an exceptionally brave and knowledgeable Iranian citizen, who agreed to my proposal to go back inside and help us locate the hostages. He was well educated and well motivated to help us. He had seen Ayatollah Khomeini destroy his country's gains toward modernization. He made a number of trips back inside Iran on our behalf, but after many trips and several months, the tension was beginning to show. I was meeting him late at night in a park outside of town. He developed a facial tick from the pressure and danger, and pretty soon both of us were nervous wrecks, but he provided us with exceptionally useful information about events inside Iran. He also provided information that helped us locate the American hostages and proved helpful designing Eagle Claw, the Iran hostage rescue attempt.

I could block out of my mind most thoughts about the danger we faced, and I was already taking normal security measures. I never took the same route to or from the office, I never came or went at the same time, and I avoided any routine patterns, whether I was going to the gym, playing tennis, or going to church. I was *very* cautious. I was also training to run a marathon, as was one of the embassy counselors, and we varied our training route and time for security reasons as well.

Then, early one morning as we were returning from a 12-mile training run, we came around a turn and headed uphill toward my house. We spotted, perhaps 100 yards away, a man in a turban and gown lying against a bank and aiming a rifle at my house. It scared the hell out of me. This was about the time my wife got up for her morning coffee, and all I could think of was that this SOB was going to kill someone in my family. I yelled to my partner, "Get to my house and take care of my family!" And I screamed bloody murder to the bastard aiming a rifle at my house.

I obviously scared him, and he got up and started running away. I closed my distance to him within 50 yards and was gaining ground. Suddenly, he scrambled up the bank, and a Volkswagen pickup truck with three people in turbans and gowns in the bed appeared. They grabbed him and made their escape.

I managed to get the license number and color of the pickup, and I got a good look at the guy. So we went to the local police with the description of the vehicle and the man with the rifle. They promised to check out our story. Several days later, we received a written report that said, "There is no such vehicle or license number in country." I can't say we were surprised, given the political direction the country had taken. But this did leave us, and me in particular, in a difficult situation. We knew that I had been targeted for assassination. We didn't report most of the details to headquarters, at my request. My chief immediately offered me the opportunity to depart country. However, I felt then, and still do today, that you simply cannot give in to terrorism. I told the chief that I preferred to stay for the remainder of my tour—I had a year yet to go. I pointed out that if the terrorists who attempted to kill me learned that I fled the country, they would simply try again with another officer. He agreed and thanked me. Later, when I returned to my office, a revolver and a box of bullets—obviously from my deputy's collection—were lying on my desk. I picked the pistol up, and it never left my side for the remainder of my tour.

That still left us with a problem—what to do about the Volkswagen pickup and the men in it? Then, one of our officers asked if I had a spare hundred dollars or two so he could ask one of our former agents in the police to check things out. So I gave him the money and license number. Two weeks later, we received a note from the former agent that the vehicle and occupants were no longer in country and would pose no further risk to me or anyone else. We didn't ask any questions.

I had to tell my wife about the episode, and I asked if she and the kids wanted to return home early while I finished my tour. She refused, and stayed with me through the end of my tour. It was a tense period, as things continued to deteriorate in the country. Six of our cars were blown up, two servicemen were killed in a bombing at a bar frequented by the U.S. military, and a policeman was shot guarding our embassy. For my part, I redoubled my personal security efforts. I changed my routes and times of activities daily. I often waited until the last minute to decide what to do, and I never accepted invitations to functions in restricted areas for the rest of my year.

The U.S. Embassy in Beirut was bombed at this time, and it struck us like a bolt of thunder. The Agency's national intelligence officer for the Near East, Robert Ames, was killed, along with several other Agency personnel. I had spent several days with Mr. Ames before his death discussing our work against targets in the Mideast, and I was devastated by our nation's loss of this fine and highly respected officer. Additionally, I was close friends with two of the slain officers, and I knew two others fairly well. This wasn't the first time I lost a friend in the line of duty, and it wouldn't be the last. This is one thing that you *never* get used to.

As with my other tours, we also had some lighter moments. In one instance, I was using the car of a local national support agent for many of my operational meetings, particularly after the attempt on my life. I kept the car far away from my residence to keep it clean. Late one afternoon, I had taken my normal surveillance detection route around town en route to picking up the car, which I had parked in a neighborhood slightly outside of town (I never parked it in the same area twice for security). It was dusk and it was getting harder for me to see things when I was about two blocks away from where I had parked the car. Suddenly, as I looked up, I saw my car being driven away. After everything else that had happened to me, I was incredulous. Surely, it couldn't have been my car. I searched the neighborhood in increasingly wide concentric circles looking for my car. Did I park it somewhere else? All sorts of scenarios swirled through my head, and I finally called the deputy and told him that my operational car had been stolen. He was also incredulous, and he asked me a lot of what I thought were silly and insulting questions like, "Are you sure you parked in that neighborhood?" "No one would have stolen your car—did you give a key to anyone else?" and, the closer, "By any chance have you been drinking for lunch, and maybe just can't remember where you really left it?"

That did it. I went home, but I didn't sleep. Fortunately the next morning I received a message from my agent telling me that a woman in the neighborhood had seen the vehicle parked overnight and called the police, who then called him and asked if he knew his vehicle was parked in that neighborhood. He was well trained and told the police that yes, he had parked it there and took a taxi home because he had drunk too much. He told the police that he would retrieve the car immediately, which he did. It was *my agent* who took my car, and he did it for my security. Later that morning, I marched triumphantly into the deputy's office and told him the details. He just waved me away, but I felt exonerated.

And sometimes funny things can happen in the midst of an operation. No matter what claims are made about our many advances in how we create, duplicate, disseminate, and destroy documents, we still make tremendous blunders on occasion. In this instance, I needed to rent a car for my operation. I had all the alias documents I needed, but just as I was ready to hand over my driver's license, I noticed that it was valid only for the operation of farm equipment. I pulled the license back, sputtered something to the clerk, and semi-gracefully said that I didn't need a car after all.

Later I discovered that I wasn't the only one with this error on their alias documentation. Things eventually got cleared up, but more than a few technical document experts were aggravated at me for making this an issue. But I did feel that this mistake needed to be brought to everyone's attention to correct the error and to get people to pay a little more attention to the details of our work.

I guess shit happens even when you're well trained, well documented, and well prepared. I had one episode during this tour that nearly blew my cover. I was working under an alias and a false identity outside the capital city and had just registered into a hotel. All went well until later that afternoon, when the manager stopped me in the lobby and told me how ironic it was that my ambassador had just checked in and wanted to invite me to cocktails and dinner. It was a serious problem because the ambassador already knew me by my true name. Fortunately, I left a message for the ambassador in my alias, stating I was looking forward to seeing him, but that I had another engagement. For the next several days, as I completed my business I took great care in coming and going from the hotel to avoid running into him.

In another funny episode I had been seeing a communist bloc party official for several months in an attempt to recruit him. It was difficult to get him alone, since his country's regulations required its officials to travel in pairs—to prevent the type of activity I was engaged in. Finally, he suggested to me at one cocktail reception that he was going out on his own to deliver some goods, and that he could stop by briefly at my home and chat with me alone. This was a breakthrough, and good news indeed. I knew that he would be coming in around dinnertime, so I had only a brief window of time to give him room to maneuver.

At about 6:00 in the evening, I saw his vehicle drive up. But as he got out and started toward the house, I noticed two other officials coming in with him. I knew immediately that somehow he hadn't managed to get out on his own. I opened the door, and he quickly and loudly said, "We're here for dinner as you suggested." The other two officials nodded and said how pleased they were to have been invited to our home. We really did have a problem, since we had no dinner planned nor enough food in stock to pull this off.

Nonetheless, my wife and I welcomed them graciously. My wife kept them entertained with drinks and a videotape of the first space shuttle landing (no tap-dancing!). I dashed out the back of the house and drove at breakneck speed to a little local restaurant. Running out of breath, I asked the proprietor what he had immediately available. He told me he was grilling a bunch of ribs for a large party. I pulled a wad of bills out of my pocket, and told him I would take them all. Given the substantial profit he was likely to make, he was more than willing. He and his staff bundled everything up, including some vegetables and salads, and helped me carry it all to the car. I sped off again at reckless speed, parked behind my house, carried the ribs in, and put them in the oven.

I walked back into the living room and announced, "Gentlemen, if you'll excuse us for a couple minutes, we'll go into the kitchen and finish preparing dinner." With that, my wife and I scurried about in the kitchen and produced a wonderful meal for the guests, but with all the nervous tension in my stomach, I could hardly eat. Oddly enough, the party official never asked how we had been able to prepare this meal for the extra unexpected guests.

In another memorable moment, I was sent off to oversee our efforts to thwart a hijacking in Malta. The airplane, with a number of U.S. citizens aboard, was stranded in a country with which we had no diplomatic relations. Consequently, it required the presence of an intelligence officer who had a reason to be in country. We noted that an international tennis tournament was scheduled to begin shortly after the hijacked aircraft landed. Since I was a noted player, I went into the country in alias and signed up to play in the tournament so I could be there to assist in our efforts against the hijackers. So far, so good. I registered at the club and went to play a few practice rounds. Then I went back into the clubhouse—a magnificent edifice built by the British during their reign. I took a locker, undressed, and walked into the shower area. To my amazement, a large sign on the shower-room door said, "Gentlemen: No boys under 12 years of age allowed with you in the shower." I showered pretty quickly, and on my way out asked the club manager about the sign. "Yes, sir," he replied, "we've had a devil of a time since the Libyans took over the club." I took my remaining showers during the tournament at my hotel. Fortunately, we were able to end the hijacking with good diplomatic negotiations and saved the American passengers.

While this was one of my most productive tours, two related management incidents are worthy of mentioning here. The first occurred about halfway through my tour. In this case, a very senior officer came out on a visit, and a small number of our operations officers, myself included, were invited to our chief's home to meet and talk to this officer. When he arrived, it was obvious that he had already had a wee bit too much of the local barley. Nonetheless, we had a relatively good dinner, with engaging conversation. However, right after dinner, the senior officer informed our host, "I would like to get these young officers together for a discussion." So we all reassembled in the living room. This senior officer then spoke on the meaning of the United States Constitution. While alternately talking and dribbling his drink onto his suit, he began, "I want to make sure that all of you engaged in espionage understand your obligation to the United States Constitution. . . ." This dragged on for nearly 30 minutes. I looked to my left, and two of my colleagues on the couch had dozed off. Our chief, mindful of the fact that he worked for this fellow, remained the only attentive one in the room.

Then the real action began. Into the room bounded the chief's over-sexed male dog. The dog ran straight to our visitor and promptly began humping his leg. It was wild, with the officer attempting to continue his lecture about the Constitution, while the chief attempted unsuccessfully to kick the dog off the poor fellow's vibrating leg. I just had to wake my colleagues for the show.

But we had not seen the last of this same dog and his companion mutt. One time when our chief was on a visit back to Washington, I happened over to his house to check on things. As I arrived, I noticed the servant trying to round up both critters into the house. I asked him if I could help, and he replied that I could, since he needed to get the dogs into the house for the phone call. Incredulous, I went inside with one of the two mutts to watch the servant hold them up to the phone one at a time. The chief had called long distance to talk to the dogs. Now I love dogs as much as the next person, but . . .

We had one of the most memorable senior management experiments at this time, during the Reagan years. Bill Casey, a man of action, believed that the CIA had grown too timid and was determined to do something about it. For some time he had been looking for a new Deputy Director for Operations (DDO), the head of the clandestine service. And, despite the fact that there were many qualified and willing candidates, he decided to bring in an outsider—with disastrous results. In early 1981, he selected a man who was a total outsider and moved him into a position in the Directorate of Administration. Casey was determined. As Bob Woodward describes it in his book, "Casey was afflicted with the disease . . . called 'I'll freshen up this place by bringing in my own people.'"[1] Now he wanted to move the man over to be the head of the clandestine service (the DO), despite substantial opposition to the appointment by the intelligence professionals. That, of course, made Bill Casey even more convinced it was the right move.

On the morning of May 11, 1981, Casey announced the appointment. The joke that made the rounds this time was that Casey was turning the CIA into a version of the TV show *Fantasy Island*, in which anyone could have whatever job they wanted. To his credit, the officer tried hard early on, but he didn't understand

1. Bob Woodward, *Veil: The Secret Wars of the CIA, 1981–1987* (New York: Simon & Schuster, 1987), p. 77.

the system, and he made lots of promises everyone knew he couldn't keep, such as more pay for case officers, more money for human spying, and so forth. Everyone tried hard to be supportive, but I knew of no one who thought things would work. Additionally, in typical Casey fashion, he had not consulted anyone in Congress. And, although the Deputy Director for Operations appointment didn't need congressional confirmation, the congressional leadership was not happy about finding out about this important appointment after the fact. A headline in the *Washington Star*, "Casey Picks Amateur for Most Sensitive CIA Job," written by a venerated CIA veteran, didn't help.[2] And the press play got worse over the next month.

But adverse press and legal issues continued until the officer finally felt compelled to resign. Casey then named a longtime professional to the job, and business went back to normal.[3]

2. Cord Meyer, "Casey Picks Amateur for Most Sensitive CIA Job," *Washington Star*, May 15, 1981, editorial page.
3. Woodward, *Veil*, pp. 140–147.

NINE

INTO MANAGEMENT

1983–1985

I was greatly pleased when I was reassigned to the territory in Asia I had come to love. I was also pleased to get another overseas assignment instead of having to work back at headquarters. I signed on to be a spy, I loved being a spy, and I could really only be a spy overseas.

Not long after I arrived I found myself back in the middle of the action. A team of assassins from North Korea had just killed a large official delegation of South Korean officials in a terrible bombing in Rangoon, Burma. They had planted claymore mines in the ceiling of a memorial to the father of Burmese independence, Aung San. When the delegation arrived to lay a wreath, the North Koreans detonated the claymores, killing seven senior South Korean officials, including two presidential advisors and four cabinet members. I was asked to fly into Rangoon to see what we could do to help apprehend the perpetrators and assist the host government.

I have seen a significant amount of damage from bombs and terrorists, but nothing prepared me for this carnage. At the bombing site, police and local officials were still picking up pieces of human flesh. By the time I arrived, local authorities had apprehended two of the assassins. One was killed trying to escape, and the second was found swimming in the Irrawaddy River, trying to make his escape. As police approached, he held a grenade against his chest and detonated it. Somehow he survived, and eventually confessed. Rumors abounded afterward that the police had extracted a confession by first addicting the survivor to heroin, and then withdrawing it. But to my knowledge, this has never been confirmed. We could do little to assist, other than provide intelligence leads for follow-up, so I returned and began my next tour.

Again, I was lucky to be where I was when a lot of action was underway. We had a large and successful number of operations against communist bloc officials, including the KGB. We also had a number of excellent officers, including several of the best female case officers I've seen.

In one operation, a female officer was doing an outstanding job collecting biographic data on a senior KGB official from a minority group in the Soviet Union. When compiled with some excellent research by headquarters, her research told us that the Bolsheviks had executed the officer's father during the Russian Revolution. We learned that the officer had experienced—and resented—significant persecution throughout his life for being a member of a minority group. The KGB official commented frequently that he was jealous of the pay and perks that Americans overseas accrued. In all, he was an attractive and vulnerable target.

Our officer focused on this target for a little over a year. Then, as her regular transfer time approached, we began thinking of how to effect a turnover to attempt to complete the recruitment. But as time wound down, we also discovered that the KGB officer had fallen head-over-heels for our officer—a difficult situation to manage. When she discovered this, she properly reported it to management. The KGB officer had been calling her late at night, talking about how much he wanted to see her, and how he missed their frequent meetings and conversations. Things got even more difficult to manage when he began to show up and knock on her door late at night, wanting to get to know her better. This was something that none of us wanted to have happen. "Hell, he wants to get in my pants," she said, "only in his dreams."

Fortunately, we had a second officer who was also in regular contact with this KGB officer and would occasionally see him at a local club, where they would have a beer or two and chat. Finally, the KGB officer's amorous advances toward our officer became intolerable. So one evening the second officer sidled up to the target and said simply, "Look, stop pestering [our officer] with your late-night visits. It ain't going anywhere." The KGB officer was crestfallen and made one last effort that evening to visit our officer's apartment, where he wailed and cried, begging to be let in. The second officer became concerned and began to walk by the female officer's apartment several times a night. On this particular night, he happened to be walking by when he saw the KGB officer enter the apartment house, and he knew what was up. After waiting several minutes, the second officer went into the apartment house and, as the KGB officer was wailing, tapped him on the shoulder. He scared the guy so much that he never bothered the female officer again. We didn't get the recruitment, but we do take care of our own in the CIA.

While the CIA kept track of the KGB, our Cold War opponent kept good track of us, too. However, they lacked the analytical skills and logic that have made our operations so successful.

On one occasion, I had begun another developmental effort against a KGB officer who was under non-official cover (NOC), and things were going along quite well. We shared a number of lunches, and he and his wife had been dinner guests at our home. As is the normal case, the KGB officer wanted to reciprocate, and told me that he had some very interesting slides to show me. I was curious, and accepted the dinner invitation.

As in many of these cases, the evening began with more than a liberal sprinkling of liquor. An excellent meal was followed with several types of Russian liquors. Finally, he trotted out a slide projector and told me, "I am going to educate you about the realities of life in the Soviet Union." This was followed by a one-hour presentation of slides of the synagogues of the Soviet Union. With each slide, he would proclaim the virtues of religious freedom for the Jews in the Soviet Union. Being a guest, I didn't argue with him and simply said that the pictures were beautiful. With the evening over, my wife and I went home—confused as could be about why he had put on this elaborate show.

I reported the details to headquarters, and we just couldn't make sense of it. I saw the fellow a few more times over the next few months, and each time he would ask, "What did you think of the slides? We treat the Jews very well in the Soviet Union." I did dispute this a couple of times, but it seemed to make no difference, and I never carried the development much further. It wasn't until after the fall of the Berlin Wall, when we acquired a number of KGB files, including my own, that things finally came together. The KGB file reported that I was Jewish. It was based on my defense a few years earlier of the Israeli ambassador, and the fact that I played tennis with him regularly. The file also noted that I had insisted that the Israeli ambassador play in the tennis tournament and, in the spirit of fair play, played as his partner in the tournament. The KGB analysis was that only a Jew would defend another Jew and thus, despite no other information corroborating my religion, concluded that I had to be Jewish. They simply could not overcome their own prejudice. Thus, when the KGB officer reported my development of him—and vice versa—his bureau set the stage for the slide show of synagogues with the belief that it would impress me enough to gain a measure of my sympathy. Later in my career, when I served in Germany, this same information was passed to the East German Intelligence Service, the STASI, who published their data about me in an exposé of the CIA. To the dreaded STASI, I was still Jewish more than a decade later.

Another story involves a Soviet journalist and suspected intelligence officer, whom I met infrequently. He was awestruck by the active red-light and bar district in town and, according to a number of reports, spent a considerable time indulging in the pleasures of both. I never much liked him, but we did have lunch together from time to time.

On one occasion, we were having lunch when the American Veterans of Foreign Wars (VFW) was having its annual convention in town. There is, of course, no more patriotic group in the world. The journalist suggested that we go down to the bar district after lunch because he wanted to visit the convention and write an article on it for his Soviet paper. I asked him, "You aren't going to that group and introducing yourself as a Soviet journalist, are you? You'd have to be nuts!" He was adamant, and I agreed to go as far as the edge of the district with him, hoping to talk him out of this crazy idea.

At the edge of the bar district were an unusually large number of policemen, who mainly discouraged tourists and the inquisitive from going into the area where the convention was taking place. I couldn't talk the KGB journalist out of going into the bar where the convention headquarters was, so I left. I later found out that he had waltzed right into the convention center where some of the lubricated veterans were raising hell, introduced himself, and showed his Soviet press credentials. According to the journalist himself, a number of the veterans proceeded to beat the crap out of him, and unceremoniously threw him out into the street. Steaming, he then approached the local police and demanded that they go back in with him and arrest the perpetrators. The police ignored him. When I saw him several weeks later, he was still steaming—and still bruised. I suggested to him that he had a terrific story to write about his reception. We met occasionally after that, but I was more convinced than ever that he demonstrated none of the good judgment we would expect of an agent.

In one of the most fascinating adventures I've ever taken part in, several of our officers had been in frequent contact with a KGB official. He was intelligent, open-minded, and had shown more than a few signs of vulnerability to recruitment. Things developed over most of a year, and with headquarters' concurrence, we fashioned a recruitment attempt. We planned to have an officer from an adjoining country do the honors due to local sensitivities with the host government.

The KGB officer was an avid swimmer who swam laps at a local club in the early-morning hours when few others were around. Our officer did his bit during one of the KGB fellow's morning swims. We offered a deal he couldn't refuse, including a substantial amount of cash, and the promise of protecting his relationship with us. He initially indicated willingness to consider the offer. Our officer made arrangements to meet again the next day to discuss the final terms. So far, so good. But unbeknownst to us, another Western service was also finalizing a recruitment pitch to the same KGB man, and late that afternoon that service dispatched an officer and made a recruitment pitch to him. They also offered him a substantial amount of cash, and made the same commitment to protecting his work as a spy for them. To say the least, the KGB fellow was both honored and scared.

The upshot was that he decided to report both pitches, and the next evening, the local Soviet Embassy decided to call a press conference and expose the wickedness of the Western intelligence services. But they made a miscalculation. They did indeed hold the press conference, at a major hotel, and they relayed, relatively accurately, the recruitment pitches made by both Western intelligence services. But—not unlike their normal understanding of events in a free-press environment—they never expected the reception they got. There was uproar of laughter and derision; they in fact made fools of themselves. The local press, and in fact several national presses, covered the event with great jocularity. The Soviets never did really understand what had happened to them in their time of indignation. Despite the fact that we didn't get the recruitment, we scored a wonderful propaganda coup, since the event was reported in every major newspaper in every country in the region. We couldn't have planned it better ourselves.

I had the great good fortune that one of the finest case officers I ever met worked for me. I'll call her Julie. She was courageous, intelligent, had excellent language skills, and had a great wit, too. I liked Julie immediately upon her arrival. She had a Ph.D. from a foreign university, but she was one of the greatest pranksters I ever met. And, she retaliated with a vengeance. I had only been in country several weeks more than she had when, one morning I sat down at my desk to read the morning traffic. There, in my in box, was an official community notice with the heading, "The Ambassador's Missing Painting!" The official notice went on to describe the ambassador's great consternation that one of his favorite paintings, *Eastern Justice*, was missing from his home following a large reception the previous weekend. It described a petite oriental lady blindfolded, with the scales of justice in her hand. I could hardly believe the notice. Who would be so crass as to steal a painting from the ambassador's residence? I put the notice in my out basket and made a mental note to mention it at our staff meeting. Then I picked up my coffee cup, looked up, and saw right in front of me—*Eastern Justice* hanging on my wall. I had a near heart attack and, as this officer and the rest of my colleagues collapsed in laughter, realized that I had been had.

Julie was exceptional—and fearless. Late in her tour, we had a terrorist walk-in. He was a Middle Easterner, and he looked exactly like Rasputin, the legendary Russian mystic. With long, shaggy hair and beard, he appeared in a flowing orange robe. Julie was on call the day he walked in, so she went down to meet and debrief him. Shortly afterward, I was called to our chief's office, where he and our chief of operations berated me for allowing a female officer to handle a terrorist. I responded that I saw no difference between risking the life of a female officer versus risking the life of a male officer, and that I considered her as capable as any officer and, frankly, better than many male officers.

Julie continued debriefing the terrorist about a plot to assassinate several members of the CIA in an adjoining country. She left him in the care of a local guard while we checked out as much as we could about his information. What came back confirmed indeed that this fellow had accurate—and disturbing—information about this plot. Although he claimed not to be a part of the plot, he did admit that he was originally in on the planning. We did not want this fellow to go loose, wandering about the country. By this time, he had met me as well as Julie, since we had to ferry messages and instructions back and forth due to the urgency of the information obtained during the debriefing. Consequently, the terrorist could identify both of us as CIA officers.

I was in touch with several officials of the local internal service—both security and counterintelligence officials. I gave them the nuts and bolts of the walk-in, and asked if they could place surveillance on the terrorist when he left our facility (they could not legally arrest him since he had committed no crime in the host country). They did better than that. He was seen being picked up by two officers of the local service. We never asked any questions after that—and I learned only upon my departure that they had detained him until both Julie and I were safely out of the country.

I never forgot the value of having friends in the local service. We had managed to thwart the plot against our officers in another country, and the good relationships we had in the host country protected both Julie and me. I also never forgot how courageous she was and how professionally she handled this as a junior officer. I still maintain that our female case officers are there to do all the jobs we ask of the male officers. Most female CIA officers I've worked with are outstanding and courageous, and would be offended to be asked to stand aside for any reason whatsoever.

But amidst all of this scrutiny, Julie continued to be a great and original prankster. I recall one case of a lead she had developed, a Chinese man with the surname of Hong. She did the usual reporting, cabling information back to headquarters, and discovered that the man's name was really Hung, not Hong. To the great merriment of the troops, and in the hopes of slipping one by the boss, Julie drafted the correction in a cable to headquarters. I was on my toes that day, and her cable, titled "Hong is really Hung," was altered before being sent out, much to the disappointment of Julie and the troops.

In another stunt, Julie went to one of the local live fish markets and had a huge live carp mailed to one of the embassy senior officials on her birthday. The official received a knock on the door and was asked to sign for a big, heavy package. When she took the present into the house and removed the outer wrapping, she found a large carp swimming around in a cellophane bag. I never did learn the fate of that carp, but Julie successfully repeated the prank several times.

In yet another legendary caper, Julie persuaded a number of us to be accomplices in her prank. We had a mutual friend, a female consular officer who, while on a tour of duty, had not seen her husband for nearly a year. Julie learned that the husband was due in country, and that the consular officer was going to the airport to meet him. So our ringleader made arrangements to have a young elephant put inside the official's home while we gathered and awaited the couple's return. Meanwhile, the elephant's handler had his hands full with the elephant, which didn't want to go into the house. The elephant ended up wrapping his trunk around the telephone and electrical wires and pulled them both down. This disabled the couple's air conditioning at a time when temperatures were over 100 degrees. The elephant also left huge deposits of dung on the front porch. The couple returned home, but we didn't jump out and yell "surprise." Boy, were they aggravated, but after some time the consular officer even forgave us.

Julie saved her best for me. To this day, she continues to insist that what occurred was not intentional, but good sources in on the planning of this one tell me otherwise. Our chief asked me to brief and care for the senior counterintelligence official of a major European ally who was passing through the country and wanted to exchange views. The chief asked me to make arrangements to go to dinner with him. I grumbled a bit back in my office and suspected out loud that the guy was going to ask me to go to the local bar and nightlife district with him, which I did not want to do. Julie wandered by and told me that a club had just opened near where we were going to dinner and gave me the card of the place, Johnny's Place. It promised on its marquee, "A good time for everyone." I didn't say anything, but stuck the card in my pocket. After work that day, I went down to the restaurant, met the fellow, and exchanged some thoughts on our business. He was in fact the chief of counterintelligence of his service, a rather high-ranking official.

Sure enough, as soon as dinner was over and I bid my farewell, he hemmed and hawed and said, "I say, old fellow, I hear there's some pretty exciting nightlife in this town. I would be very grateful if you would take the time to give me a tour of some of the more racy spots."

Just what I didn't want to do. Then I remembered the card I'd placed in my pocket. I took it out and told him that I would meet him at Johnny's and have one drink with him. Since he was being driven and I had my own car, we agreed to meet at the bar. Traffic turned out to be horrible that night, and to make matters worse, I couldn't find the side street the bar was supposed to be on. If I couldn't find it, how would he?

By the time I had gone around a complex set of one-way streets nearly 45 minutes had passed, and still no sign of the bar. As I came back around, I noticed a large house with a neon sign that said "Johnny's Place" with an arrow pointing down a dark alley. I illegally parked my car and hustled down the dark alley. Sure enough, there was the sign, Johnny's Place. I went inside, and it was nearly pitch dark. I sat down at the bar and ordered a double Scotch. As the music cranked up, I could see in a mirror some dancers on a stage behind me. I took a long pull on my drink, turned around, and nearly choked. On the stage were five or six male entertainers, dressed in women's underwear, gyrating all over the stage. I looked to the side and saw that there were no women in the place—it was a gay bar. I jumped up and ran out of the door, and the doorman ran after me yelling, "Sir, sir, we have little boys upstairs!"

"Get away from me, you pervert," I shouted. I got in my car and drove home to consider the options: first, the CI chief may not have found the place; second, he may have found the place and like myself was uncomfortable there; third, he may have found the place and liked it. I then considered the fourth option—he was disgusted and would call my chief in the morning to report this development. After a sleepless night, I went to the office the next morning and got a call from the fellow.

"Say, terribly sorry, but I couldn't find the damned place. I wanted to apologize for leaving you stranded there, but I finally just went back to my hotel. Very sorry." I accepted his apology and hung up the phone only to see Julie and several others standing in the doorway.

"How'd you like the place?" she said, and we all laughed for hours.

I was later to become involved in the sad drama of locating living prisoners of war (POWs) in Vietnam. This was to be a growth industry of substantial size, and at times borderline exploitive of the unfortunate families who harbored what would turn out in each case to be a false hope of finding their loved ones alive.

The first volleys of the CIA-and-DIA-(Defense Intelligence Agency)-are-hiding-evidence-of-live-sightings mantra that would haunt us for over a decade began with several publicity-seeking congressmen leveling the charge. Word came out to our large intelligence community that everyone involved in the collection of intelligence was to pull out all stops in finding information about any living POWs. This kind of pressure inevitably leads to fabrication in the shadow world of intelligence. In this case, one of our defense attachés debriefed a contact who provided him with bones that he claimed were human remains that he had acquired. He sold these to the attaché along with some other details of location and so forth. The attaché decided to send the bones home for inspection and unfortunately just put them in a paper bag and sealed them in a diplomatic pouch that was heading out on its long and meandering way home.

All hell broke loose when headquarters found out about this. The defense attaché got a screamer from his headquarters about the insensitive handling of this. And all members of the American intelligence community received personal orders from the ambassador that henceforth, all such remains would be handled with respect and would be dispatched directly back home, with an escort. This was the beginning of numerous POW task forces.

When I was the chief of the East Asia division a decade later, we were still responding to fabricated reports of live sightings of POWs. This was the beginning of a very trying time in which we routinely had walk-ins with duplicated dog tags, ID cards, and bones, expecting payment. Within months, we had quite a collection of duplicate tags, ID cards, and other relics—all evidence to be checked out piece by piece. During the course of a decade, not one living POW turned up from all this intelligence and evidence. This broke the hearts of many families, but made the career of at least one congressman, who exploited the families for his own political gain.

And, related to this, I had my first encounter cleaning up after a bad operation. A retired lieutenant colonel from the Green Berets had made a reputation mounting rescue operations in search of POWs in Laos. He had gotten a lot of publicity, with absolutely no results. He made several fruitless trips out to the area, generating only protest from the local government concerning his illegal activities, but no POWs. On one occasion, his outfit reported that he was engaged in a firefight with Laotian troops after barely crossing the Lao border, a reckless and pointless action.

Every officer has his share of nut cases. My favorite was a walk-in I interviewed. After hustling him out of sight so he wouldn't be seen if he did have important information, or if he might have potential to become a reporting source, I went through the early drills: Did he know anything about a harmful attack against U.S. interests or U.S. persons? Could he verify who he was? The Q & A session was routine and uneventful until I asked him, "What information do you have for us?"

He leaned back, opened his mouth wide, and said, "You see these back teeth? The Russians are sending radio signals out, and my teeth receive them. I can tell you anything you want to know by walking by the Russian embassy and listening to their conversations. I want to be a spy." I did the normal checking, and we didn't have anything to back up his story. I thanked him for his efforts and sent him on his way. I then sent a cable out to warn other CIA facilities about the fellow in case he showed up there, which he did—at several other locations.

One other episode nearly ended my career. My headquarters had just selected me for a new assignment. I was, to say the least, very pleased. It would come with a promotion into the senior intelligence service ranks, and signaled that headquarters considered me ready to be a top-ranking officer.

Before it took effect, one of our most senior officers came through the area on a routine trip, and our chief held an informal reception for him, which was a terrific opportunity for our younger officers. While chatting over cocktails, the senior officer noted that I had been in a particular country on my previous assignment and asked what I thought about the ambassador there. With my guard down I answered, honestly, "He's a real horse's ass. He never understood what was going on in his own country, and he didn't have a clue how to use the good intelligence we were providing."

The officer erupted. With his face reddening, he shouted, "You are talking about the closest friend I have on this earth." At that point, everyone but the two of us left the immediate area—including our chief. I have always had one inviolable rule—no one will shout at me. So, I looked at him and said, "I'm sorry you have such a horse's ass as a good friend, but what I told you was the truth. If you wanted to hear something else you should have told me he was your friend before you asked the question." The chief came over, and things went downhill from there. He led the officer away, and I left early.

TEN

HOME AGAIN—EAST ASIA

1985–1988

I had been assigned to a senior position in one of our most prestigious and important operational components in East Asia Division as a China operations expert. Things had been going well for me. I was active and in a good managerial position that still allowed me to deal directly with my real love, espionage.

Shortly thereafter, we had an agent in an African country who had done exceptionally well for us, but the country was in the midst of civil war. Our agent had been offered exfiltration (secretly getting him out of country for his safety), but he chose to stay in place and report. We decided I should meet him in person, present him with a medal for his service, let him know we were appreciative of his decision to remain in place, affirm our willingness to exfiltrate him, and review our plans for that emergency.

For operational reasons, I was to travel in "black"—that is, in another persona. Unfortunately, we twice overflew our airport in the country's capital. When we discovered it had been closed in the fighting, we decided to land at a remote military airport several hours outside the capital. It turned out that this airport was in the hands of Russian troops who were supporting the Marxist government against the rebels. The airline informed us that we had the option of staying there until the capital airport reopened or flying back to our point of embarkation. I fussed around, stating that I was there as a private businessman and that my business there was apolitical. They let us into the hut at the airport as they considered what to do.

I needed to get into town, so I asked the local Soviet commander if there were some way I could get into town. He offered a handful of us a ride on a Soviet military truck that happened to be taking reinforcements into the city. He warned us of the possibility of rebel ambush, adding that he could not vouch for our safety. Because I had to get into town, I took the risk and rode with the Soviet troops. The risk was worth it because I had made a commitment to an agent who had taken greater risks for us. I have to admit I was worried, but I was also faintly amused at the thought of a Soviet commander transporting a CIA officer into town to meet an agent. The two-hour trip turned out to be uneventful, and I made the meeting with the agent. When I presented him the medal he actually wept. I explained to him that, since the medal had his name on it, we had to take it back and keep it safe for him. He understood, and went on to further distinguished service to the United States.

I was working with an exceptional chief in 1985 when we discovered the first case of one of our own spies working for the Chinese Intelligence Service. On November 24, 1985, the Year of the Spy, the FBI arrested Larry Wu-tai Chin, a CIA employee, and charged him with espionage.

I received a call on Sunday evening, November 24, that the arrest was imminent. I was instructed to begin to compile a list of the kinds of questions we would ask him about his spying activities. I worked most of the evening.

Chin, born in Beijing, was a naturalized U.S. citizen whose espionage dated at least back to 1949. He had been working in some capacity for the United States since 1943, when he was an interpreter for the U.S. Army. During the Korean War, he had been sent to Korea to interrogate Chinese POWs. Already a Chinese spy, he was hired in 1952 by the CIA to monitor foreign news media, radio, and television programs for intelligence analysis. He served at a number of broadcasting sites and at various posts around CIA headquarters. Not to understate the case, he did massive damage to our China programs. Along the way, he admitted to receiving at least $180,000 for his treason, but our estimate was that he had received over half-a-million dollars. The investigation also uncovered the fact that he and his wife owned at least six condos and one house.

Chin appeared relatively cooperative when his trial began in January 1986. He was convicted of espionage, conspiracy, and tax evasion on February 7, 1986, and faced the possibility of two life-without-parole sentences, plus 83 years for good measure.

On the evening of February 20, I was told to be prepared to go the next morning to the jail in Alexandria, Virginia, where Chin was being held. I was to go with an FBI representative to begin preliminary questioning to do a damage assessment.

But I never got the opportunity, because that same evening Wu-taiChin committed suicide. Rather than betray his Chinese intelligence handlers, he had put a plastic bag over his head and suffocated himself.

Wu-tai Chin wasn't the only one who was brought to justice that year. In an incredible series of espionage events, the following transpired:

- In early 1985, KGB Colonel Oleg Gordievsky was rescued by the British Intelligence service from under the noses of the KGB in Moscow.
- On May 17, Edward O. Buchanan, USAF, was arrested for spying for the Soviets and East Germans.
- On May 19, John Walker, former navy petty officer, was arrested for spying for the Soviet Union and running a major espionage ring. Shortly afterward, his son, brother, and close friend were also arrested.
- On July 11, CIA employee Sharon Marie Scranage was arrested for spying for the Ghana Intelligence Service.
- On November 2, KGB defector Yuri Yurchenko re-defected to the Soviet Union.

• On November 21, Jonathan J. Pollard, a naval intelligence analyst, was arrested for spying for Israel.
• On November 24, Ronald Pelton, former National Security Agency analyst, was arrested for espionage.
• Sometime in late 1985, Edward Lee Howard, former CIA officer under surveillance by the FBI, made his escape to Moscow.
• And on December 20, Randy Miles Jeffries, a congressional courier, was arrested for espionage.

It's a small wonder that 1985 became known as the Year of the Spy. It put the American intelligence community in substantial turmoil. Only later did we find out that CIA officer Aldrich "Rick" Ames and FBI Agent Robert Philip Hanssen had begun their treason working for the Soviet Union that same year.

Inside my own office, things didn't improve for me when my boss departed on an overseas field assignment. When he left, I inherited in his stead one of the worst managers I had in all my time in the Agency. This fellow believed in the opposite of my previous chief's policies: I was to make no decisions on my own, and he wanted us both to be in all the same meetings together.

I complained to him that I found this a terrible waste of our time and resources. And it added two hours per day to our work time, since he also insisted on seeing every bit of paper that came into the office—but only after I had initialed that I had seen it. Fortunately, I escaped, but again, not without paying a price.

In the meantime, I had been present as an expert on China when the DDO was hosting a lunch for the newly appointed Ambassador to China. It was a good appointment, of a senior State Department officer whom I knew, and who held the CIA in high regard. During the luncheon, the ambassador-designee asked me an operational question. Before I could respond, the DDO interjected with a patently false answer. After the luncheon, I told the DDO I objected to his lying to the ambassador, whom I felt had a statutory right to this information. "Shut up and do what you're told," he responded. I knew what I had to do.

And I did it. The ambassador-designee had lined up a series of briefings prior to taking his post. Toward the end of my briefing, I gently corrected the answer the DDO had given the ambassador at lunch. He smiled and thanked me. Later, as we finished the Q & A session, he told me privately that he was concerned that his spouse didn't really understand all the security measures that would be required once they took their post in China. He asked if there was any chance we could chat with her informally. We agreed, and arranged a lunch during which we provided her enough information about Chinese counterintelligence to let her see the seriousness of the situation. We stressed that she and her husband would be the subject of considerable attention by the Chinese internal security apparatus. Our conversation appeared to be helpful, since the ambassador later called to thank us. This is another example of the close cooperation we have with our State Department colleagues.

It didn't take long for the retribution from my previous assignment in Asia to filter down. Within six months, I was called in by the chief of the East Asia division and told, "Your assignment as a chief is in trouble upstairs." It was about the senior officer I had offended with my comments about his closest friend being a horse's ass. I didn't take this news very well, and I was forced to consider my options, including resigning. But before I made a decision, one of the more understanding senior officers in the Directorate, a close friend to the DDO, called me in for a chat.

"Look," he said, "we both know your assignment as chief is finished. There is no way that the DDO is going to forgive you and let you have that assignment. However, I know you are one of our finest officers, and here is my pledge to you. I am going to succeed the current chief of East Asia. I plan to move you to a key position, but out of the line of fire. If you hang on, and do the kind of job I know you are capable of, I will guarantee you a shot in two years at another senior assignment."

I was impressed with this senior officer's honest, straightforward approach. Although I didn't know him well, he was a military-academy graduate and had a reputation in the hallways as a man of integrity. So I told him yes, I would do that, and that I appreciated his honesty.

I made the move, but my immediate supervisor was enraged. He claimed, falsely, that I had schemed for the new assignment behind his back. I asked him whether or not the new chief of East Asia had mentioned to him his desire to move me to another assignment. He acknowledged that he had but felt I owed him my loyalty and wanted me to turn down the assignment.

I explained that I felt the assignment was necessary to salvage my own career, but he would have none of it. "Clean out your desk and leave today," he commanded. I could hardly believe my ears. Our secretary was beside herself and tried to intervene, pointing out to him that this was not fair. He looked at her, then at me, and told me, "I am taking a walk to get a cup of coffee. Don't be here when I get back." I told the secretary not to worry, that I would be out before he returned, and I moved out in one hour. I took the other job, and it turned out to have been the best thing I could have done. I felt vindicated and was active again. Moreover, once more my belief had been confirmed that the Agency would ultimately do what was right and honor those who stood up for their beliefs and told the truth, however unpalatable.

My next great adventure took place in one of our more isolated posts in Southeast Asia. Fighting between rebels and government forces had broken out in the capital. We were considering evacuating personnel down the river that ran through the city. My mission was to go out, make an evaluation, and ensure that the appropriate evacuation plans were in place. Our facility was relatively small, but very enthusiastic. They had already been through the worst stages of occupation by another country, a small civil war, and martial law. The American embassy had already drawn down its personnel, and the ambassador had grown quite fearful of the situation. Consequently, he had ordered that no one venture around in the country, and he was also opposed to our planning an evacuation, as it would send what he felt was the wrong signal to the local government.

Our people had done their jobs. One of our staff officers had been a Special Forces medic, and had already put together a contingency kit for the possible evacuation. He had also assisted in the acquisition of an old diesel-driven steamer of about 40 feet in length, and had hired and trained his own engine-room technician. Additionally, he had scrounged around and salvaged enough doors from old armored cars around the city to sufficiently armor the boat. And he, the engine-room technician, and our deputy had made one trial run upriver to where they would pick up personnel for evacuation, and they had made one trip downriver to an appropriate drop-off point as well.

It was reminiscent of the movie *The Sand Pebbles*. They asked me if I wanted to make a trial run, and I couldn't resist, so I agreed—even though it was obvious that everything was well planned and in place. I mentioned it to my headquarters, which advised me against making the trip. The ambassador was also opposed, insisting that my personnel and I were disobeying orders just by venturing outside. I told him that our personnel had done what they were there to do, and that I would likewise carry my responsibilities, which included going out on a test run. He suggested that he was going to report me to the Secretary of State, but I suggested to him that he didn't want to explain why neither he nor his State Department colleagues had been unable to report accurately about the local political situation. In the end he grumbled, "Go ahead, but don't blame me if you get shot."

The trip on the old diesel up and back down the river through areas that had only recently taken fire was thrilling. The crew knew where rebel troops had gun emplacements and navigated out of their range. In all, this was another great example of the Agency's capabilities and the courage of its officers.

Another important event occurred as I was preparing to leave the area. Our people had been instructed to do all we could to find the headquarters of the leader of the rebel government established by the invading force. No one had yet been able to locate it. One of our junior employees, a 28-year-old woman, approached me in a hallway and said, "Sir, I think I know where the hideout is located. Would you like to go see if we can find it?" I was most impressed. I questioned her and found that she had set up an operations room and loaded it with equipment to intercept communications from the rebel government. She made all the calculations to triangulate the information from signal intercepts. Coupled with some coded information, she had determined that the headquarters of the rebel force was located about 25 miles outside of town. After that, I told her I would be delighted to accompany her, even though martial law was in effect. She brought around a four-wheel-drive Toyota Land Cruiser, and I hopped in. We went only six or seven blocks when she saw a roadblock just ahead.

We were in the second vehicle, and she asked me, "Do you want to go ahead?"

"Sure," I told her, meaning to proceed to the roadblock only. As we watched the vehicle ahead, we saw that the roadblock was set up to search for hand grenades, many of which had exploded in the marketplace the previous day. I watched in amazement as the police searched the vehicle ahead of us and uncovered two handguns and one automatic weapon, only to give them back.

We moved into the roadblock, and my partner asked the obvious question, "We noticed you found two handguns and one automatic weapon concealed in the car ahead of us, and yet you gave them back?"

"Well," responded the officer in charge, "we were only searching for grenades."

"We don't have any either," she responded and drove around the barrier and accelerated. I waited for shots to ring out, but the guards just stood around and scratched their heads. I didn't say a word.

We drove nearly 30 miles out of the city, into a remote jungle area, when we came upon some barbed wire emplacements and a paved road leading into a huge compound. The headquarters was within a hundred yards of where she thought it would be. We wrote down the information and returned back to the city, where we reported the location to a very satisfied headquarters. I congratulated the woman and later helped her get her choice of onward assignments. She understood that hardship was part of the business, and she treated it as routine.

But it was also during this assignment that I begin to see the changes coming in the Agency. The one thing that stands out most is that author Tom Clancy gained access to the Agency building and to either Agency files or knowledgeable Agency personnel to write his novels. We received an administrative notice one Thursday stating: "Those personnel under cover should avoid the entryway and first floor between the hours of 0900 and 1400 on Friday, as Tom Clancy and Harrison Ford will be in the building to do research and film portions of their upcoming film." Times where changing. That Friday, between the hours of 0900 and 1400, our secretaries were nowhere to be found. They were all down in the lobby hoping to catch a glimpse of Harrison Ford.

ELEVEN

OVERSEAS CHIEF

1988–1990

I finished the longest tour that I had ever done in headquarters. I restarted my career and was ready to move on. The chief of the East Asia Division delivered to me an assignment as chief in a major Asian country. I was delighted, and we moved out for my new post.

The best job in intelligence is chief of a CIA facility. Nothing compares in regards to responsibility, authority, and independence. The CIA chief is not only the Director of Central Intelligence's representative, he is also the ambassador's right-hand man. I was well prepared to assume the job.

On my first day, my capable deputy came to me with a significant operational proposal that was bold and risky—and if the operation failed or was uncovered in advance, it would have undoubtedly resulted in my early recall. The operation involved placing a bug into the offices of a communist bloc nation's trade mission. A decision was needed immediately. He left the proposal on my desk, and we agreed to meet after I had a chance to study it.

I remember reading through it, and all of a sudden it hit me—that I was the final authority in this matter for the first time in my career. It was both an elating and a sobering realization—there was no one else to make the decision. I re-read the proposal several times, called him in, and told him to proceed. We carried out the operation successfully several days later.

I was also selected for the Senior Intelligence Service (SIS), the highest ranks within the Central Intelligence Agency, several months later. My rehabilitation was complete, and my career once again on the move.

In most cases, our chiefs are declared to the local internal and external intelligence services—that is, the senior intelligence officials of a country are told in advance that a CIA officer will arrive to be in charge. The reason is to encourage cooperation on issues of mutual importance, such as the proliferation of weapons of mass destruction and terrorism. The Agency provides in many cases intelligence support to the local government, where appropriate and where it is in conjunction with U.S. policy objectives.

I was declared in this case, and I had just come into country after a major flap had developed. The local government had just PNGed (expelled—persona non grata) a State Department officer for activities incompatible with his presence. Actually, the officer had been carrying out his legitimate activities under the mantle of human rights, but the local government was convinced he was a CIA officer attempting to penetrate the opposition movement. As a result, they expelled him, causing a major crisis in our relations with their government. There had even been some talk that I should not proceed to my assignment, but after consultations, the senior officers at the State Department and the CIA decided it would be best to keep the channel of communications between the CIA and the local government open during this crisis.

But the director of the local internal service delayed my official meeting with him to teach us a lesson. Finally, I went for my first official meeting with him. He was an arrogant, bright, politically astute confidant of the prime minister. I showed up at the appointed time, and was escorted to his outer office. His secretary said he would be right with me, but I waited 30 minutes even though the secretary interrupted him several times to remind him that I was there. One of the times she popped her head in, I saw him putting a golf ball into a glass. When she told me after another 30 minutes that he would be right with me, I stood up and told her to tell her boss I had returned to my office. I told her to tell him that, should he wish to make my acquaintance, he could call me and make an appointment to come to my office—if I had the time.

She was aghast, and urged me not to leave. But I had had enough. By the time I got to my car, a breathless aide to the director ran up and said the director requested my immediate presence, if I would be so kind. I went back up and was escorted immediately to what I can only describe as an icy reception. The director looked at me and said, "Let me give you two pieces of advice: Don't turn right on a red light because it's illegal here, and don't attempt another penetration of the government."

I told him, "Unfortunately, you and your government had it all wrong. The officer you PNGed does not belong to me. And I will never lie to you." I bid farewell and went back to work. We immediately nicknamed the director "Red Light" and it stuck.

I later learned that Red Light asked his colleagues around Asia about me. He told my deputy that he believed and trusted me. In an odd turn of events, he then asked me to play golf with him. I did, and we became regular golf partners. He never really lightened up, but by the end of my tour, our joint cooperation had expanded considerably, and we accomplished a significant amount. I had also revalidated one of the rules I formulated early in my career—never lie to a friendly intelligence service. There were times that I would tell them that I simply couldn't comment on something, but that I would never lie to them. In the shadowy business of espionage, oddly enough, reputation is very important.

One day, an attractive female officer, whom I'll call Marlene, came to my office and, in a very routine fashion, said she needed some advice. Flattered, I asked her to step in, and I would see what I could do to assist her.

She told me she needed some clarification about reporting what we call close and continuing relationships. We as an Agency had put into place some stringent rules regarding ongoing relationships with foreigners. If the foreigners were of operational use, they were already being reported. If they were just social contacts, they still needed to be reported once a year. Marlene had always done a great job cultivating good relationships within the mission and within the foreign community.

I told her I would be glad to take a look at any contacts she had, and I asked her to tell me a little more about the circumstances of her request. She looked me straight in the eye and said, "I'm screwing an Australian fellow, but I don't really like him and so I don't know if I have to report the relationship." I almost fell off the chair. I swallowed hard and said in what I hoped was my best professional voice, "Well, in this case I think you report it as a close contact regardless of whether or not you like the fellow." She thanked me for the advice, went out of the room, and wrote it up.

One lesson I learned was to never underestimate the technical capabilities of a foreign intelligence service. We had been badgered for months by headquarters with a proposal to get our host country liaison partners to help us place some modified beaconing equipment into boxes heading for a notorious weapons proliferator's camp. I had already rejected several proposals that, when described to me, didn't seem sophisticated enough to avoid detection.

I did agree to let a team come out and demonstrate to our partners that we had modified equipment that was sufficiently sophisticated to avoid detection by the proliferator. I should have seen trouble coming. The team that came out was headed by one of the most arrogant and useless officers I had ever encountered. He made the presentation, announcing, "No one besides the CIA is capable of detecting our modification." Red Light was present for the presentation; he called one of his technical specialists in.

"Do you mind if I ask him to find the modification?" asked Red Light.

"Nope," said the head of the team, "they'll never find it."

It took Red Light's technician less than five minutes to uncover and unravel the modification. The operation did not proceed. I never forgot it when some of our specialists would tell me, "No one can do this but us."

I had the opportunity to work with the host country's Chief of the External Service quite closely on a number of important covert action projects. The chief, whom I'll call Ethan, was a close confidant of the prime minister. Ethan was also one of the most senior intelligence officers in Asia. He had influence well beyond the borders of his own country.

And, I had the opportunity to work with two politically appointed ambassadors in this posting. The first, by his own admission, had purchased his ambassadorship. I got along well with him, although he bullied many of his own staff. We established a good relationship from the start. He asked me frequently to be his golf partner, but I tried to limit the amount of time I spent out of the office with him. He was a multimillionaire, and he was used to having his own way. He loved to bet heavily on his game. When we played as partners, any hole we lost was, in his eyes, because I didn't play the hole properly. He was overbearing, and I managed to avoid a conflict with him, but it was hard. I learned while we played golf that he had purchased his ambassadorship by contributing $15,000 to the Republican Party coffers. He told me during one outing that he had routinely sent envelopes with $5,000 to each senator and representative of his state, just to prime the pump for an ambassadorship.

His wealth led to a funny incident. United Nations Ambassador Vernon Walters, formerly Deputy Director of Central Intelligence, came through town. The ambassador asked me to join him and Walters for lunch. Walters held court as he generally did, and it was a fascinating experience. Walters was a most gracious man, and since he and I both spoke Chinese, we talked a lot about the region in Mandarin. Walters was interested in my views of the Asia region. The ambassador bristled a little at all the attention Walters was focusing on me. When the bill arrived, the ambassador picked it up. Walters protested that since he and I were government employees, we could not allow the ambassador to pay for our lunches. The ambassador looked at Walters and said, "There's a very good reason why I am going to buy lunch." When Walters asked what that could possibly be, the ambassador, still with the check in his hand, said, "Because I am very rich."

Walters looked at me and said with a grin, "I think he has a very good point, don't you?"

As chief, I was responsible for briefing visiting congressional delegations—CODELLS as they are called. CODELLS are the responsibility of the Department of State, and cause of a lot of anxiety among the department professionals. CODELL members expect every courtesy imaginable—and some that are unimaginable.

One in particular stood out for the mean-spiritedness of the delegation leader. The delegation consisted of six or seven senators on a typical fact-finding mission. The capital city where we were located was known for good shopping. The delegation arrived on time and came into the U.S. Embassy. The country team assembled to brief the delegation. (The country team, which generally consisted of the various heads of government agencies at post, is the ambassador's principal advisory team.) The ambassador began the briefings, and five minutes into it the delegation leader snapped, "We don't need any briefing. What we need is to get to our hotel and get some free time."

With that, they departed—but not until they stopped by finance first and picked up their travel and expense money.

A vice president also came to visit. If anything, their visits cause even more anxiety than the CODELLS. The only thing the vice president asked was when he could get a tee time. He was a two-handicap golfer and managed to cut short some of his official calls to get a few holes in. He greatly aggravated our local government officials in the process.

He also expected everyone to be photographed with him. I told the ambassador that I had no intention of standing in line to have my photo taken with the vice president. The ambassador asked me to do so as a favor to him, and I agreed. And it was memorable. As the photographer snapped the picture of the vice president and me, the VP yelled "Next" and shoved me out for the next victim. For some reason, my hand went behind me just as the photo was taken, and it appeared that I was hanging on to my wallet while standing next to the VP. Wouldn't trade it for anything.

I was fortunate that a second ambassador was appointed while I was there. He was a wonderful man, very astute, pleasant, likeable, and very much devoted to doing a good job. He, too, was a dedicated Republican. He had a distinguished career as a governor, and clout in the Republican Party. One of the first dignitaries to visit him was the Chairman of the Republican Party. The ambassador held a large reception with a receiving line.

My wife and I had something in common with the ambassador. He had a male Welsh corgi named Oliver. We once had a corgi of our own and knew and loved the breed. As my wife and I passed through the reception line, Oliver appeared and stuck his nose right up my wife's skirt. The ambassador appeared quite embarrassed and said to us, "Oh, I am so sorry. Oliver has this terrible habit of sticking his nose up women's skirts." I blurted out, "Don't worry, Oliver and I have a lot in common."

The ambassador almost came unglued and for the remainder of the reception went around saying, "Did you hear what Floyd said?" We got along terrifically.

The government there was always on a campaign of some sort—Keep the State Clean, Support Your Local Government, and so on. My favorite was War On Piss! Residents of the capital drank copious amounts of alcohol when they were out in the evenings, and as they made their way home, they did what males have done for centuries—emptied their bladders in the great outdoors. It was a real problem. Most people lived in block apartment housing (as Pete Seeger's song stated, they all lived in "boxes, little boxes all the same"). The government investigated the problem and discovered that women were doing the same thing. The solution was to declare a war on piss, which was headlined in the press daily. When an unfortunate was caught in the act, the papers would run a column with their photo in the Photos of Shame section.

But the offenders couldn't be beaten so easily—they would just find less conspicuous places to relieve themselves, away from the prying eyes of the authorities. And the most inconspicuous and convenient place to urinate was in the apartment blocks' elevators. People would simply find an elevator in the nearest apartment block, empty their bladders, and leave.

Which resulted in even more government propaganda. The government even installed urine detectors in apartment-block elevators, and the detectors really worked. By trapping the culprits behind closed elevator doors and setting off an alarm, the authorities were able to apprehend a number of men and women over the next several weeks. Their photos ran on page one of the local newspaper. The war on piss was a regular issue for our country team report. I would occasionally send my deputy to attend the meetings just so I wouldn't have to hear the latest developments.

During one country team meeting, someone asked if urine detectors were installed in our elevators. Without thinking, I said for all to hear, "I can assure you they don't have one in our right elevator." There was dead silence, and the ambassador, laughing, instructed the political counselor, "Don't report that to Washington." The ambassador told the story to every delegation that came to town.

I was promoted a second time toward the end of this tour, and I was also offered a position in the Operations, Resource, and

Management Staff in the Directorate of Operations. There I would work with money, planning, conduct operational reviews, and exercise oversight over covert action. On one of my visits home, I met the chief of the unit, a very experienced and able officer, who would become my mentor. I would learn many things that I had never been exposed to before.

TWELVE

HOME AGAIN—
INTO THE SENIOR RANKS

1990–1992

When I was recruited for a position in the Operations, Resource, and Management Staff (ORMS), I didn't know what to expect, but I wanted to learn how money was acquired for programs, how Congress fit into the equation, and how programs got reviewed and dropped. I also wanted to learn about the CIA's most secret covert action programs.

I was selected for the job by the head of the unit, whom I'll call Jake. Early on, he introduced me to the greatest finance officer the Agency has ever produced, a woman we called Moneypenny—after the secretary in the James Bond movies.

Moneypenny took me in and taught me everything she could about the finance end of the business; she had absolutely no guile or jealousy. I had a reputation for being exceptional at operations, and she could have resented my move into the top ranks of her office. Instead, she did everything she could to help me learn things quickly. Moneypenny briefed me on how her office and how congressional committees were run, and she taught me how to obtain funding from the comptroller's office.

The head of the unit, Jake, was perhaps the most politically astute officer I had met in the Directorate of Operations. He instinctively knew when something was going to rile either our congressional committees or the CIA's upper ranks, and he headed off trouble before it began. He would frequently walk by my office and say, "Get your coat, we're going to Congress," or "We're going to go see the DDO." Jake didn't have to take me along, but he did. If we were dealing with something sensitive, he would often say, "You're not supposed to be in this meeting, so just sit back and be quiet and learn." And learn I did.

Jake's savvy was legendary. Our office facility was due to move to the new CIA building. As usual, the engineers came through to divvy up office space. Jake was at the time a very senior officer, an SIS-04 (Senior Intelligence Service)—the equivalent of a full general. As the engineers laid out the boundary for his office, Jake grabbed the head engineer and told him that he would soon be promoted to an SIS-05, and would thus be entitled to a larger office. The engineer agreed and increased the size of Jake's office.

I developed an excellent working relationship with Jake, and I accompanied him to many funding-request meetings. After a while, he'd send me to do the work. I learned quickly how to present funding proposals for operational problems and plans, and I became quite good at it. With all my experience operating overseas, I was able to put problems into perspective pretty easily. By the end of the first year, I had assisted the Agency in getting millions of extra dollars for its programs.

After another promotion, I was designated one of two Meritorious Officers of the Directorate of Operations. Moneypenny was the other. This was a clear message to the Directorate of Operations of just how important our senior resource staff jobs were.

I was moved up to deputy after my first year in ORMS. I didn't expect any more promotions and started thinking about a new job after two years on staff. Then Jake had a family emergency and went on leave, so I was moved up to acting chief of staff for nearly the last year of my assignment. I continued to learn how to use the power of that position. As with my operational life, I always tried to be fair to everyone and do everything for the right reason.

As a Senior Intelligence Service officer, I also developed an appreciation of why the CIA does such a good job when compared with other organizations: The Agency encourages its senior officers to speak their mind. Occasionally, we're penalized for it, but in general the Agency is terrific about encouraging people to speak up.

A good example occurred during my time as acting chief of the Operations and Resource Management Staff. Bob Gates was Director of Central Intelligence (DCI) at the time. He held a large meeting with all headquarters Senior Intelligence Service personnel to review business and do strategic planning. Perhaps a hundred of us were present, including Bob's deputy director of central intelligence, at the time a navy vice admiral, and a newly appointed associate deputy for military support to operations, a major general.

The room was filled with huge egos, and Gates raised several controversial issues to stir the pot, foment new ideas, and generate meaningful discussions. Officers stood up in succession and bluntly told the director that they didn't like this or that about what he was doing. This was brainstorming at its best.

I noticed our two senior military officers in heated private discussion. Finally the vice admiral stood up and lectured the rest of us because he and the major general were appalled by a perceived lack of respect from those who questioned the director's programs and comments. In what could have been an awkward moment, Gates quickly stood up and said, "Gentlemen, hold on to your seats. You will learn that, in the CIA culture, we encourage this kind of give and take." It was, in my mind, one of Gates' finest moments. The conference was a success, largely due to the open and challenging nature of the meeting. And, it was quite a learning experience for the two military officers, both of whom went on to have distinguished tours at the CIA.

In this post, I spent quite a bit of time with Congress. The DDO, Tom Twetten, was a thoroughly gracious man with a difficult job. An antiquarian book collector and a Mideast specialist, Tom always looked out for his people. He never made a big thing about it, but when tragedy struck and people needed support, he was there. When a young colleague died of leukemia, Tom quietly boarded a plane to the Midwest, attended the young man's funeral, and offered his condolences to the family. In another case, he arranged for an officer who was dying of cancer to be awarded the Distinguished Intelligence Medal at his bedside. I accompanied Tom on the trip, and I was really moved to see how much comfort the officer and his family got from the DDO personally visiting their home to award this man his well-deserved medal.

On one occasion, Tom was called to testify at an annual budget presentation. He had to testify before, among others, the Senate Select Committee on Intelligence (SSCI). Two members of the committee were real jerks. One was a senator from the Midwest who had a staffer rumored to be a disaffected case officer. During the meeting, this staffer fed information to the senator that seemed to aggravate him, but we were able to manage the situation.

Another jerk was a senator from the East Coast—a total arrogant ass. He had demanded that the DDO appear before the committee to justify several items in the intelligence budget request. Tom and I went down to the senate chamber and met with the committee members—all but the East Coast senator. We waited and waited. Finally one of the other senators, embarrassed to keep us waiting, suggested that we start. We had just gotten to the first few items when the senator showed up. He sat down in his chair, told us to continue, and said he'd catch up. He then pulled a *Newsweek* magazine out of his folder, sat back, and read it as the DDO testified. The DDO kept his calm and presented his testimony. I was enraged by this senator's discourtesy.

That year's budget contained additional money to conduct espionage. A number of senior DO officers were sitting around figuring out how to put more people on the street to conduct espionage. These would not necessarily be full-fledged case officers, but people with specialized skills whom we might utilize only once or twice. The big issue was what to call them? We couldn't call them case officers, because they weren't case officers. One of our senior officers made a unilateral decision that would haunt us.

As you probably know, the intelligence world employs non-official case officers (known as NOCs), who are under cover other than as U. S. government officials. Unfortunately, the officer decided to call them case officer collectors (COCs). A most unfortunate acronym. Our budget proposal went to Congress requesting monies set aside for NOCs and COCs, a term we pronounced as "knocks and cocks." In addition to the sexual tone of COCs, we also took heat for our Dr. Seuss request. Soon several little ditties appeared about NOCs and COCs and sox. Funny, but we did get the additional funding—and changed COCs to something else.

In the early 1990s, the Agency entered what is now referred to as its touchy-feely period, which quickly got way out of hand. It was a time when any CIA officer could vent their spleen against the "fighter pilots" of the Directorate of Operations—the case officers. They demanded to get promotions just as fast as case officers did, and they demanded recognition and management assignments. All this despite the fact they couldn't compete in the spy arena with the case officers.

And they took over the whole personnel system of the CIA. People who had never taken a risk in their lives wanted—really demanded, in fact—that they get the same benefits as if they had. It was the beginning of the devaluation of the human intelligence collection system.

Then one of the great CIA tragedies struck. I was sitting in a staff meeting early on the morning of January 25, 1993, when I heard the sound of gunfire—far away, but it was gunfire for sure. My first thought was that a sniper was somewhere in the woods surrounding our headquarters. Minutes later, we all learned that Mir Aimal Kasi, an immigrant Pakistani, had walked calmly along the line of cars waiting on Highway 123 to turn into the CIA compound, killed two employees, and badly wounded a third with an automatic rifle. He then calmly walked back to his car and sped away and out of the country. It was a horrific incident and stunned many of us. And it hit close to home—one of the dead was my physician and the other was married to one of my finance officers.

Terrorism, which we had known so often overseas, had now moved into the United States—and directly in front of our high-security compound. It was sobering, and many people still bear the scars of that tragedy. As for Kasi, it took many years but he was finally apprehended due to a terrific operation involving our overseas stations, the FBI, the U.S. Marshals, and some friendly help from the Pakistanis. Kasi was brought back to stand trial and was summarily executed in 2002.

But the job dealing in resources and with Congress taught me a lot. I was briefed on virtually every classified experimental program that the CIA had. The CIA has researched, developed, and deployed many cutting-edge maritime, air, and ground vehicles, including remote unmanned aerial vehicles (UAVs). At that time, these technologies were very sensitive and still in the initial stages of development. And I got some opportunities of a lifetime—to fly a modified version of a UAV to evaluate its performance and capabilities; to go out with the maritime craft; and to drive the earthbound vehicles. The Agency had modified some of the aircraft to hold two people—one to steer and one to take photographs, in order to later determine whether the craft would be manned or unmanned.

So one morning I crawled into the vehicle with one of its developers, and we went up for a flight. Did it ever bounce around. At one point I actually took over the controls, but I did decline the offer to do the landing in favor of an experienced officer. But it was obvious that the vehicle would best be unmanned—and that it had a tremendous capability to gather intelligence. I did the same with the maritime vessels and the land-based craft. There were many other such projects that remain secret, and the American public needs to know that one of great benefits they get from having a CIA is the work it does in cutting-edge technology and techniques. The CIA leads the world in its innovative research-and-development work.

Just as we had gotten over the shock of Kasi's attack, on the morning of February 21, 1994, the FBI arrested CIA officer Aldrich Ames for spying for the Soviet Union. The news swept through the organization like wildfire, and people couldn't believe their ears. *One of our own* had done massive damage. I won't go into great detail since so much has been written about Ames. But the damage was significant:

Ames passed to the KGB (and later the SVR) the names of 11 of the U.S. government's spies in the Soviet Union/Russia. Due to his treachery, 10 were executed and the other spy spent years at hard labor before being pardoned by Yeltsin.

He disclosed the techniques of our double agent program.

He identified hundreds of our officer's names and many agent names.

He provided a stack of top-secret documents over 20 feet high.

He passed unknown numbers of computer disks, each containing thousands of pages of information.

For his treachery, Ames was paid over U.S.$1.5 million, with another million in a European bank. The Russians even had a dacha set aside for him, which, fortunately, he never got to use. In a plea bargain, he got life in prison.

This episode triggered events that continue to plague the CIA to this day. In the aftermath of the Ames debacle, the polygraph test, supposed to be done every five years, turned into a witch-hunt. Polygraphers were stung by the fact that they had passed Aldrich

Basketball All-Star 1958

1st Lt, Germany 1965

At the University of Oregon 1962

At the Berlin Wall 1966

First landing 1968

Leaving home for the CIA 1967

Training in jump gear 1968

Studying Chinese 1970

Building a bridge 1973

*Refused visa because
of my hair 1974*

Playing at the Bicentennial 1976

My band 1977

*Jogging on the
Great Wall 1982*

*Receiving promotion
from DCI Woolsey 1993*

Receiving DIA Director's Award 1998

*Season's Greetings
and
Best Wishes
for a Happy & Prosperous New Year*

Lt. Gen. Khin Nyunt
Secretary (1)
State Law And Order Restoration Council
Union of Myanmar

*Christmas greetings from
Gen Khin Nyunt of SLORAC 1994*

*Ozaukee news article
2000*

Ames even while he was spying for the Soviets. From then on, the polygraphers were on the hunt. The result, in some cases, was almost unbearable interrogation techniques. And there were a lot of inconclusive cases, in which the polygrapher could not call the officer clean or conclude positively that they were practicing deception. Inconclusive—by the time everyone realized what a mess we had on our hands, hundreds of employees were put into this category. They couldn't get assignments, and they couldn't be promoted. This created animosity throughout the ranks of the Agency and also led to the requirement that all CIA employees file financial disclosure forms. On these forms employees declared their total assets, including houses, jewelry, stocks, cars, and so forth. The financial disclosure requirement intruded significantly into everyone's life.

After two years, I was ready for a new operational assignment. To my great surprise, one Friday afternoon the DDO called me to his office and asked me, "How would you like to be chief of the East Asia division?" I was stunned, thrilled, and honored, but mostly stunned. A dozen or more officers out there were senior to me, and they would be thrilled to be a division chief in the Directorate of Operation—one of the best jobs in the Agency.

The holders of the key area division jobs in the DDO—Europe, Asia, Africa, Latin America, and the Soviet Union—were known throughout the Agency as the "Barons," which gives you some idea of the stature they held in the business.

I told the DDO that, of course, I would like the job. I also told him that I really wanted him to think over his offer, and that, on Monday, if he still wanted me, I was ready to take it. The DDO was perplexed, and I told him there would be obvious sniping about me being promoted over senior officers for the job, and I wanted to let him have a weekend to think about it. "I'll be damned," he said, and agreed. I fretted and fussed all weekend, and, thankfully, bright and early on Monday morning, I got a call from the DDO telling me to make preparations to move over to East Asia as division chief.

THIRTEEN

CHIEF, EAST ASIA—ONE OF THE "BARONS"

1992–1994

I spent two years as chief of the East Asia division in the CIA's Directorate of Operations (DO). It was a time of great change in the way we did our business. The Berlin Wall had only recently gone down, and with it, the normal operating methods with which we had become so comfortable. Many countries had tolerated a large CIA presence because they saw us as an indispensable part of their own protection against communism. So, although in many cases they would have preferred a reduced CIA presence, they understood that we were united against a common enemy. But when the Wall went away, people took a second look and began to worry about our size and what we were really doing there. Our DDO was cognizant of this issue, and one of his charges to me was to re-validate our presence in Asia and make any needed changes.

To do so, I effected many changes in the way we did business in Asia, and most of these remain in effect today. I received another promotion, this time to Senior Intelligence Service–04, and I remained there until retiring in 2001.

Senior management can make a tremendous difference in the success of any good operating component. I was lucky to secure the services of three fine, operationally oriented senior officers. One was an expert on China—I'll call him Dave—who also saw and understood the need for change in the way we operated. Dave implemented a number of new ideas in how we conducted our espionage. A second officer, I'll call Bob, was a colleague who had been a chief of facility himself twice. Bob came in, took over a new account, and distinguished himself. The third, let's call him Seth, was an officer who had also tangled with the same DDO who had cancelled my first chief's appointment. As with me, Seth lost an assignment essentially for the same reason I did—telling the truth to someone who didn't want to hear it. So Seth had been shoved aside to a meaningless assignment. When I learned he was available, I went to the new DDO and got him assigned to be one of my deputies. (I was proud several years later when Seth was himself appointed as chief of the East Asia division). I was also served exceptionally well by putting in a bright, witty senior officer I'll call Judy as my executive officer. Judy had worked for me once before, and she was a person of impeccable integrity. Judy would inevitably be the first to tell me if she felt we were doing something inherently wrong. (I was proud that she became one of our senior chiefs of facilities following this assignment.)

I was also lucky to have one of the State Department's finest officers, Ambassador Winston Lord, as my counterpart at the Department of State. I had known Winston when he was ambassador to China. He had performed exceptionally well there, and he knew and understood the strengths and weaknesses of intelligence. As with the other division chiefs, I had frequent and immediate access to my counterpart at State, and we received great support from Winston.

I can best tell the story of my two years as chief of the East Asia division in a series of vignettes. Following 1985, the tumultuous Year of the Spy, the treachery within our own organization had not totally ended. The Agency had discovered in April 1991 that one of our secretaries, Virginia Jean Baynes, had been copying documents to pass to a man named Joseph Garfield Brown. She had befriended Brown at a karate class. Brown would then pass the documents to

Philippine government officials for money. Baynes confessed when confronted and identified Brown as her cohort.

Seth, Bob, Dave, and I held a meeting in early 1992 to set a trap to lure Brown back to the United States, where the FBI could arrest him. Here was the ploy: We would openly advertise in Philippine newspapers that the CIA was looking for someone to instruct its agents in self-defense tactics. While most thought it implausible, sure enough, Brown sent in an application. In an exchange of official correspondence with the CIA, he was asked to appear for an interview. Brown dutifully paid his own way back to the United States.

On December 27, 1992, the FBI arrested Joseph Garfield Brown at Dulles Airport as he returned from the Philippines and charged him with spying for the Philippine government.

"Hey," he shouted as he was being cuffed, "I'm supposed to be going out to the CIA to work there."

Baynes was given a 41-month prison sentence.[1] Brown pleaded guilty to conspiring to commit espionage and was sentenced to almost six years in prison.

One of the duties of the division chief is to keep in touch with the field, which is best done by traveling through the region. I made a number of long trips out to Asia to meet with the troops and, where appropriate, with local officials.

One of my first trips was to a South Pacific island where a dictator ruled with an iron hand. I arrived, met with our own personnel, and to my amazement found I was invited to address that country's national security council. This was unprecedented, and I accepted. I met the key members of the government and was invited to attend a ceremony in which the local liquor is prepared fresh—and consumed in great amounts. Local custom was to crush kava root mixed with a little water in a large wooden bowl with bare feet, and then consume it on the spot. After the first drink or two, I forgot about all the bare feet involved in preparing the brew. I made it through

1. *The Counterintelligence Reader,* Vol. 3, Frank J. Rafalko, ed. (Washington, D.C.: National Counterintelligence Center [NCIC]), p. 407.

161

more than the usual amount and was offered good wishes and promises of eternal cooperation.

Another early trip was to visit our great allies, Australia and New Zealand. Both have excellent intelligence services with whom we were and are quite friendly. It's a relationship that works for both sides. I was fortunate enough to be able to spend enough time to see both countries in some depth. The Aussies are wonderful people, as those who have visited the country can testify. I was able to get to the outback, and it's spectacular—just like in *Crocodile Dundee*.

One of the high points of the trip was a visit to southern Australia, where I had a beer at a local bar with a kangaroo. Well, the Aussies didn't give the kangaroo a beer in my presence, but I was pretty sure the kangaroo was no teetotaler. I did have breakfast with the kangaroo the next morning—he had corn flakes.

New Zealand was also spectacular. Like the United States, varied geography abounds—high mountain peaks, deserts, glaciers, and the badlands, where a notorious New Zealand bandit named McKenzie rode, plundered, and killed. At the peak of the badlands, McKenzie and his dog were hanged after being apprehended. As the story goes, McKenzie was so bad they hanged him *and* his dog. Puzzlingly, there's a statue in memory of McKenzie's dog on the spot—but none of McKenzie.

But it was in lovely Queenstown where I almost (but not quite) became the first CIA officer to bungee jump. The young New Zealand lad escorting me said he had instructions that I could do anything I wanted. So we drove to a towering bridge above a rushing ice-cold river where bungee jumpers would tempt fate. Although my escort assumed I wanted to jump, I suggested that we watch for a few minutes before I made the plunge. As I watched, a man who must have been in his 80s wrapped the cord around his ankle, stepped off the platform, and plunged head-first toward the river. Just inches from the rushing water, the cord did its job, and he bounced back up to just about touch the bridge. I wasn't that nervous, but how was I to tell this lad that I didn't want to do what the 80-year-old daredevil had just done? I was rescued by a young Filipina, who stepped in line ahead of me and prepared to jump. The guy in charge weighed the woman, adjusted the cord's length, tied it to her leg, and told her to jump.

Jump she did, and after plunging downward she took an unintended dip in the river. The guy in charge must have weighed her incorrectly. Worse yet, she flew back up, and up, right past the launch platform. But she missed the platform; if she hadn't, things might have turned tragic. After seeing the Filipina's near miss, the lad yanked me away and said he didn't think his superiors would be too happy if I got seriously injured.

As with other businesses, the CIA sometimes recruits flawed individuals. One case involved my executive officer, Judy, coming to me and saying that she had been working with some of our reports personnel, and that they had reason to believe that one of our highly touted young officers had fabricated intelligence reports on his previous tour. This young man spoke several languages and had been promoted early in both his previous tours. He had been held up as a model for other young officers, and as a model for successful CIA recruitment of minorities. These circumstances made this a difficult case.

During her research, Judy discovered that one of the officer's previous chiefs had indeed suspected the same thing and had reported his concerns through sensitive channels. But nothing was done. Judy assembled a team whose investigation showed that details of the officer's reports came from a source that was demonstrably elsewhere during the time the officer was reportedly meeting him and gathering the intelligence. Their research also turned up one or two other instances in which the officer had falsified the meeting or the intelligence. I took this information up to the DDO, who had been one of the officer's patrons and one who twice had endorsed his early promotion.

Understandably, the DDO was most upset and said he was certain that some mistake had been made. He then told me the life story of the officer—that he was an orphan and a graduate of a prestigious school, who had made his way up through life's difficulties and ultimately into the CIA, where he was a role model for minorities. I told the DDO I understood the sensitivity of the problem, but it was imperative that we take immediate action. The DDO agreed, reluctantly, and concurred in my plan to reassign the officer to a job outside the CIA headquarters to limit his access to classified information while I conducted a full investigation. Further, I asked the DDO for permission to immediately call the officer in, inform him of what we had discovered, and turn the matter over to our office of security. The DDO concurred in all these actions.

I called the office of security and arranged for a representative to be present when I met with the officer. I told the officer that we had serious suspicions that certain pieces of information he reported had been in fact fabricated. We had a tremendously long session. The officer first denied the allegations and then later acknowledged that he elaborated on parts of the report. He later admitted he had not even met the agent who allegedly provided the report before sending the information in. The officer said, "This is not a serious matter—other officers do this all the time." He also maintained that I was discriminating against him because of his race. We had built enough of a case to turn the case over to the office of security.

Just as the officer was leaving, I asked the security officer whether or not I had the authority to inform the office of security not to let the officer return to classified buildings until the matter was resolved. The security officer said that I did, and he would strongly endorse this action. I informed the officer that his access to classified information would be denied while the matter was under investigation.

In a strange turn of events, that evening I went to a ballgame in Baltimore. I was paged through the stadium loudspeaker system and told to call our headquarters. I called and was told that, upon leaving, the officer had gone straight up to the DDO office to complain about what I had done. I was ordered to call security that night and remove the hold I had placed on the officer's security clearance and to permit him back into my division while this matter was sorted out. I refused to do so. The DDO then had a senior officer call the officer of security and restored the officer's clearance. The officer gained entry back into the headquarters compound the next morning.

I went back to the DDO first thing the next morning and got the clearance lifted again. Eventually, the office of security did their investigation, and the officer in question acknowledged that he had fabricated a number of intelligence reports at two of his previous postings. We sent out a memorandum to the entire intelligence community in effect recalling all of the reports that this officer had produced.

As a postscript, we also found that the officer had not graduated from the college he claimed, that he was not an orphan, and that he had invented other stories about his background and his credentials. After an exhaustive process, the officer was fired for cause. It was a sad case, but it also reconfirmed to me that the Agency would take the actions necessary in such a case. In the Agency we work hard to maintain the integrity of our workforce and our product.

One of the great things about being the chief of East Asia division was Asia's diversity. From metropolises to tiny hamlets to city-states, Asia has it all. In another great trip, I went to a poor country in the north that had not seen a lot of Americans. Our goal was to solidify a relationship with the country, which had been in the Soviet sphere until the Berlin Wall collapsed. My mission was to help this country move toward the West.

From the moment I arrived, I was treated as a VIP. On the schedule was a hunting trip, but I don't hunt, and I tried unsuccessfully to get it cancelled. This was a delicate diplomatic situation. Our ambassador lobbied me hard to go on the hunt, and pointed out that it would offend our hosts if I declined. So I reluctantly accepted.

We boarded a rickety old Russian helicopter, and after we took off I noticed barrel after barrel of aviation fuel right inside the chopper next to ours. Two hours into the flight, I found out why—we were refueling en route. The copilot left his seat—which didn't comfort me either—came back with a rubber hose in his hand, stuck the hose in one of the barrels, put the other end in his mouth, gave a great suck, and siphoned gas from one of the barrels into the tank of the helicopter. My escort told me not to worry, that this pilot was their most experienced—he had crashed several times and knew how to do it properly.

Much to my dismay I learned that we were to actually hunt *from the helicopter*—a bizarre and dangerous practice if ever I saw one. One of the men strapped on a harness, hooked a safety line to the inside of the chopper, and leaned way out the door. Someone handed him an automatic weapon—an old Chinese-made AK-47— and he would fire away at any animals rounded up by the pilot's maneuvering. The whole thing still bothers me, but they managed to kill a large moose for dinner.

After dinner, I went to my tent and saw two sentries with AK-47s standing outside. I entered the tent and found out why— they had hung the remaining moose meat in my tent to keep it from freezing overnight. (Our hosts slept in the helicopter and we had the VIP tent—a traditional yurt.) One of the sentries told me they were there to protect me against wolves or bears that might catch the scent of the meat.

I slept fitfully, and heard a clink every now and then. The temperature plummeted to 40 degrees below zero, and I had never been so cold in my life. I woke up several times thinking I might be freezing to death, and each time I piled on yet another wolf hide for warmth.

When I finally got up at daybreak, I found empty vodka bottles littered outside my tent. The sentries had stayed up all night and drank copious amounts of vodka. I didn't know if I was in more danger from the drunken sentries or the wild animals.

166

My hosts gave me an AK-47 and told me to take a morning walk, that a special breakfast would be ready when I returned in about an hour. I enjoyed my stroll and soaked up some of the territory's immense beauty. And after I returned, ready for a special breakfast, I discovered my host's version of the breakfast of champions—*mooselips and rice*. I could barely get it down—and did so only with the help of some morning vodka. The problem wasn't *what* I was eating, it was that it was unchewable. It was like trying to eat one of those rubber worms that fishermen use as bait. I finally got it down, and enjoyed the remainder of the visit.

But my tenure as chief of the East Asia division was not all fun. I had one run-in with the DCI. As chief of the division, I sat in on any and all covert action activities that were being reviewed in Asia. In one case, I disagreed violently with the action being proposed, which would have involved the possibility of the loss of life of natives of the country that was to be the target of the covert action.

The briefing was long and detailed and had a military option. It was this option I objected to. I was not against using force, but in this case there were more negatives than positives. After the briefing, the DCI went around the room asking for comments and support for the program—which he strongly endorsed. The first four or five senior officers were heavily in favor. I took the plunge and outlined my opposition in a clear, crisp fashion. Following my comments, the senior DI Asian representative—a great mind and a great Asian analyst—agreed with me.

We were the only two who didn't like the plan. I was the senior DO officer responsible for Asia, and my friend was the senior DI officer involved. Without our concurrence, the plan could not go forward. I took a fair amount of direct abuse, including some snide comments about my lack of manliness. But I held my ground. In the end, the proposal was defeated. A number of the participants later called to tell me that they really agreed with me and were pleased the covert action proposal didn't go any further. I told each one that I thought less of them, and that I didn't believe for a second that they had changed their endorsements. They had the opportunity to say no in front of the DCI and declined to do so.

This certainly reinforced my lifelong opposition to covert action. I oppose it not because I think it's unnecessary, but because in my experience it's typically been a poor substitute for good policy, plus, it almost always becomes public. So it's neither covert nor good action. There have been examples of worthwhile and successful covert actions—such as in Afghanistan—but they are in a slim minority. Covert action should always be the last choice—if it's a choice at all.

The Vietnam/Laos POW issue from a decade ago still bedeviled us. I oversaw a special task force, created by my predecessor, just to keep up with congressional requests for files and information about live sightings. They continued to come in by the score. We even built a mockup of Son Tay, the area where a famous raid to free POWs took place (of course, no POWs were there). We worked on imagery, when people suspected POWs were hiding in shadows in photos. We chased down dozens of sightings of the infamous couple known as "Salt and Pepper"—purportedly two army soldiers, one black and one white, who decided to stay behind and fight with the Vietcong. Although it can be argued that we were morally obligated to do everything we could do to locate POWs, these efforts never led us to a single live POW. Millions of taxpayer dollars were spent responding to the congressional mandate, which unfortunately continued to give false hope to the unfortunate families of those missing in action.

On a lighter note, my deputy, Seth, and I managed to snag great seats to a Baltimore Orioles game on opening day—right next to the first-base dugout. The stadium was packed, and security was everywhere, since President Clinton was to throw out the first ball of the season. The crowd was predominantly Republican because when the president walked out to make the first pitch, they booed mercilessly. It was embarrassing.

I went to buy a couple of beers, and when I turned around, a CNN cameraman and reporter thrust a camera and a microphone in my face and asked, "What do you think about the crowd booing the president of the United States?"

On worldwide television, I answered that I thought we all needed to understand that the image of the president appearing at a ballgame is something we should all respect. The president under-stands that running the country is like running a baseball team. Each person counts, and it's the solid team effort that finally deliv-ers the winning game.

The reporter stopped the camera, looked at me, and said, "Wow, that's fantastic. We'll use it tonight."

I turned to Seth, who shook his head and said, "I think I'm gonna puke." I acknowledged that maybe I had laid it on a little thick but felt it was OK. That evening, CNN broadcast my comment worldwide every hour on the hour. For the next several days I got dozens of cables from my officers in Asia kidding me about being at the ballgame while they were defending our way of life.

As a division chief, I inevitably got more involved in office politics than I had in any other assignment—and never more than during the Chinese immigration flap. Sometime in June, a cargo vessel had grounded itself right off Manhattan. Immigration authorities found over 100 illegal Chinese aliens who were smug-gled into the United States. The story made the evening news for a week, and all the major media extensively covered this trade in human cargo. And things quickly escalated into a crisis.

The president directed all government agencies to work together to get to the bottom of this scandalous affair. The DCI called the chief East Asia analyst and me to his office. He wanted to know what we knew about illegal Chinese immigration. We told him the truth—it was not an issue we covered, it was in the bailiwick of the law enforcement community. The DCI ordered the analyst to write a piece on the subject and told me to order all my people in the Far East to report whatever they could on the subject.

When customer interest gets ahead of organizational structure, we make fools of ourselves. My people all told me what I already knew—they didn't cover this issue, and information on illegal Chinese immigration was routinely reported by the State Department and by the legal attachés (overseas FBI reps). Dutifully, they gathered what they could from all sources, including our embassies, and reported it in to me at headquarters. Our headquarters analysts then wrote a big piece, and everyone appeared happy. That was, until the FBI director chastised his own overseas personnel for not reporting as we had. The overseas FBI legal attachés read our reports, and recognized it was mostly their reporting that our overseas personnel had sent in over the years.

The legal attachés were furious at the various CIA chiefs for compiling and sending in their reporting. And my chiefs were none too happy with me for upsetting the delicate relationships that exist overseas between the intelligence and the law enforcement communities. In other words, we had managed to report duplicate information and turn out an analytical piece on it. The fuss finally settled down. But I never forgot the lesson—sometimes the customer is wrong in demanding a particular product from a particular producer. The divisions of labor between intelligence and law enforcement are delicate and exist for a reason. They function best when clear divisions of responsibility and good lateral communications are established. We need to remember this as we continue to react to the events of September 11, 2001.

The division chief travels with the DCI whenever he goes abroad. During my time as chief of the East Asia division, the DCI traveled a lot. On one long trip to Asia, we traveled in a VIP compartment that was crammed into a C-140, an aging aircraft that spent a lot of time in the shop. Since we had to cover so much distance, we had to refuel in flight, and this was quite an exercise. I developed a great appreciation for the men and women of the U.S. Air Force who take on these duties. Everything got tense as we refueled because there is minimal margin for error. We, the receiving aircraft, flew in the jet stream of the tanker aircraft above us, and we really got tossed around. One of the troubles with the C-140 VIP configuration was it is windowless. So we got tossed around but had no window or horizon to help us achieve equilibrium and overcome motion sickness. I managed to keep my dinner down, but not everyone else was so lucky.

We approached the landing zone of our first stop. I got out of the VIP container, went to a window, and saw some kind of liquid rushing out of the plane's belly. Our hydraulic system had ruptured, and all the mechanical equipment, including the landing gear, was affected—and we were still in the air. A team assembled and cranked the landing gear down by hand. As we approached set-down, the pilot told us over the intercom that we had no brakes.

So we made what the pilot called a white-knuckle landing. Touching down, we overran the runway and finally coasted to a safe stop hundreds of yards past the normal termination point. We got everything repaired, but the part of the hydraulic system ruptured a second time on a subsequent stop. And finally someone got the good idea to find another aircraft to complete the trip.

On our third stop, I renewed my acquaintance with the head of the local intelligence service, who had become a good friend over the years. He invited me to his home late one evening to have a beer with some of his younger officers and have a leisurely conversation about our business. I agreed, but I made a mistake—I should have told the security officer traveling with the DCI party I was going out and would be returning late.

So I talked with his younger officers, and noticed it was getting really late. My friend drove me back to the hotel, and I asked him to drop me off at the entrance. He did, waved goodbye and sped off.

Only then did I discover that, for security reasons, entrances to the hotel had been sealed off when the DCI party went to bed. I could not get back in. I tried every entrance to the hotel—all with no luck. I had no phone or phone numbers, so I couldn't call anyone. I thought of tossing stones at windows, but remembered that the security guards were armed, so I discarded that idea. One hour of great anxiety later, a laundry truck pulled up to deliver fresh linens. I told the driver my problem, but he refused to let me go in with him. As we argued, one of the hotel maids saw the commotion. I pleaded with her to let me in, but she told me it would cost her her job. I appealed again, this time with a solution. She would leave the door open for one moment and then walk down the hall. If I made it in, she had no role in it. I made it in, and slept soundly.

Our next stop included a visit to the demilitarized zone (DMZ) in Panmunjon—site of the United Nations Control Commission and the front line for U.S. forces. It was a most impressive site, as many who have visited there can testify. It was February, and we stopped there in sub-zero weather. We had the normal briefings, and went to get a peek at North Korea from the most advanced post manned by a U.S. soldier. We were bound up in parkas, and our briefer told us how tough the soldiers stationed in the DMZ were. The outpost soldier stood ramrod straight. I looked over behind him and saw a frozen used condom. I almost fell over. I nudged the DCI, and pointed to the frozen condom. He looked and laughed and said, "Wow, these guys are really tough."

As the division chief in the CIA's Directorate of Operations I had the opportunity to provide intelligence and information directly to the customer. In a briefing of then chief of staff, General John M. D. "Shali" Shalikashvili, Shali asked for a detailed account of how we were doing against North Korea. The DCI sent a senior Directorate of Intelligence analyst, Marty Petersen and I to the Pentagon to brief him. We were escorted into the office and introduced to General Shalikashvili. I looked around the room, which was filled with other generals and a horde of colonels. I turned to Shali and said, "General, I apologize, but I cannot provide you with all the information you need with all of these people in the room. We will be discussing very sensitive sources and methods, and I am sure that many of the people in the room do not have a need to know." The general turned to me and asked if his G-2 (intelligence) could stay. I said of course he could. The general cleared the room. We provided the chief of staff with an overview of our operational capabilities and analytical observations about the North Korea threat.

The general asked very precise questions and was an eager listener. We finished in about an hour and got up to leave. The general stopped us and said, "I just want you to know, on behalf of our armed services personnel, how much we greatly appreciate the sacrifices you in the CIA make daily to make our world a safer place, and to protect the very valuable lives of these soldiers. Thank you both." I was very moved and very proud to be an officer of the CIA.

In the secure room of the Senate Select Committee on Intelligence, our oversight committee, Senator John Warner and several other members requested a briefing on Asia. Again, Marty Peterson and I went down and briefed the committee. As we were getting up to leave, Senator Warner asked if we could stay for a moment, as he had something else he wanted to ask the two of us. We stayed in the room, and the other senators departed. Senator Warner had just won re-election in a tough battle after breaking with the Republican Party. He refused to endorse the candidacy of Oliver North of Iran-Contra fame as a candidate for Virginia's other Senate seat.

Senator Warner looked straight at us and said, "I know I will get a straight answer from the CIA. What do you guys think about what I did to Ollie?" We were both taken aback. I said, "Senator, if I could have voted for you twice, I would have." He laughed and said, "Yeah, that's what I thought." Warner thanked us for our service to the country.

As a division chief and a senior officer, you occasionally get sent on special missions. The U.S. government was concerned about the safety of one of history's great heroes, Aung San Suu Kyi, the daughter of the man who had led the Burmese independence movement, General Aung San. By 1988, Burma had been under military rule for decades. When Aung San Suu Kyi returned to Burma from exile to tend to her sick mother, she evolved into the leader of Burma's democratic movement. She got two things for her efforts: she won the Nobel Peace Prize in 1991, and she was placed under house arrest upon her return from accepting the award. Despite this, she was democratically elected in one of the first real open elections in Burmese history. Shortly after the election, the treacherous military junta ruling the country, known as SLORAC—the Council for the Restoration of Democracy—a misnomer by any definition—overturned the elections and put her under house arrest.

By the time I became chief of East Asia division, Aung San Suu Kyi had already been under arrest for some time. She continued to attract a huge, loyal following, and the military regime considered her dangerous to their desires to continue to dominate the country. All U.S. efforts to free her led to naught. We downgraded our presence there to a *chargé d'affaires,* and recalled the ambassador in protest. The decision was made to send me to see the leader of the junta, Lieutenant General Khin Nyunt—who was also the head of their intelligence service—on a secret trip while in the region on other business. One of my chiefs in the region made secret arrangements. The rules were that no publicity would accompany the visit. I arrived in country, and prepared for the meeting. I was picked up by an armed detachment of soldiers and taken to a government building. As I exited the car, flashbulbs popped all around me. It was obvious the regime had ignored the agreement of no publicity.

I went into the meeting, and had a most difficult time with the General. I was photographed several more times, and left with nothing accomplished. This was a great disappointment. It took me several days to get over the failure of my mission. The heroic Aung San Suu Kyi remains under restraint by the group of thugs running the country. Numerous other public and non-public missions, including a U.S. presidential envoy, have likewise failed to free this beacon of democracy.

As a senior officer, I was offered the opportunity to participate in an Agency-wide executive seminar. This program exposed our senior officers to various think tanks to challenge our traditional ways of thinking, and to develop our cadre of executive officers. It was fun, exceptionally stimulating, and one of the great programs the Agency offers. The seminar sessions were spread out over more than one year.

For one seminar, we visited a well-known leftist think tank— the first time a CIA group had made such a visit. We were a small group, with 12 experienced senior officers. In the midst of briefing us, their director stopped and said, "Ladies and gentlemen of the CIA, we have a surprise for you." With that, in walked Oliver Stone. Being Oliver Stone, he immediately went on the offensive, accusing us as CIA employees of "attempting to overthrow governments, killing innocent people," and so forth. It almost started a riot. Stone backed off a bit when we attacked his films, particularly *JFK*.

"Well," he said, "if you want me to tell the true story, then I insist that you simply give me all your files, and I'll decide what's true and what isn't true." It was a rough session for him, and for us.

At one point, I asked him directly, "How can you live with yourself—passing *JFK* off to our kids as if it were really history?"

Stone leaned back and said, "Hell, I don't care if it's true or not. I'm simply in the entertainment business." Oliver Stone will never get another nickel from me.

FOURTEEN

GERMANY—
BACK INTO THE FRAY

1994–1998

My assignment as chief, Germany, came about in a strange manner. I had been asked to select a post from among several excellent possibilities. The chief of European division had already asked for and been selected for Germany. I was asked to fly to Europe, and upon return, select the country that I preferred. I visited several places and was most impressed with them, but I had not come to a conclusion. I was en route home and stopped in Great Britain to take care of some business. While there, I received a phone call from the DDO.

"Congratulations!" he said.

"Thanks," I responded, "what for?"

"You have been selected as chief of Germany," he said, saying he would explain when I got back. So, I wound up with the German position that I didn't ask for. Throughout my entire career, I never asked for a specific assignment, nor did I turn any down. We all serve at the pleasure of and for the need of the service. But in my view, that attitude has unfortunately changed with the current generation.

When I returned to the United States, I learned that the position in Germany had opened up for a number of reasons. Primarily because the officer who had been selected to be chief, Germany, had visited the country, and his wife hadn't liked the country or the assignment. So he declined the assignment.

The DCI called me in and said, "I want you to go out and fix Germany." I understood the DCI was talking about justifying the CIA's significant presence there, now that the Cold War had ended. Four years after the collapse of the Berlin Wall, little had changed. Our European friends and allies, Germany included, were no longer willing to turn a blind eye to our activities now that there was no common enemy. I understood my instructions and began preparations. For my part, I was delighted. I served in Germany while I was in the military, and both my ancestors and my wife's ancestors came from Germany.

But there was one political problem. Several weeks before, the U.S. ambassador to Germany, Richard Holbrooke, a strong, demanding, and outstanding diplomat, was informed that the other officer was to be assigned as the chief, Germany. I had known Holbrooke from previous years when he was undersecretary for Asian affairs at the Department of State.

One afternoon, our associate deputy director for operations (ADDO) called me and told me to go with him to meet Ambassador Holbrooke and tell the ambassador I was coming to Germany instead of the other officer. We met Holbrooke and talked as we walked. The ADDO then gingerly told him that I was to be the chief and not the other officer, whom the ambassador had already met. Holbrooke exploded. He ranted and raved about our inability to make up our minds. He calmed down a bit, turned to me, and said, "Look, Floyd, I know you are a senior officer, and I like you. But how am I to interpret this change?"

I thought for a moment and said, "Dick, if I were you, I'd look at it as an upgrade from the previous appointee."

Holbrooke looked at me for a moment and burst into belly laughs. "Damn," he said, "you'll do just fine." We got along great from that point on. Unfortunately, his time in Germany was limited, and he moved back to Washington and on to distinguish himself as the U.S. ambassador to the United Nations.

The CIA prepares officers for their overseas work. I was offered several months of German language training, and after arriving in Germany I spent two months in full-time training at a private institute. Although I wasn't totally fluent, I worked in the language and certainly traveled everywhere without difficulty. I also read the newspapers. I still remember the longest word I learned—*die Deutchedonausampshipfahrtgesellschaftkapitinskabina* (the cabin of the captain of the ship which sails the Donau for the ship company). I also learned how strict Germans could be. I went into a small restaurant and ordered (in German) a ham-and-cheese sandwich.

"Nope," I was told, they do not have ham-and-cheese sandwiches.

"Do you have ham sandwiches?" I asked.

"Yup."

"Do you have cheese sandwiches?"

"Yup."

"OK, take the ham and take the cheese that you make each sandwich with and make me a ham-and-cheese."

"Nope." So much for German flexibility.

I worked hard on my language study. In addition to the ham-and-cheese-sandwich caper, I also had an educational experience regarding German sun worshipping. One afternoon, the sun peeked out during a particularly cool spell, so I took my language books and headed for Wannsee Lake—like almost every other German in the vicinity. Approaching the beach, I noticed two signs in German—one said "Beach" and the second said "Frei Korper Kulture." The only word of the second three that I knew was *Frei*, meaning "free." So, I took that fork in the road. The trek toward the beach was about a mile long. I started down the beach toward a point on the far western shore where I had arranged to meet someone. Up came a lifeguard.

"Take 'em off, buddy." To my horror, he was stark naked. When I demurred he said, "You come to the naked beach, you get naked." *"Frei Korper Kulture,"* I was to learn, meant "Nude Beach." On top of that, I was lily white while all the people on this part of the beach were completely tanned. I lamely said to the lifeguard that I only wanted to walk over to the western side. "Take 'em off," he said again. So I took 'em off! I heard nothing but giggles as I displayed my tennis tan—face, arms, and legs tanned, and everything else pure white. I made it to the western side, put my trunks back on, and met my friend, without offering any explanations.

During the preparations afterward in Washington, I had one of the most memorable meetings in my life—a personal meeting (along with several other officers) with a man named Jan Karski. We visited the Holocaust Museum in Washington D.C., and as a special event, we were scheduled to meet Karski in person. I knew about Karski's service in the Polish underground during World War II. I had read his terrific book, *Story of a Secret State*, which recounted his activities—among them, his meetings with Churchill and Roosevelt to tell them the news of the Holocaust.

We were ushered into a small room and introduced to Karski. I sat spellbound as he took us back in history and described his flight to London to bring the news to Churchill, and then by Lancaster bomber to the United States, where he finally got to see President Roosevelt and relayed the same information. Karski's descriptions of his meetings with and descriptions of these two great leaders were fascinating. Karski didn't hide his feelings about having been rejected by those leaders. I remember well that at the end of the session he reflected and said, "I no longer carry any animosity about these events. After all, who could expect the two leaders of the free world to take this kind of incredible information seriously from a Polish captain in the underground?" I understood his point. I greatly appreciated this rare opportunity to be taken back in time by a person as great as Karski.

We wound up in Bonn, then the capital of Germany, and found a beautiful home overlooking the magnificent Rhine River. We strolled with our dogs along the Rhine in the evenings, stopping for a beer or a glass of Mosel wine. The Germans say their country is *"Hund freundlich und kinder feinlich!"* or "Great to dogs and terrible to children!" And it's true. We took two dogs to Germany and they were treated royally. They went on trains with us, into restaurants, and once even into a movie theater. But they are expected to behave, and ours did. Germany isn't hard to like for dog lovers.

"Fix Germany!" It was a tall order, and it brought me face to face with the man the Germans called "008"—Minister Bernd Schmidbauer, the coordinator for intelligence for the German Chancellery. Fascinating, handsome, controversial, full of himself and the need to prove himself, and absolutely taken with his role as the coordinating head of German Intelligence, the minister was more than a handful to deal with. And he had one fatal flaw common to many spook wannabes—he had no in-depth knowledge of what intelligence really could and could not do. Thus, he often expected intelligence, particularly the CIA, to bail him out of difficult situations.

Which leads me to the Mouse caper. The minister had been dealing for several years with a shady ex–private detective named Mauss. This operative had inserted himself into a number of intelligence operations that typically failed. He also fabricated much of the information he had provided to the minister. In this case, an unfortunate German citizen was a hostage in South America. The minister dispatched Mauss to go down and bribe the captors to release the hostages. However, Mauss was also known to the local government as corrupt, and had made illegal contact with the group holding the hostage. He was arrested and jailed for his efforts. At this point, now in trouble, the minister came to us as he generally did, and asked us to intervene to get both the hostages and Mauss released. I told the minister there were several things wrong with this: First, U.S. government policy against paying for hostages

181

precluded this. Second, even if we did attempt to help, it was unlikely it would do any good, since we had no real influence with this South American country's government.

The minister was furious and retaliated by leaking a story that the U.S. Ambassador to the country where the hostages were being held was unwilling to help. Washington called me about the minister's dealings. I told headquarters this was just another case of the minister digging himself into a hole and wanting us to get him out. The incident unfortunately escalated. The U.S. Ambassador in the South American country went public with his sentiments about the minister. The minister, irate about what the ambassador had said about him, then again called me in. I took the opportunity to tell 008 that what the ambassador had said about him was true, if unfortunate. This series of events escalated for several months before the hostage was finally released. Mauss did some jail time before being expelled from the country.

Another of the minister's not-so-clever episodes involved his use of some intelligence that we had provided to him. In this case, the minister, who was also a member of the parliament, was taking a stand against corruption in one of the former Soviet Bloc countries. He asked me about that corruption, and I provided him with some classified information with the clear stipulation he could not use it without first securing my permission. "OK," he agreed.

In the morning paper I saw a picture of the minister holding up a few sheets of paper that looked suspiciously like those I had given him. Sure enough, the article in the open press clearly stated that the information provided to parliament by the minister came from the CIA. More calls from my headquarters and more explanation about the minister ensued.

These were not isolated events, but were regular occurrences during my four years of dealing with the minister on a regular basis. The minister was quite capable of generating trouble in his spy games. The most public caper was the minister masterminding the "plutonium affair," as one newspaper dubbed it. In short, the minister was concerned about fissionable materials making their way into the hands of terrorists and other criminals. The intelligence agencies of both the United States and Europe took the issue very seriously. There were a number of scams going on throughout the world with red mercury (a Soviet-developed nuclear bomb component) being offered for sale. These were well known.

To be helpful, I gave 008 information about the scams and fabricators. He ran a sting operation. Unfortunately, as part of the sting, he directed the shipment of a small amount of plutonium onto a German aircraft that was due to land in Munich. News of the scheme leaked out, and the German Green Party—exceptionally environmentally aware—had a field day with the minister.

The minister was intent in playing his 008 role to the hilt on the worldwide stage. He got involved in the Mideast and Southeast Asia, in addition to Europe. This inevitably involved some scheme, and he would then turn to me to get the CIA to bail him out. I know that the minister knew that we couldn't or wouldn't help in many cases, but he wanted to build up a record demonstrating that we didn't help him when he needed it for leverage.

In one irritating encounter, I confronted the minister with the fact that I knew that information he provided was false; he responded, "I liked your predecessor better because he would agree with me and tell me what I wanted to hear." My relationship with 008 was proper, and in total, productive, and I maintained with him the same policy I maintained with other intelligence services— never mislead or lie to them.

In another encounter with 008, a senior officer who desperately wanted a tour back in Germany pestered me for over a year. He spoke fluent German, but I turned him down for potential chief or deputy jobs in Asia while I was chief of East Asia division. Simply put, he was a first-class annoyance, and pretty much everyone saw this. I told him frankly that I had no intention of allowing him in Germany.

This officer was present during one of 008's trips back to the United States, and was involved in briefings that we had set up. I didn't know until later was he had the gall to directly approach 008 in a men's restroom to lobby 008 to persuade me to assign him to Germany. And 008 was smart enough never to raise the subject with me. What the officer didn't know was that one of our German desk officers was in one of the bathroom stalls when the officer made his men's-room pitch to 008. The officer took notes on the entire episode and gave them to me. So after 008 left for Germany, I sidled up to this officer and commented, "Oh, by the way, 008 asked me to ensure that your appeal to him in the restroom was rejected." I thought he'd fall right through the floor. He never got a German assignment.

One of the great pearls of wisdom I gleaned during my career came from an officer who was in charge of sorting and routing the traffic to our various offices. "You know," he said, "whenever I want to know something, I just go sit on the can for a while. Sooner or later somebody will have a discussion in the men's room that gives me more information than I get from all our town hall meetings." Indeed!

Not long after my arrival, a VIP visitor who had traveled all over Germany arrived. So I availed myself of one of my senior management officer's services, we'll call her Stephanie, who knew Germany inside out and spoke fluent German. The official party arrived late in the afternoon, and Stephanie assisted with interpreting and ensuring that everything was on track. Since she and I had never met, and since we had some down time before the evening meal, she suggested that she come to my hotel room a half hour before dinner so we could get to know each other. I agreed, answered the door when she knocked, and invited her in.

Stephanie sat down, and I poured her a glass of white wine. To mask our conversation (just like in the movies), I turned on the TV. To my great embarrassment, a porno channel came on, with people writhing and moaning with pleasure. Stephanie shrieked, and I fumbled around with the remote, but the moaning got even louder, so I finally just yanked the plug out ot the TV. Stephanie was bright red, I was red, and we were mightily embarrassed. I asked her to meet me later downstairs. I wasn't sure what would happen next. Fortunately, as I sat in the lobby waiting for dinner, she came in, sat down, and ordered a glass of wine and a beer for me. She then turned to me and said, "Did I pass the test?" and we both laughed until we had tears in our eyes.

Stephanie eventually became my deputy. She was a fine officer, dedicated, a terrific writer, and had a keen sense of humor. For my part, my embarrassment was still not quite over. When I checked out the next morning, I discovered an exorbitant charge for a pornographic movie on my bill. I tried to explain it away, but everyone just laughed.

One of our first big visits was an important DCI visit. We visited the former East Germany as part of the trip, and to keep a low profile, we traveled by bus with our German hosts. We visited a small city and toured some of the historic sites. Naturally, we had a large security contingent with us. Try as they might to blend into the crowds, they still attracted attention, hopping off the bus first to check out security, wearing ear pieces for their radios, and talking into the sleeves of their coats.

We picked up an elderly woman who was our guide and translator and explained the local history of things as our tour progressed. At each stop she was held back while the security people got out of the bus first and surveyed the landscape. Finally, at one point, as the DCI and I exited the bus, she remarked, "Wow, you must be someone important to have all this security."

To the horror of the German security people with us, the DCI said, "You see, I am the director of the CIA." Our hosts were aghast.

The woman, however, simply turned to him and said, "Oh sure, and I am the Queen of England."

And then there was the near-arrest of my driver/bodyguard. On a mission to a nearby country, and unknown to me, my driver decided to carry his weapon. He was properly licensed, of course, and as I discovered later, he had indeed properly notified the airport authorities he intended to have the weapon transported aboard the aircraft. He had not told me that he planned to do this, and we had never before traveled with weapons.

He didn't tell the airport authorities at the check-in desk that he was packing (carrying a gun). We separated for some reason, so I checked in and waited for him to come through the security checkpoint. All of a sudden, I heard alarms going off, and I stood up and saw my driver up against a wall, with two policemen pointing their weapons at him. The clerk at the desk activated the alarm when she saw the weapon in his briefcase. There was nothing I could do but watch. Finally, just before we were to board, they released my driver after numerous phone calls had verified his story about who he was and that he had secured advance permission from the airline to carry the weapon. Two German policemen escorted us personally onto the aircraft and to our seats. No one spoke to either of us during the entire flight.

During one visit by a group of senior secretaries, I told my driver to use our official car to drive the women to the airport in comfort. It was a warm spring day, and the driver decided to have a little fun and turned on the car's seat warmers. An hour later, they arrived at the airport all sweaty and ragged. No one had wanted to mention that they were getting hot flashes, and it wasn't until they arrived that they noticed that the seat warmers were on.

I had more than my share of hard times during my tenure as chief. Much of it could be attributed to the fact that the German equivalent of *Time*, *Der Spiegel*, ran an article that listed me as the chief of the CIA in Germany. The fact that they included the line "the mastermind of the CIA located on the Rhine" did little to help. Exposure like this did several things: First, it generated a whole series of calls from other German papers and media, as well as from the U.S. media. *Der Spiegel* in particular posed the question, "What are all these spies doing in Germany?"[1] Secondly, it resulted in crank calls and threats as well.

I simply turned over all calls to the embassy. I got great support from the embassy press officer, who answered all requests with: "It is U.S. policy not to comment on intelligence matters." After a while, the calls stopped. This incident also resulted in the publication of my name as a CIA officer in a Russian-sponsored book, *Headquarters Germany*.[2]

The exposé *Headquarters Germany* named a lot of officers and units correctly, but perhaps worse, listed hundreds of people who had no CIA affiliation whatsoever. In my own case, the information contained nothing new—in other words, it was a rerun of information that the Soviets had put together. One of the premises of the book was that "the CIA is still operating in [Germany] despite the dissolution of East Germany, the Soviet Union and Communist systems in Europe."[3] That resulted in a great deal of unwanted publicity about what the CIA was doing in Germany, and created demands for lists of names and other information from a number of sources, none of which the U.S. government provided. And once this started, it became a regular ordeal. Every several months, the local German media ran old articles again and again. I knew the Russians were behind this. We confirmed that, on several occasions, the author of a given article would be a known Russia agent of influence.

Congressional delegations, the secretary of defense, the secretary of state, the vice president, and the president all came on official visits while I was chief in Germany. It took a great effort to accommodate this succession of VIPs, but the visits were very important. They demonstrated to the Germans that we were interested in them

1. *Der Spiegel*, No. 12 (1997), pp. 34–36.
2. Klaus Eichner and Andreas Dobbert, *Headquarters Germany* (Berlin: Edition Ost, 1997).
3. Tomas M. Troy, "Headquarters Germany," Book Review, *Studies in Intelligence,* 1998, p. 30.

and helped keep the Atlantic Alliance strong after the confusion of the end of the Cold War.

As our government wrestled with what U.S. Intelligence could and should do in the post–Cold War period, a commission was appointed to study the issue and prepare a report for the president and Congress. After a considerable amount of work had been done, the commission visited Germany to talk to our allies about their views.

Most commission members were on the President's Foreign Intelligence Advisory Board, or PFIAB. The members of PFIAB are generally from the private sector—men and women who serve out of loyalty and have already earned their fortunes. We had dinner with the delegation at a local restaurant and drank several bottles of fine German wine, for which I was stuck with the tab. In the end, the Commission prepared its report—a full, thoughtful, well-presented analysis of the U.S. Intelligence needs in the twenty-first century.[4]

There were difficult times in Washington and in Bonn. During my stay in Germany I worked for four different Directors of Central Intelligence (one was acting director for over six months). Additionally, I had three different ambassadors and one chargé d'affaires through this same period. So every time I turned around, I had to brief a new DCI—and his staff—on what was going on. This was terribly disruptive, and had its effect on the morale of the Agency in general. I was fortunate, however, that for approximately three years of my time, the deputy chief of mission of our embassy, J. D. Bindenagel, was an expert on Germany. I promised him early on he would not be surprised by anything the CIA or the intelligence community would do in Germany—subject of course to my not being surprised myself. We worked out a very good relationship. If he needed to see me, I would drop everything to be available, and should I call and ask to see him, he would do likewise. I didn't schedule the normal weekly appointments, because I didn't believe in wasting either his time or mine. I was sorry to see his tour end during my

4. *Preparing for the 21st Century—An Appraisal of U.S. Intelligence,* Report of the Commission on the Roles and Capabilities of the United States Intelligence Community, March 1, 1996, U.S. Government Printing Office.

final year, and believe that in addition to a good professional relationship, we had a good friendship.

All the changes going on caused great anxiety in the Agency. Senior leadership changes were everywhere. John Deutch had just been appointed and confirmed as the new Director of Central Intelligence by President Clinton. I had met Deutch before, when he was deputy secretary of defense and I had accompanied a senior delegation to meet with him.

On his first day at the CIA, I was headed for a visit at headquarters. As I prepared to turn into the parking lot, I noticed a big, black armored Cadillac on my tail. It followed me into the guest parking lot, and out of the car stepped John Deutch. He was walking into CIA headquarters for the first time as the new Director of Central Intelligence. I parked my car, got out, and walked over to him and reintroduced myself. I congratulated him on his confirmation as DCI. He remembered me, and asked that I walk with him so we could talk.

"What would you say if I told you I wanted to close all of our operations in Europe?" he said. I told him I would suggest that we should re-examine where and how we were doing our business first, and then make decisions regarding closing or reductions. He mulled this over as we approached the southwest entrance together at 8:20 a.m., the peak time when employees came into the building. Dozens of people I knew were gawking at me as I walked in with the new DCI. I turned to leave when he took me by the arm and asked me to ride up with him in the DCI elevator to his office to finish our discussion.

I did, and we had a good chat. Afterward, I went to the office set aside for me and made a number of appointments. The chief of the German area ran up and said, "The DDO wants to see you right away. What were you doing with the new DCI?" I went up to the DDO office and told him that I had simply walked in with the director. The DDO was all a fuss but accepted my explanation. For the next month, including after I had returned to Germany, rumors were all over the place that Deutch had selected me to be the next DDO—a subject that never came up in our conversation. It illustrates how much anxiety his appointment caused in the Agency.

I got along well with Deutch—he asked me if there was anything he could do for me, and I told him an early visit to Germany to demonstrate the importance of our relationship would be very helpful. His first foreign visit as director was to Germany.

We entered what I called the silly season in a big way. It began innocently enough, but soon turned into a personnel management nightmare. Those on top and new to the business decided that what was wrong in the Directorate of Operations—as demonstrated by the Aldrich Ames case—was the DO culture. They were alarmed by what they saw as a sharp division of the DO into layers—with the case officer cadre considered the pointed end of the spear. They believed that case officers looked down on other skilled officers in the Directorate, such as reports officers, support personnel, and the like. Further, they believed that this had to be changed and replaced with a culture where everyone was valued for what they did. By extension, they established functional groups of officers who were all promoted and paid at the same rates. This was designed to break down what they called case-officer mentality, in which those who did the real spying, the case officers, allegedly saw themselves as the fighter pilots of espionage. The culture-killing measures reached their peak, and we were left with a totally unworkable personnel system. Everyone was allowed to bid for any job they wanted, without any restricting qualifications, such as the need to speak a native language or have area knowledge.

The result was a flood of people applying for positions well out of their experience or qualification range. They all had to be interviewed, which required careful notes including justifications for why they were not selected. If it were a highly desired country, say Australia or France, 50 people would apply for every position in hopes of getting one. This inundated the personnel assignment process to the point where it could barely function—and it placed a huge number of people into positions for which they were eminently unqualified.

After several years, there was an alarming drop in the number of good recruited spies coming into the fold. As stated in recent remarks from Congress following the tragedy of 9/11, this led to the realization that the DO is broken and must be fixed. We have come full circle, and it appears that the DO is struggling but back on its way to full staffing. But these were lean years, and the damage will take more years to be fully repaired.

These events affected us in Germany in a big way. First, I had precious few good linguists, as many of my language positions were filled with people with no languages other than English. And this wasn't just true in Germany—it was the case throughout the entire organization. Unfortunately, I had to send more than a few people who weren't getting their jobs done home. It wasn't that they weren't trying—they simply didn't have the expertise to do the job that they were sent out to do. And it was impossible to tell this to headquarters, since they were the ones who killed the culture and made the assignments.

It was not only the DO that suffered. I sent home a number of people in support positions, because they just couldn't do their jobs. During one trip back home, a senior administrative official told me, "You know, there is a cloud hanging over you for sending so many people home." I was aggravated, and pointed out several cases in which the individual I had sent home had arrived in country without the necessary professional knowledge to do their job. I didn't enjoy sending anyone home, but the work had to be done. We had security specialists overseeing finance officers; information management specialists overseeing communicators; and many non–case officers occupying case-officer positions. The Agency was becoming dysfunctional from its attempts to give everyone the opportunity to do just about any job.

And this was true at top levels of management as well. Many in the upper echelons were non-intelligence careerists, who proceeded from the assumption that, since the Agency was in trouble, it must be because those who formerly held high office didn't do things right. No attempt was made to find out why things were done the way they were. We got again another DDO who was not from the clandestine service. Using four-letter words frequently, he would make calls issuing instructions that no one would carry out. I knew within a few months of his appointment I was going to make plans to retire.

Headquarters mandated change, mostly without consultation, and certainly without much thought in advance, which reached incredible levels. A few examples will suffice:

I received a call telling me a new officer was being assigned to my area. I learned that she was being assigned to protect her from her husband, who was due to get out of jail and had sworn to take revenge on her. I almost exploded when the caller continued, "This way, if he comes out to pester or harm her, you can have the local German authorities arrest him." I told the caller that Germans had no such authority until someone broke German law, in which case it would be too late to protect the woman. I told him that, for her own safety, she should stay home, and I suggested a headquarters assignment. I won the battle by pointing out that sending someone overseas for protection was insane.

An officer was sent out who had requested an overseas assignment in the belief that it would make her current boyfriend miss her, realize that he loved her, and then propose to her. Shortly after her arrival, the boyfriend found another girlfriend, and our employee requested reassignment back home.

One of our officers had arrived from a denied-area posting with his family in tow. It was his second marriage, and he had a stepson with him. The family was dysfunctional, and we wound up refereeing several fabulous family fights, including one in which the son was choking his mother. In another episode, the father had gotten into a fistfight with his son, and wound up with broken eyeglasses and cuts on his face. As this agent approached the end of his tour, I suggested none too politely to headquarters that an assignment back home was in order. There this family could get the counseling and help they desperately needed. The results? The family was assigned to another overseas posting.

A senior support officer arrived. He was indeed an expert in his field, but he was unilateral—that is, he had never had opportunity to expand and learn the full side of the support craft. I wrestled with this case as morale in his section reached rock bottom. Finally, headquarters reassigned the officer back into his field, where he once again excelled.

One of my managers/case officers had carried out an extremely complex technical operation that was well conceived, difficult, time-consuming, and against a priority target. She, and I, were very proud of it, and she received accolades by the dozen from those who benefitted from the operation. Incredibly, division management seemed perplexed by the operation. In fact, as I discovered during a trip to try to explain it, they actually thought the operation was done by someone else and ignored the officer involved. I attempted to get an award for this officer, and had all the technical support experts lined up. She never received any recognition for her efforts. Again, it was typical of the difficult time we were going through.

And there were other cases. The *Washington Post* reported on March 10, 2000, that a retired CIA officer was being given an award after being "the highest ranking CIA official fired in a scandal."[5] I need to fill in the disturbing circumstances of the firing.

While the DCI was on an official visit to Germany, he instructed me to contact the officer via secure phone and ask that he come to our locale to meet. I am sure that the officer expected some sort of reprimand. The scandal in the press had described a series of activities in Latin America that had taken place nearly a decade before and involved some questionable support to local insurgents who had been working against the elected government with alleged CIA backing. As a good officer, he took the call and made immediate arrangements to fly down for the personal meeting with the DCI. He was serving at the time, in the summer of 1995, as the chief in another European country. He was an outstanding officer, and a former division chief. I was, as were many others, exceptionally fond of him. He was senior to me in the SIS ranks, and had been one of the people who had quietly offered me advice and counsel as I took on increasing responsibilities in the organization. I always found his advice sound, and he was exceptionally conscious of the feelings of others.

He arrived and was told to wait at the hotel where the DCI was residing, as the DCI and I were out with some local officials. I knew the meeting was set for 9:00 p.m. and that it was about a 15-minute drive from the restaurant to the hotel. At 8:30, I suggested that we needed to tie things up for the DCI to make his next appointment. The DCI was in no hurry, and even had more desserts sent in.

At 8:45, I wrote a note to the DCI, "The officer is waiting at your hotel per your instructions." The DCI turned to me and said, "Let him wait." I was *upset*, and went to the DCI's aide and said that we needed to be moving and that it was inappropriate to keep this senior officer waiting.

The aide commented, "Let him sit—he isn't going to like what he is told anyway." That was my first indication that he was going to be fired. Despite my protests, the dessert lingered on. We finally left after keeping the officer waiting over an hour. In the end, some justice was done when the officer was presented after retirement with a medal for his service to the CIA and the U.S. government.

There were more cases like this. The point is, the personnel system, which the CIA had willingly torn down, was replaced using concepts that simply didn't work well in the occupation of spying. The term BOHICA (bend over, here it comes again) was used with each new absurdity.

I forwarded some information we had acquired from the Germans alleging that a U.S. company was breaking sanctions against a Mideast country. The information alleged that one or more U.S. government officials knowingly turned a blind eye to the events. I knew that this was explosive, but I doubted the legitimacy of the information and noted that when I sent it in. Within two days, I received a heads-up from a colleague at headquarters: "You need to know that the director and the White House are planning to send a special envoy out secretly without your knowledge to deal with the Germans on the information."

With that tip, I called headquarters and found out, after much hemming and hawing, that, yes, a special envoy was coming out to see the Germans, "but we'll keep you posted on what he finds out. Don't tell the ambassador or anyone else."

This was unheard of, and I refused to follow their instructions. I told headquarters that I had no intention of allowing a special envoy to meet with the Germans on an intelligence matter without my being present. Further, I told them that I would personally brief the ambassador on the impending visit.

Later that day, I received a call from a lawyer representing the U.S. government officials who had been accused of overlooking the breaking of sanctions. He asked if I could protect them. I told him that I would protect no one and that his request was totally inappropriate. I received several other calls suggesting that I wasn't helping my career any. Finally, I called headquarters and told them that unless this matter was handled properly, I would resign. Shortly thereafter I was assured that I was the point of contact, and was told to brief the ambassador and set up the meetings. As it turned out, my suspicions were correct—the information alleging the misdeeds of senior U.S. officials was incorrect, and we were able to conclusively prove it.

The appointment of unqualified people to senior positions began to wear me out. The frequent changes in DCIs and all the personnel movement in the ambassadorial ranks made conducting our business even more difficult. This led to a tremendous emphasis on no flaps—that is, it's better to not do something than to risk doing something and having it go wrong. Given that we were in the midst of serious work against organized crime, narcotics, and terrorism, it was a formula for mediocrity. And this approach coincided, due to the lack of senior experience at the top, with the belief that headquarters is the place where the action is, and more and more operational positions moved to Langley from the field. CYA (cover your ass) became the byword, and the Agency became extremely risk averse, as Congress itself was to acknowledge by 1999.

With a great deal of disgust I found out that an operation in a country neighboring Germany had come unwrapped, and headquarters was looking for someone to blame. I got a tip from a colleague at headquarters that, although I had only peripheral involvement, the chief of our division was conducting a secret investigation with one of his deputies with the idea of laying the blame at my feet. An officer had been arrested, and the division chief showed my photo to him several times to get him to match me with the police photo of the person they claimed was behind the operation. This officer held his ground and refused to make the false identification. Unknown to the division chief, this officer had known me in the past. It was a colleague of this officer who had called and informed me of the subterfuge in my own organization. This is all too symbolic of what went wrong with the Agency during this period.

There was additional shock and disappointment when we learned on November 16, 1996, that another CIA case officer, Harold Nicholson, had been arrested for espionage—again, for working for the Russian Intelligence Service. In this case, Nicholson had been an East Asian officer for most of his career. I knew him tangentially, and he had been a senior officer at one of our field stations. He was at most an average officer—certainly not the high ranking and successful officer the press portrayed him to be. Fortunately, given his mediocre performance, I had turned down his request for an extension and a chief's job when I was chief of the East Asia division. I didn't have any particular insights, I simply felt he was undistinguished and perhaps burned out. I didn't know the truth at that time. In this case, many of the fixes that had been put into place after the Ames case paid off. Nicholson had trouble with three polygraph examinations in 1995, which led to further measures, such as background financial investigations, surveillance, and surreptitious entry into his car and residence. Nicholson had worked for the CIA in Manila, Bangkok, Tokyo, Bucharest, and Malaysia, where he offered his services to the Russians in 1994. Over the next two years, Nicholson was paid over $180,000 for his treachery. His motivation was simple—money. As the plea-bargaining progressed, Nicholson was cooperative as we found the damage he had done. In addition to what he could tell the Russians from his overseas assignments, along the way Nicholson had been assigned to our secret training facility, and had passed to the Russians the names of everyone who went through the facility during his two-year assignment. Due to his cooperation and a plea bargain, he was sentenced to only 23 years in prison for his treachery.[6]

But things did end on a high note for me. George Tenet was confirmed as the new DCI in July 1997 after President Clinton's nomination of Anthony Lake went bad. I had known Tenet since 1990, when he was the staff director of the SSCI and I was working in the resource management staff. He was bright, energetic, and experienced in intelligence. It wasn't long afterward that Tenet reached out and persuaded a legend in espionage, a true professional, and a good friend of mine, Jack Downing, to come out of retirement and become the new DDO. Jack had been chief in China twice, deputy in Moscow, and a former DDO division chief. He spoke fluent Mandarin and Russian. This was like a great reprieve,

6. *The Counterintelligence Reader,* Vol. 3, Frank J. Rafalko, ed. (NCIC) pp. 354–363.

197

and an audible sigh could be heard throughout the DDO. We could once again begin operating again in a professional mode.

And we did begin to operate again. But a lot had been destroyed in the process, and now, nearly six years later, we have still not totally recovered. But we are on the way.

As my tour approached its end, I was involved in one last important operation. George Trofimoff, a retired army colonel, sold his country down the river, spying for the Russian Intelligence Services for nearly 25 years. He was finally arrested on June 5, 2001, but the operation to net him began long before. This operation involved the very best of U.S. intelligence cooperation with all agencies and at all levels. Contrary to a lot of press play, the CIA most often cooperates fully—and successfully—in investigations concerning national security. Trofimoff was convicted and will spend the rest of his life incarcerated for his treachery.

I worked hard to ensure that the critically important U.S. military intelligence units in Germany got their fair due. I had maintained my United States Army Reserve commission, and had just completed 20 years of service before I got to Germany. The military people all knew and appreciated that, and it gave me credibility with them and helped me coordinate intelligence activities in Germany. As my time in the CIA ended, I was stunned—and proud—to be awarded the Defense Intelligence Agency Director's Award in a great surprise ceremony. It is the highest honor granted civilians by the Defense Intelligence Agency.

While in Germany, I had the opportunity to meet a number of figures of historical importance. The first, and perhaps the most interesting of all, was an 80-year-old woman who ran one of the great restaurants in the then-capital of Bonn. Her name was Rita Maternus, and she alleged that she had been the mistress of none other than General George Patton. She was stunning for her age, and it was obvious that she had been a knockout in her younger days. She was a legend, and she frequently drank enough of the local wine to get up on the bar and show off her legs. She would say how much George had liked them. She was exceptionally fond of Americans, and if she was around when you brought in a large party, she would frequently send a bottle of the best champagne. The staff took good care of her and made sure her glass was never empty. The restaurant had been one of the last places to fall to the invading Allied forces in 1945, and one booth has a lampshade signed by pilots of the last squadron of the Luftwaffe heading out on what they assumed would be their last mission.

I met Felix-Christoph, the son of the noted General Reinhard Gehlen, who, among other accomplishments, headed the West German Bundesnachrichtendienst (BND, or Federal Intelligence Service) from 1956 to 1968. A mirror image of his elegant father, Felix was confident, pro-American, and grateful for the help the United States had given his country in the fight against communism.

I also had the pleasant opportunity to meet the son of Field Marshal Erwin Rommel, Manfred Rommel, while visiting Stuttgart and acquiring a couple of collector's items from the Afrika Korps. Manfred Rommel was the mayor of Stuttgart, Germany. He had been mayor for some time, and was reaching the end of his statutory term limit. He too was pleasant, and was particularly interested in maintaining the good relationship the people of Stuttgart had with the U.S. Forces, Europe (EUCOM). The mayor had an excellent relationship with a whole series of EUCOM chiefs. I met him at several receptions as well as informally on several occasions. He was particularly grateful for what the United States had done in keeping the Soviet Bloc at bay. He talked about how the people of Stuttgart had been fortunate to have been liberated by the Americans, and contrasted that with the occupation by Russia of what would become East Germany.

In my role as the CIA chief in Germany, I attended three years running of the Wehrkunde Conference, the largest gathering of defense ministers in the world, held annually in Munich. I met the fellow who started it all—Baron von Kleist—famous for his opposition to Hitler, which also landed him in prison. The Baron, as he liked to be called, fit all the images that imperial Europeans like to project—a white mane of hair, sartorial splendor, and domineering personality. He ran the conference with an absolute iron hand, never hesitating to tell a speaker to hurry up, sit down, or yield the floor. He even once told his own defense minister to be quiet while another defense minister had the floor.

One of my favorite people in Germany was Rainer Kesselring. He had dropped the "von" from his father's name. He was, indeed, the son of the famous Field Marshall Albert Kesselring, and was very much his father's son. Kesselring had risen to become vice president of the German Federal Intelligence Service, the BND. He was a man of great integrity, and it was a pleasure to do business with him. He was extremely accommodating and did a great deal to further the cooperation between our two intelligence services and our two countries.

I was offered the opportunity once to meet the daughter of the infamous Reichsmarshall Hermann Göring. However, I was informed that she, as were the children of other Nazi leaders, was still suffering from the unimaginable horror of living with the legacy of their fathers. I opted to pass on this opportunity, but I still regret not meeting her.

I was quite fortunate with the new CIA leadership in place. Both the DCI and the DDO asked me which senior position I would like. I responded to both that I now had 33 years in the CIA and that I had long believed that there is a time for senior officers to step aside and let the next generation develop their own leadership for the good of the Agency. Ever since I assumed the leadership mantle, I had promised myself—and those who worked for me—that I would not hang around past my time. Finally, I explained to both the DCI and the DDO that I simply loved working in the field, and felt I had done all I could in senior positions at headquarters. It was time to either retire or to consider becoming a CIA officer in residence (OIR) at a major U.S. university. To their everlasting credit, both the DCI and the DDO immediately encouraged me to teach at a university for two years before retiring. Thus, I accepted the OIR offer.

I loved Germany then, and still do. Where else could you get the official title "Botschaftsrat fur Koordinierungsangelegenheiten der Vereinigten Staaten Von Amerika"? The Germans can indeed be difficult, but they are also very predictable, and blunt. You know where you stand, and they will tell you the truth.

Germany has been, and still is, one of the best friends the United States has had, and we take the country for granted too often. A good example is the speed and deliberation with which the Germans took on an important role in the Bosnian theater of war. It was a hard decision for them, given their history, but they stepped up to the responsibility and did it well. They were, and are, a responsible, important intelligence ally, and I was proud to develop useful and meaningful relationships with them that continue to today. I am proud that I continue to receive birthday cards and Christmas greetings from many of the official Germans with whom I dealt. Relationships are what it's all about.

FIFTEEN

OFFICER IN RESIDENCE— A SCHOLAR

1998–2001

I returned to the United States and took up my assignment as CIA officer in residence (OIR) at Marquette University in Milwaukee, Wisconsin. I had wanted to participate in the CIA's officer-in-residence program— sponsored by the Center for the Study of Intelligence (CSI)—when I first became familiar with the program after my return to headquarters in 1988. When I was asked to consider a major chief's job in early 1994, I did so with the understanding of the DCI that I would apply for the OIR program after completing my three-year assignment. As things developed, I was asked to take a fourth year, and did so upon the agreement with a second DCI that I would then be considered for an OIR assignment. Finally, under yet a third DCI, I applied from overseas duty prior to completing my chief's assignment and was selected for the position at Marquette University.

I had voiced my interest in one of these teaching assignments to three different DCIs, who were knowledgeable and supportive of the program and were positive and verbal in their support of my participation in it as a senior officer. That said, there was an incredible bureaucratic process involved in submitting an application from overseas. For reasons that never were clear, it seemed impossible to use an electronic cable format for the application—it had to be submitted in a formal letter—which I could not do from overseas due to security requirements that we use aliases in all reporting, and the application had to be in my real name. Fortunately, the German support desk, in particular the patience and great assistance of a secretary on that desk, helped me submit the paperwork as if I were at headquarters itself.

There were a number of considerations once I began the process of applying for the program. To begin with, since the Center for the Study of Intelligence (CSI) has no positions or any budget for its own OIR program, I needed a sponsor. Despite the support of three different DCIs for proceeding with this assignment, I found resistance within my own operating division. The chief there refused to sign off on the assignment. Fortunately, his boss, the deputy director for operations (DDO), Jack Downing, was in favor of the assignment, and it proceeded forward.

In general, the CIA sponsors officers under this program for two-year tours on the faculties of participating colleges and universities. The objective is to promote broader understanding of intelligence roles and missions, closer collaboration with the academic community, and to make contributions to the scholarly study of intelligence. CIA officers are visiting faculty members and teach and serve as a resource for faculty and students. The program began in 1985, and the CIA has sponsored officers at over 50 academic institutions, including Harvard, Princeton, Ohio State University, Clemson, and Marquette, to name a few. The program has been a huge success, with more universities asking for CIA officers than we can provide. And this success is demonstrated by the fact that over 200 universities currently include intelligence and intelligence-related subjects in their curricula.

I selected Marquette for two reasons: first, they had been asking for an officer for nearly four years; second, the DCI, George Tenet, was anxious to get someone out to Marquette and to the Midwest. During the application process, I visited Marquette and was warmly welcomed by the history department and the College of Arts and

Sciences. Also, one of the great scholars of intelligence, Ralph Weber, was on Marquette's faculty and had been pushing for the program. He and I hit it off very well during my initial visit, and I knew I would have his support. Weber had previously served as a scholar in residence at both the CIA and the National Security Agency. He knew well the unique parts of my business, and I considered that a tremendous advantage.

I spent three months prior to moving to Milwaukee working out of the CIA Center for the Studies in Intelligence—sort of the CIA think tank. The CSI oversees the Agency's program to send senior officers to major universities to teach subjects related to intelligence, and it also has the CIA history staff. The history staff has seven to eight doctorate-level history professors whose job it is to research major historical events in the Agency's development and produce studies, both classified and unclassified. It is, by any standards, a remarkable jewel in the CIA organization. The staff there, including Brian Latell, head of the CSI at the time, did everything they could to prepare me for my teaching assignment. I had access to anything I wanted, and I prepared several draft syllabi for the staff at CSI to critique. By the time I arrived at Marquette, I was fully prepared for the transition into academia.

I decided, having been away from the academic world for such a long time, that it would be to my advantage to arrive in time for freshmen orientation. And by the end of the week, I knew some of the school's history, where things were located, and I came to know and appreciate the philosophy of Ignatius Loyola that forms the basis of Jesuit education.

Most OIRs are given the first semester to get comfortable and prepare their courses. Nevertheless, I was indeed busy. Dr. Weber had me guest lecture one of his history courses. Another professor, Dr. John Krugler, had me make a presentation on the Vietnam War. Things then blossomed. The local chapter of Phi Alpha Theta, the national history honor society, asked me to make an evening address to the local chapter. It was right before Halloween, and so I titled my talk "Spooks, Who Needs Them?" It was a great success, with a packed house, including the chair of the history department. My contacts and reputation blossomed.

I gave a presentation on Vietnam to a history class. I followed up with a film and lecture on Vietnam, again for Phi Alpha Theta. I did this lecture with a professor who taught a course in the history of Vietnam. Basically, our presentation was to show the film *Good Morning, Vietnam* and then have a discussion about the film. My colleague, who had never been to the Far East, was a Vietnam trivia expert, and between the two of us we managed to generate a huge amount of interest. The film was two hours long, but the audience stayed an additional hour just to ask questions and talk about the film. The next morning a delegation of students who had attended the lecture showed up. They said the presentation had opened their eyes—that their parents, of the Vietnam generation, had never discussed Vietnam with them. They said they considered learning about the Vietnam War of great importance. My first semester was fruitful, and I was off to an excellent start.

The chair of the history department, Father Steve Avella, gave me great latitude to prepare a history course, *The History of Foreign Intelligence*. He gave me tremendous support during my tenure. I learned a lot from him as well, and he was always available for me to discuss ideas for my course. He told me, "You are the expert in intelligence, teach the course any way you want to." Likewise, Dean Thomas Hachey of the College of Arts and Sciences gave me full support, and, of course, Ralph Weber was always on hand to provide wise guidance as I proceeded. The course was offered for upper-division and graduate-level credit. We set a goal of enrolling 12 to 15 students, and the first time the course was offered 14 students enrolled. The course went very well, and enrollment kept growing over the next two years—24, then 34, students, plus a long waiting list.

The librarian, John Jenz, is a history buff. He allocated $1,500 for me to select books on intelligence for the library. I put together a must-have list and a would-like-to-have list. Even though my wish list exceeded the budget, John ordered every book I requested. Together we built one of the best libraries on intelligence in the Midwest. As my tenure progressed, I sent John a note whenever a new book came out that I thought was important, and he would add it to our collection.

As I got the hang of teaching at the college level, Father Avella asked me to consider taking advantage of my Asian experience and asked me, during my third semester, to teach a survey course on Asia. I taught it also at upper-division and graduate levels. In my last semester, we added an advanced colloquium in intelligence, which was quickly overenrolled, and I wound up teaching two sessions to accommodate the interest. It was very rewarding to watch the growth of interest in intelligence over the two-and-a-half years I was at Marquette.

I received great help from the CIA in support of my teaching. As I put courses together, I decided to tap into the vast resources of the Agency for a couple of expert guest lecturers. The deputy chief of CSI lectured on congressional relations; a sitting DO division chief talked about his experiences with Aldrich Ames; a military officer from DIA spoke on military intelligence; and senior DI analyst Marty Petersen came frequently and lectured on intelligence estimates and how they reach the president.

One of the really spectacular events was a visit from General Oleg Kalugin, former Director of Counterintelligence for the KGB. I approached Kalugin at a conference on intelligence in Berlin, and he agreed to come to Marquette and present to my students a picture of intelligence direct from a historic enemy—the KGB. He also made an evening address to Phi Alpha Theta.

Kalugin's visit stirred up great enthusiasm at Marquette. Dean Hachey was so enthusiastic that the college picked up the General's stipend and expenses. Kalugin's presentations were knockouts. I asked him to present an opponent's view of the CIA, and the students loved it. Kalugin defended the KGB's operating methods, and thereby validated all that I had lectured on about the KGB. He made a standing-room-only presentation in the evening, which drew high praise from the dean.

I gave the keynote address on history and the intelligence officer at Phi Alpha Theta's annual initiation dinner. At the request of the CIA office of public affairs (OPA), I made a presentation at Brookfield Alternative High School on the myth and reality of the CIA.

I also helped teach a few class periods of historical methodology, a course for upper-division and graduate students. I did presentations on how to use the Internet for research, oral-history interviews from the Vietnam War, and I helped another professor teach his What Is History? course.

Marquette has a substantial ROTC program, with the navy, air force, and army all well represented. The head of ROTC asked me to talk to the graduating seniors about future threats and taking care of yourself overseas. And for the next two years, I lectured to graduating ROTC seniors. I received warm praise for the realism of my presentations, and these young men and women better understood the unique risks they would undertake as U.S. officers abroad.

The OIR program brought me great personal and professional satisfaction and the opportunity to attend conferences on intelligence. During my time at Marquette I attended three conferences sponsored by the Center for the Study of Intelligence, and one sponsored by the Defense Intelligence Agency (DIA). The first was at DIA, in Washington, D.C., on the teaching of intelligence. It put me back in touch with some old friends, and gave me access to new ones involved in my new craft—teaching intelligence. The second conference, this time about the U-2 spy plane, was held at the Bush School of Government and Public Service at Texas A & M University. The CIA had declassified a large number of documents concerning the U-2 spy plane, and a few of the original pioneers told their fascinating tales about the U-2 program. One of the original test pilots talked about what it was like to fly this highly unstable experimental aircraft.[1] It was a great conference.

At a sideline reception at the Bush School, I had the great pleasure of meeting Colonel Ryszard Kuklinski—the man who had been a CIA agent on the Polish army general staff during the crisis in Poland in 1980–1981. Kuklinski had made his escape as the Polish Intelligence Service closed in, and remained in the United States. I had an interesting private meeting with him. Kuklinski continued to wear a disguise to protect his identity (he has since died). Some in Poland, especially many Polish dissidents—the very people Kuklinski's spying helped the most—consider him a traitor. Others see him as one of the great heroes in Polish history.[2]

I traveled back to Berlin and attended the first of two conferences on intelligence and the Cold War. In Berlin, I met scores of old friends, and some adversaries. I met for the first time Colonel Oleg Gordievsky, a defector from the KGB. He had been a British intelligence agent in London, and one of the spies who had probably been exposed by Aldrich Ames. Under hot pursuit, he escaped from Moscow to freedom. He gave a featured speech on what freedom meant to him. I managed to spend quite a bit of time with him. His tales of his harrowing experiences are contained in his book, *Next Stop: Execution*.[3]

The second conference on the Cold War was at Texas A & M's George Bush School of Government and Public Service. While there, I accepted an invitation to participate in a conference later in the fall at the Bush School: North Korea—Engagement or Confrontation?

1. Gregory W. Pedlow and Donald E. Welzenbach, *The CIA and the U-2 Program, 1954–1974* (Washington, D.C.: Center for the Study of Intelligence, 1998).

2. Douglas J. MacEachin, *U.S. Intelligence and the Polish Crisis 1980–1981* (Washington, D.C.: Center for the Study of Intelligence, 2000).

3. Oleg Gordievsky, *Next Stop: Execution* (London: Macmillan, 1995).

Because of my extensive experience in East Asia, I moderated one of the panels. I again met former President George H. W. Bush, who attended the conference. I had briefed him when he was Ambassador to China, and had met him once also when he was director of the CIA. I was pleased to be invited for private cocktails at his apartment at the Bush School, and I was surprised as I went through a small receiving line. He recognized me immediately, and said, "I don't need to be introduced to this guy—he briefed me when I was ambassador." I couldn't have been more puffed up or more pleased. What a gentleman.

One of the stipulations in OIR assignments is that we can't actively recruit for the CIA while on campus. We are permitted to answer requests from students for information that will put them in contact with the appropriate career offices at the Agency, however.

One of my students asked to see me about his interest in the CIA. He came to my office and hemmed and hawed a bit. Finally, I told him to come to the point. He said he was worried about taking a polygraph test, which he understood was required as part of the process of getting into the CIA. I told him yes, it was, and I said that we all go through it. I told him the most important thing is to be truthful. I also told him that the CIA understood we were all young once, and growing up sometimes involves doing things we wouldn't want our parents to know about. I told him that the CIA accepted this as part of what makes us individuals. I told him if he was hiding something serious, such as the commission of a felony, he would be ruled out.

No, he said, it wasn't a felony. He was under probation for something he had done. Not knowing what he was talking about, I told him he would have to tell our security people about it, and I hoped it wasn't serious. He turned red and told me he was caught streaking naked across the basketball court during one of the major Marquette tournament games last year. I managed not to laugh out loud, and assured him unless he was a frequent streaker, it probably wouldn't rule him out. He said that he had learned his lesson.

The Center for the Study of Intelligence sent a message to all their OIRs that they were sending a few publications out to each of us. One day, I walked into my office and was confronted by an angry history department chair who asked me why I had all those books and publications sent to the history conference room. I assured him that I had done no such thing. He walked me into the conference room where 24 large boxes of old CSI publications were strewn about. Sure enough, on top was a shipping note saying they all came to Marquette at my request.

I could use maybe one copy each. Most of the materials were old and outdated. I could use some for research, but I couldn't even get the library to accept the rest. It took me the next six hours to carry the boxes down to my small office—stacking them up against the walls in rows that almost blocked my only door. I spent six months quietly disposing of the materials in trash containers around town, although I briefly considered just tossing them in the Milwaukee River.

One aspect of the OIR assignment aggravated me greatly. Like many other SIS officers who take these assignments, I agreed to downgrade my senior position to GS-15 status, with pay retention. They explained to me this was simply a formality to free up badly needed senior positions for operational spots. I had no problem with that. After all, I intended to retire after this assignment, so I saw no harm in it.

Not quite! I was not told that the personnel system operates with downgrading as a punitive action. Although that was not intended in the OIR assignment, that is how the finance end of it turned out. Because of the punitive interpretation by bureaucrats, I was unable to get the pay raises Congress set aside for our officers while I was in the OIR program. I complained about this, as did many other OIRs, and everyone was sympathetic. It never changed.

It was not Congress' intent to downgrade the OIRs. But in the end, the officers in charge of supporting the OIR program rectified this unintentional injustice, and my SIS-04 rank was reinstated just as I retired.

As my second year as an officer in residence wound down, I faced the decision of whether to retire or seek other work in the CIA. Both Marquette and the CIA asked me if I was interested in a third year, and the history department chair asked me to plan an advanced course on intelligence. I thought a lot about it. I liked the work I was doing, I felt I was being productive, and the students responded enthusiastically to learning about intelligence from a practitioner's view.

I agreed to a six-month extension, to be followed by full retirement. I now had over 35 years of government service, almost 34 with the CIA. I reached the maximum pension over a year ago, so I was really working for very little. And the leadership at Marquette changed—and not for the better. The position of dean of the College of Arts and Sciences was filled for over a year with an acting dean while the university searched for a qualified replacement. In addition, the leadership of the history department changed. The new chair was the antithesis of his predecessor. Everything had to be routed through him for approval before anything got done. Several examples will suffice. The new chair required that all requests for library acquisitions go through him. I told him I had an agreement with the librarian that I could forward my requests directly to him. I told the chair that I saw no reason to complicate the process, and, frankly, I was a better judge of what was a good library acquisition on intelligence than he was, yet he would not recant his demand. Secondly, he asked me to prepare an advanced course on intelligence. I agreed, but told him it that I would require substantial resources. Most of the teaching material I was using needed to be duplicated, since there was no real textbook that would meet my course requirements. He agreed.

The course had a lengthy waiting list, so the chair asked me to consider teaching two sections. I agreed, and again asked for substantial assistance. He assured me this was no problem. We filled two sections for the course. However, several days after I began the new course, after all arrangements for classrooms and other needs were filled, the chair stopped the secretaries from duplicating the materials I needed for the students. I taught the course without all the materials I felt were necessary. I decided right then I would retire after the semester was over. I had no patience for this type of bureaucracy. And as a final aggravation, the chair held all staff meetings at 3:00 on Friday afternoons so the faculty couldn't go home early. This particular department chair displayed all the traits of a poor leader that I had rebelled against throughout my entire career, and my decision was made. After the semester, I retired.

I still support and believe in the OIR program. I am proud to have been a part of it. I also retain my fondness for Marquette University, which provided me with this unique opportunity. My OIR assignment was one of the most rewarding and productive of my 35-year career. The thirst for information about the CIA and intelligence is enormous, and I believe we need to expand the program and respond to the public interest and support for the CIA and intelligence in general.

SIXTEEN

RETIREMENT, OR LIFE AFTER DEATH

2001–

I always promised myself, my family, and those who worked for me that when I got my promotion to GS-13 I wouldn't hang around past my time. I distinctly remember discussions when I was a junior officer about senior CIA folks who simply stayed around too long. "What's that old fart doing here?" "I thought he was dead—maybe he is." And so it went.

I remembered when Bob, one of my deputies when I was chief of the East Asia division, and I went on a trip to Boston. We had both been promoted the day before. As we sipped a beer in our hotel room, we talked a lot. I had come from a dirt-poor family; he was an orphan who never knew his parents. We considered ourselves compatriots, and we were friends for the next 20 years, even though our assignments seldom crossed. As we sat there, we made a vow: No matter what happened from then on, we declared ourselves to be successes. We both made the elevated rank of GS-13, and it was a significant event in our lives. I lived up to that vow, and he did too.

As I filed for retirement, I made several trips back to Washington and discovered that the CIA decided to do away with the executive dining room at headquarters. This was part of the plan to make all of us equal. The executive dining room was now the employee dining room, really an expensive cafeteria open to everyone. One table in the employee dining room was designated as the retiree corner. It seated six of our distinguished alumni, all over the age of 70, who met every Tuesday and expected their table to be waiting for them. Now I respect tradition, but I went up to have lunch, and every seat was taken except at the retiree table. I didn't know the tradition, and sat down there. Wow! You would have thought that I left the proverbial you-know-what in the punch-bowl. A number of the old farts showed up, and I knew something was wrong. I knew every one of the guys sitting at that table, and when the last person showed up without a seat, I said that I had to take a phone call and left. As I left, I heard a lot of snickering, and someone who knew me said, "Sir, you can't go to that table yet. You need a drool cup to sit there." That reinforced my commitment to retire while I still had some respect.

Realistically, in any other occupation, I would have had many good and productive years left. I was only 59 years old, and had 36 years of government service. But I lived up to my promise to myself: quit while you're on top, while you're feeling good about yourself—before they start calling you "an old fart who doesn't know when to quit."

A number of recent retirees told me that once you retired from the CIA, offers of all sorts would pour in. Frankly, I suspected this was true—but only if you retired in the Washington, D.C., area, where the Beltway Bandits absorb huge contracts with the U.S. government and make their money utilizing our former officers, who retain their top-secret clearances.

So I was surprised when, three days after retiring on January 3, 2001, I got my first few messages asking if I was available. It was astonishing. One pharmaceutical firm asked if I was available to be their director of security for their Asian operations. It was indeed an attractive offer—a base salary in the six-figure range, plus lodging in New York and in an Asian capital of my choice. The problem was they wanted me to be responsible for their operations in China, Taiwan, the Philippines, Indonesia, Singapore, and Malaysia. I told them that this was mission impossible. No one, myself included, could do the job requested. So I turned them down. One week later, they called again and asked if they could renegotiate the salary. I told them one last time that it wasn't the salary, I just didn't believe they were serious in looking at security—that, simply put, no one could do the job they were asking to be done. I asked them to remove my name from consideration. I don't think they really understood my reasoning.

Shortly thereafter I received an e-mail asking me if I might be interested in "a private firm with a government contract looking for experienced investigators. Training to be provided. $25 per hour starting salary. Part-time work." Since I was now retired, I thought this sounded pretty good because I didn't want to work full-time again. I sent a positive note in, and was asked to travel to their corporate headquarters, spend four days being trained in their methodology, and then go on a one-year contract, renewable year by year. I went to their training session, and I discovered, as I suspected, it was vanilla work, or investigative work designed to avoid running up big bills. Nevertheless, I took a one-year contract to be a contract investigator to see how it would work out. I was one of only three people out of a class of 50 to be issued immediate credentials.

Basically, I investigated people for security clearances. Over the next year, my worst fear came true—I was working almost full-time. I learned that my employers were mainly interested in clearing out a huge backlog so they could keep their cushy government contract. They operated on the cheap, and I terminated my contract after one year. But I fulfilled my part of the contract—I worked through their entire Wisconsin backlog. I learned again what I already knew about the world of background and security investigations—most of us know very little about our neighbors. During the year, I discovered cases of bad debts, spousal abuse, and generally unacceptable behavior by many needing security clearances to do their jobs. There were more problem cases than even I would have thought possible.

Two other things occurred after I retired. The CIA established a reserve cadre of retired people who kept their security clearances in case the Agency needed to ask people back to active duty (as has been the case since September 11, 2001). They asked me if I was available for the reserve, and, of course, I said I was. I was told the director of the reserve program would take care of processing the clearances. Six months later, I returned to headquarters on other business and discovered that the director hadn't gotten around to processing my clearance. I started from scratch and filled out all the forms again. And this after 35 years of work. I figured this didn't bode well for the reserve program, and told them that if I were called, I would serve, but I wouldn't volunteer.

My next offer was from a major European manufacturer of armored security vehicles, which offered me a salary three times greater than my highest CIA salary. They wanted me to move to Europe to carry out the work from their headquarters. My wife and I decided we wanted to stay in the United States for a while to spend time with our kids. Plus, I wanted to do some writing. So, we turned the offer down, reluctantly.

I continued to see signs that all was not well at the CIA. Traditionally, CIA employees are given a retirement medallion, and people typically received one within 90 days after finishing their service. Six months into my retirement, I had received nothing indicating that I had retired, other than a reduced paycheck. I called several times to inquire about the delay, and finally asked to speak to a supervisor. After much fussing, a supervisor told me, "Sir, we have no record that you ever worked for the CIA. Consequently, we cannot send you a medallion." I did finally get my medallion, but it took a couple more calls to get it.

Meanwhile, I returned to the CIA as a guest lecturer at the newly formed Kent School of Intelligence Analysis. The idea of establishing a professional school for analysts came from Marty Petersen, who had served as the chief analyst on China, and later was the director of the office of East Asia analysis. Marty and I had traveled together with the DCI when I was chief of the East Asia division. Marty was exceptionally astute, and particularly effective at briefing foreign dignitaries. He moved on from his Asian analyst positions to become associate director of intelligence, arguably the number-two analyst in the business. There he proposed the creation of a school to professionally train our analysts, much as we have always done with our case officers. The DCI enthusiastically supported it, and the school has made a major contribution to improved analytical product. I made two trips to lecture in two different courses, and was enthusiastically received on both occasions.

Several months after retiring, I received a call from Cardinal Stritch University, a Franciscan university with about 6,500 students in Milwaukee, and only eight miles from my home. They asked if I could put together and teach a course on intelligence and foreign policy for their political science/history department. The dean of the department, Terry Roehrig, discussed it with me. He was very persuasive, and Cardinal Stritch was extremely flexible in allowing me to schedule my hours around other commitments. I agreed and began teaching in fall 2001. The class went quite well. I got to know and respect both Dr. Roehrig and others at Cardinal Stritch, and they treated me well. Cardinal Stritch has a well-thought-out development plan and also one of the best PR departments I have seen.

Then came the terrible events of September 11, 2001. Cardinal Stritch asked me to address the student body about the incident—to help them cope with it and understand the underlying causes and consequences. They also asked if I could speak to the local news media about 9/11. I agreed, because after 36 years in the business, I felt obligated to do anything I could to offer people some modicum of understanding about this tragedy.

The demands for me to speak exploded. Over the next six months, I did 13 television/commentary appearances, six newspaper interviews, and four radio talk-show pieces. Further, I participated in a panel appearance at the Wisconsin Institute for Peace Studies, and made additional presentations at Marquette, Cardinal Stritch, and numerous service and civic organizations. I was honored as well by being invited to deliver the 2002 commencement address at Cardinal Stritch—probably the only CIA operations officer ever to deliver such an address.

I am pleased to have contributed to people's understanding of 9/11. Being able to help like this reinforces my belief in the relevance of the CIA OIR program, and in the importance of the American public having an opportunity to understand what the U.S. intelligence community and the CIA are all about.

Building on my 9/11 lectures, Cardinal Stritch invited me to teach a new course on international terrorism. Due to intense interest, the course was overenrolled, so they broadcast it live on TV to three other private universities in Wisconsin.

SEVENTEEN

MANAGING THE AMBASSADOR
AND THE
INTELLIGENCE COMMUNITY

I want to offer a few thoughts on the role of the chief of the CIA overseas in relation to the broader intelligence community. The chief holds a powerful position, with authority given directly from the DCI, who in turn receives his authority from the president. The ambassador is often consulted about a designee for the position, but he does not have the authority to approve or reject the assignment. This is important, because it frees the chief from spending too much time satisfying the ambassador, and frees him to report and present intelligence without fear of reprisal. This arrangement works well, and most ambassadors get along well with their CIA colleagues. There are exceptions, but in general, good ambassadors understand the value of this arrangement and use the CIA and its product quite wisely.

One of my ambassadors loved to get our intelligence—and the more controversial it was, the more he liked it. I recall an instance in which we received some reporting from an excellent source saying that the local government leader intensely disliked our ambassador. One of my officers argued that we dared not show this piece to the ambassador. I immediately decided that we would—this was just why we had the independence we did. I knew that this had to be handled discreetly. I arranged a private session to show the information to the ambassador myself, with no other copies to be distributed. I was concerned about his reaction. The report in question said the senior government minister involved referred to our ambassador as "an a——e."

I handed him the report. He hemmed and hawed, and finally chuckled and said, "Wow, this is terribly useful. All I hear from the rest of my staff is how much he likes me. Keep this kind of stuff coming so I know what I'm really dealing with." He knew the importance of real feedback and used it to craft his future dealings with that local official.

It is critical to guard the independence of the CIA and for the chiefs to tell it like it is. One ambassador I worked for continually tried to change this arrangement. He told me several times he was thinking of demanding that he be allowed to write my fitness report. (We received one annual evaluation from our headquarters each year.) I told him that he was free to offer whatever evaluation he wished, but my future did not depend on his evaluation—the DCI was my ultimate boss. He and I got along well; he just didn't like me being so independent.

This same ambassador arrived at his posting after a long political wait. He immediately set out to cow all the heads of agencies at the post at a special meeting. It was a big gathering—the official community was really large. The ambassador kept us waiting 30 minutes, then strode into the conference room and simply said, "I just wanted to gather all of you together. My DCM [deputy chief of mission] will listen to what you have to say. There is nothing that any of you could tell me that I don't already know." With that, he got up and left the room.

I waited a few minutes, then put my papers together and headed for the door. The DCM asked me where I was going, and I said, "If it's not important enough for the ambassador to be here, it is not important enough for me to be here either. I'll send my deputy over." And I did.

MANAGING THE AMBASSADOR

The ambassador called me to come up and see him. He started to fuss with me, and I explained my position—I recognized he was the number-one American in the country and I had responsibilities to him. I suggested, however, that our relationship depended on two things: complete honesty and trust between us, and the fact that I would move heaven and earth to see him whenever he wanted to see me. By the same token, I would never bother him unless it was something he really needed to know. We talked this out for a while.

He told me he didn't like the fact he didn't know the names of our agents. I told him the reasons behind this. I also told him that I would never let him go into a meeting with one of our sources without warning him in advance that he was about to meet with one of our sources. He accepted this as fair. He said he felt he should decide what we were to report on instead of headquarters making that decision. I explained how the requirements system worked, and that the entire policy community, including the secretary of state, vetted the requirements that came to us.

This same ambassador tried one end run on me. He took the liberty to call and make an appointment with the chief of intelligence in the local government. He didn't tell me he had done this, as he should have. I got a call from the local chief, who told me he considered the call from the ambassador inappropriate, and he would not meet with the ambassador unless I was present. I took this case to the ambassador, who was greatly embarrassed that I found this out. He sputtered about the chief calling me, and I let him off the hook. "Sir," I said, "this man is very important to us, so I would like to suggest you keep the appointment, and I will simply meet you there and join you for the meeting." The ambassador concurred, and never excluded me from any meetings with intelligence personnel for the remainder of our time together.

Ambassadors are generally appointed from two distinct groups: professional diplomats, and political appointees. The political appointees can be either major monetary contributors to the predominant political party or former members of the legislative branch or governors. Both can be great ambassadors—or jerks. Most ambassadors take their jobs very seriously and try to do the best they can. I was very lucky in my career, and had a mix of both political and professional appointees. Frankly, I never had an ambassador I did not respect, or could not work with. Working with an ambassador is a two-way street, and our CIA chiefs need to keep in mind that ambassadors are very uncomfortable with the independence and power that our chiefs have. I always felt it was our job to make them comfortable. Every ambassador I ever worked for finally appreciated that we were the one part of the embassy whose charter was to tell the truth, however unpalatable it might be, and that we had no political ox to gore. Despite occasional differences, we've been working this way for over half a century, and it works well.

But we must maintain our independence. In the rare cases in which we discover something wrong, we must take firm action to right it. When I was chief of the East Asia division, I dealt with 26 different ambassadors in Asia. I tried to meet each one personally and give them the time they wanted and needed with me, as well as the respect they deserved.

On one occasion, however, I had to step in forcefully. In one of our Asian capitals, a State Department employee was declared persona non grata for activities incompatible with his position—a euphemism for being caught spying. In this case, however, he was neither a CIA operative, nor was he doing anything outside his official charter. The local government was absolutely convinced he was spying, and threw him out of the country. This caused a major crisis in our official relationship with that country.

Our chief in country reported to me that, despite the crisis in relationships, he was still in touch with our counterpart in the internal security department of that country's intelligence service. Meanwhile, the host government's foreign policy folks refused all contact with our ambassador. I told him to keep our contact open and see what could be done to help defuse the situation. Everything was fine so far.

However, our ambassador ordered my chief to go to the chief of their intelligence service and tell them that the United States wanted to defuse the situation. I had no objection to this. We establish all these good relationships to be used when needed. However, after our chief did so, I read a sensitive cable from our embassy there reporting, "The local government has sent us indications that they wish to defuse this situation." This was plainly not true and gave the false impression that the local government was caving. I called our chief, who told me that the ambassador indeed did send the cable over his objections. I sent a cable to our chief and told him to show it to the ambassador. In it, I frankly told the ambassador that he needed to either send in a statement with the real facts of the meeting, or else I would go to the State Department and tell them that his cable was incorrect and I would relate events as they really occurred. The ambassador was livid, but he did send the retraction. The crisis blew over, and our reputation for telling the truth survived.

The CIA does everything it can to help the members of our embassies abroad. We hold individual briefings for all heads of agency; we often invite their spouses in for special talks about their countries; and we work a lot with military attachés assigned overseas. We run special courses to explain our mission to them and assure them we're there to support them. We stress that we aren't there to compete with them. In all, our relationships overseas are generally very good.

It occasionally takes a firm hand to retain the statutory position our chiefs have as the ambassador's point man on all intelligence activities in their assigned country. Most ambassadors strongly endorse openly and publicly that they expect all intelligence activities to be coordinated through and approved by the chief. For the ambassador, it's one-stop shopping, but sometimes the shopping cart turns down the wrong aisle.

In one of my overseas assignments, we had a large military presence. I always got along well with the military, which I both admired and respected. I served in the Army Reserve for over 20 years and pulled active duty tours every year, which gave me some real clout in dealing with the military. In one case, where I was chief of facility, I called a meeting of military intelligence representatives stationed in the country to coordinate our activities to ensure we weren't duplicating efforts. Things went well until one army colonel stood up and said in a direct challenge, "I appreciate what you're trying to do here, but I think I need to tell you that I don't work for you, and I will decide what issues to coordinate through you and which ones I won't." The room was silent, and I asked the colonel if he had a finance officer.

"Yes, why?" he responded.

"Because," I said, "you need to draw enough money to get your ticket home tomorrow." He was stunned. I told him he could make whatever phone calls he wanted, but he would either live up to his responsibilities to coordinate activities under my authority from the DCI, or I would make three phone calls. First, I would call the ambassador and tell him the colonel was leaving short of tour. Second, I would call the DCI and tell him to expect a call from the army. Third, I would call his boss in Washington and tell him why the colonel was taking the next flight home. After a short break, the colonel stood up and said he had reconsidered, and he looked forward to being a part of the team. From that point on, I had no trouble coordinating activities with the military.

I traveled a lot as the representative of the DCI and the ambassador, and I left most of my organizational work to my assistants. I believe that being physically present—and available—to community members is a critical part of being a chief. I learned early on that you can gather more information by walking around and being available than by any other means. And I learned that it is critical that our chiefs not be desk bound. For that reason, I always declined having a coffee pot in my own front office. I preferred wandering the halls to get my coffee, so I could chat with the staff. This way I frequently came across issues I would never have heard of if I had stayed at my desk.

EIGHTEEN

THE DIRECTORS OF CENTRAL INTELLIGENCE

1967–2004

I worked for 11 Directors of Central Intelligence and one long-term acting director during my 34 years with the CIA. This averages one director for every three years, which is too short to adequately meet the intelligence community's needs.

I would like to offer a few observations about the DCIs I served under. In order of appointment:

Richard Helms (June 1966–February 1973)

Helms was the DCI when I started at the CIA. In simple terms, he was a revered professional who had risen through the ranks. To those of us in the clandestine service, he was one of us. We knew he understood our unique mission and the difficulties we faced. I didn't personally know Helms, although I briefed him on several occasions when he was a member of the President's Foreign Intelligence Advisory Board (PFIAB). But I served the first part of my first over-seas tour under him. And I clearly recall the publicity when the CIA retiree's association paid his $2,000 fine for a perjury conviction in 1977, which was the result of his not testifying accurately about what he knew about Chile, due to valid concerns about sources and methods. I recommend Tom Powers' terrific book *The Man Who Kept the Secrets* for an excellent account of Helms.[1]

---

1. Thomas Powers, *The Man Who Kept the Secrets: Richard Helms and the CIA* (New York: Simon & Schuster, 1979).

James Schlesinger (February 1973–July 1973)

I was fortunate to be stationed overseas during the short, turbulent rule of James Schlesinger, who has the distinction of having the shortest tenure of any DCI in history. It was the first time during my tenure that we had a DCI who didn't want to be there—and it showed. Schlesinger came to the job as a Washington insider. He had previously held posts at the Atomic Energy Commission, and had been deputy director of the Office of Management and Budget in 1971. Further, and this surely led to his appointment as DCI, Schlesinger, under instructions from President Nixon, had conducted a comprehensive review of the intelligence community. He came to the job with strong views on what needed to be done.

Schlesinger put out a directive for all CIA employees to come forth with any information they had about illegal activities. Many did, and many officers were fired. By the time Schlesinger was done, he had fired over 7 percent of the CIA workforce, most of them from the Directorate of Operations. This was my first experience with the ups and downs of CIA personnel and budgetary allotments. This took place under the title BALPA, meaning balance of payments. In truth, it resulted in a significant reduction in our intelligence collection capabilities, even for the very short period that Schlesinger was DCI.

Schlesinger went on to be secretary of defense—a position he was interested in. But he was unceremoniously dumped by President Gerald Ford, along with William Colby at the CIA, Nelson Rockefeller as the vice-presidential candidate, and Henry Kissinger as national security advisor, in what was dubbed the Halloween massacre in November 1975.

William Colby (September 1973–January 1976)

Colby was a veteran of the Office of Strategic Services (the OSS) during World War II. I first knew of him when he was chief of the Far East division (now East Asia Division), and he was one of my predecessors in this position. I recall meeting him the first time early in my career while he was briefing a large group of us at the Agency auditorium. He was known as a humorless man, fascinated by statistics. I can still remember people at the briefing groaning and rolling their eyes as Colby punctuated his presentation with more statistics than anyone could possibly absorb. I was never high enough in rank to have any dealings with him as the DCI. Two excellent books I would recommend by Colby are: *Honorable Men*[2] and his book on the Vietnam War, *Lost Victory*.[3]

Colby was disliked by many CIA veterans because he revealed CIA family secrets to Seymour Hersh, the distinguished columnist for the *New York Times*, who subsequently published all of Colby's revelations, nearly 700 pages in all, in the *Times*. Others disliked Colby for his willingness to make full disclosures to the Church Committee, which conducted a congressional probe of the CIA. The result was the establishment of permanent congressional over-sight—anathema to many intelligence professionals at the time.

The family secrets were a revelation, not only to the American public, but to most of us in the CIA as well. Certainly those of my generation had no real knowledge of the barrage of abuses presented in the media on a daily basis. The Agency's own internal review of the abuses consisted of 693 pages of possible violations.

There was a further schism in the CIA when, in 1974, Colby made the decision to refer the testimony of former DCI Richard Helms about events in Chile to the Justice Department. Justice took legal action against Helms, who was convicted of perjury. I never felt that Colby deserved all the criticism he got for all of this. In reality, the CIA, and certainly the American public, are much better off with a properly supervised intelligence apparatus than they were when oversight was a wink and a nod between the DCI and powerful congressmen, as was the case from William "Wild Bill" Donovan to Colby.

2. William Colby, *Honorable Men: My Life in the CIA* (New York: Simon & Schuster, 1978).
3. William Colby, *Lost Victory: A Firsthand Account of America's Sixteen-Year Involvement in Vietnam* (Chicago: Contemporary Press, 1989).

The mysterious circumstances of Colby's death remain unknown to this day. An excellent boater and swimmer, he disappeared while paddling down a Maryland river in April 1996. His body was recovered on May 6, 1996. Naturally, this set off a series of rumors, and the conspiracy buffs had another preposterous story—that CIA officers with grudges against Colby had him killed. It did a real disservice to Colby, his family, and the CIA.

George H. W. Bush (January 1976–January 1977)

I was overseas during all of George H. W. Bush's short tenure as DCI. I met and briefed him one time when he was ambassador to China and had good vibes about him. It was clear he really understood intelligence and how to use it. In addition, there probably has never been a DCI who was loved as much as Bush was. I met him several times since his tour as DCI, and he remembered who I was, even though my dealings with him were rather routine. He remains revered in the CIA, as demonstrated by his frequent appearances at headquarters and by the CIA building being named the George Bush Center for Intelligence.

Stansfield Turner (March 1977–January 1981)

I was lucky to be overseas during the first part of Stansfield Turner's tenure as DCI, and unlucky to be home during its finale. Simply put, neither President Jimmy Carter nor Turner had any use for human spying. It was clear early on that they much preferred the antiseptic approach of both spy satellites and intercepting communications. The fact that electronic intelligence is spying, just like human spying, seemed to make little difference. And Turner fired over 800 CIA case officers overnight. Many of them, like myself, were fluent in exotic languages; most were mid-level in grade; and all had overseas experience. Turner's cuts set our human intelligence networks back for decades.

Reportedly, Turner was cutting CIA bloat left over from the Vietnam War. No question our ranks had swelled during the Vietnam era. But a more reasoned, careful approach could have avoided all the damage to our human collection efforts, not to mention the instantaneous alienation of over one-fourth of the CIA. Incredibly, Turner was reportedly stunned by the hostile reaction to the mass firings. More incredible still, in his book *Secrecy and Democracy*, Turner complains about the lack of human intelligence during the Iran hostage crisis. I recommend his book for those interested in the history of and dealings with terrorism during this time.[4]

William Casey (January 1981–January 1987)

A friend of mine and former chief, Near East division, Frank Anderson, probably said it best about the tenure of William Casey: "Casey was both the best thing that happened to the Agency, and at the same time, unfortunately, probably the worst thing that happened to the Agency."[5] Anderson's comment captures well the essence of this unusual DCI with direct access to the most powerful man in America, President Ronald Reagan. Casey was the first DCI to acquire cabinet-level status, giving him more power than any DCI since the legendary William Donovan.

I had a number of dealings with Casey. None was more interesting than the day I received a phone call from the DDO asking, "You speak Chinese, right?" I said I did and was told to report to the DCI suite to interpret. I knew a high-level Chinese defector was in town, and I had, in fact, helped arrange a personal meeting for him with the DCI. So I was prepared. I asked only one question: "Who will be in the meeting?" I was told it would be Casey, the defector, and myself. In I went.

Dozens of chapters have been written about Casey's personal appearance—rumpled suits, mumbled words, and so forth. I won't

4. Stansfield Turner, *Secrecy and Democracy* (Boston: Houghton Mifflin, 1991).
5. Frank Anderson, *The CIA: America's Secret Warriors; Part I: The Brotherhood/Betrayal*, The Discovery Channel, 1997.

dwell on that, as I knew going in that understanding the DCI could sometimes be challenging. One Senate Select Committee member once commented, "Bill [Casey] doesn't need a scrambler—no one can understand him anyway." And, as Bob Gates notes in his fine book *Out of the Shadows*, Casey did what he typically did—he opened the door and yelled, "Three martinis!" and the meeting got underway.

Unfortunately, after just a few words of introduction, with me interpreting from the defector to Casey (Chinese to English), and from Casey back to the defector (English to Chinese), the martinis arrived. Casey handed one to our guest, toasted him, and then grabbed a handful of peanuts, shoved them into his mouth, and continued talking. As he did so, peanuts fell onto his tie, and when he bent over to pick up another handful of peanuts, he spilled a good portion of his martini onto his shoes. With a mouthful of fresh peanuts, Casey continued the conversation. It was a real struggle, but we made it through a half-hour session. Our defector was moved to tears at the reception by the head of American intelligence.

On the way out, Bob Gates stopped me and asked how things went. I said they went fine. "How in the world did you understand the boss enough to do the translating into Chinese?" Gates asked.

"I didn't," I said truthfully, "I just told the fellow what I thought the director should have said." We all laughed, but the mission was accomplished.

Casey continued to get us in trouble with his penchant for operating on the edge, often in spite of advice to the contrary. Casey wanted those around him to be activists and find ways around obstacles. He parceled tasks out to whomever he wished, and we were forever cleaning up after him. I recall once when one of Casey's favorites, the head of the task force working the Iran-Contra operation, came to see me to order me to seek a contribution for their secret fund from our Chinese counterparts. I told the officer, who had been a classmate of mine in training, that before I proceeded, I needed to know under whose authority this request was coming. And I wanted to know whether or not it had been agreed to by my immediate boss, the chief of the East Asia division, and by the DDO. I was told that no, neither had been consulted, nor did they need to be. My colleague told me, "You don't need to worry about that—I'm doing this on Casey's orders."

I told my colleague that I had no intention of responding to this request. First, I said, the Chinese would refuse such a request, and it would damage the valuable relationships we were carefully building. Second, I said I wouldn't work in this uncontrolled way. My colleague was furious. "Buddy, you don't know who you are refusing," he shouted. Nonetheless, I told him I would respond once I received the request properly. He stomped out of my office, and I never heard another word about secretly soliciting funds. I had no idea of the extent of the Iran-Contra disaster. My colleague was later convicted and fined for perjury for falsely testifying before Congress about the whole mess.

Casey had a way of reaching out into private industry or anywhere else and pulling someone in to do special tasks. It was a messy way of doing business, and we ultimately paid the price for it. And so did the U.S. military. Embarrassed by the Desert One fiasco during the Iran hostage crisis, and encouraged by Casey, the military longed for the chance to set up their own version of the CIA. They did so, and established a program called Yellow Fruit. Although it began with the best of intentions, Yellow Fruit worked in the cavalier, outside-the-system process that Casey liked so much. I knew one or two mid-level military officers involved, although I had no idea of what they were really doing, or of the scope of the eventual scam. But Yellow Fruit wound up embarrassing the entire U.S. military command structure when it was found that over 300 million taxpayer dollars were missing. Eventually one colonel and two lieutenant colonels were convicted by a court-martial for their roles in the diversion of funds and sentenced to Leavenworth. Interestingly, one of the people involved in Yellow

Fruit's unraveling was retired Lieutenant Colonel "Bo" Gritz of the Vietnam POW escapades. Tim Weiner's book, *Blank Check: The Pentagon's Black Budget*,[6] has a detailed chapter on Yellow Fruit. I can recommend two books about Casey: *Veil: The Secret Wars of the CIA 1981—1987*, by Bob Woodward,[7] which is quite flawed, and *Casey: The Lives and Secrets of William J. Casey*, by Joseph Persico, which is quite excellent.[8]

William Webster (May 1987–August 1991)

I was a fan of Bill Webster as DCI. Judge Webster inherited a terrible public relations mess when he arrived, and in my estimation, he did a terrific job of restoring the CIA's image. I was one of his chiefs during this time, and I had a number of dealings with him. I remember well one of his first press conferences after his confirmation as DCI. One reporter asked him, "Judge, having spent your career enforcing the law, how can you now take over being head of an organization whose mission is to break the law?"

Silence followed, until the Judge replied, "We at the CIA don't break America's laws, we break the laws of the other fellows' countries." It was a tremendous boost to all of our morale.

In William Webster, we had the antithesis of the management style of his predecessor, William Casey. The Judge was laid back and delegated everything. He surrounded himself with good people, listened to them, made decisions, and let the rest of the staff do their jobs. Some have accused him of being too aloof, but I never found that to be the case in my dealings with him.

I recall one good example. I brought back a very senior intelligence official from the country I was assigned to. He had tremendous influence in his government and was also the close confidant of the prime minister of that country. I scheduled him for a call on the DCI. It was to be a most important meeting. Thirty minutes before the meeting, I received a call from the DCI office asking me to come up

6. New York: Warner Books, 1990, pp. 172–98.
7. New York: Simon & Schuster, 1987.
8. New York: Viking Penguin Books, 1990.

and meet with the DCI before I brought the guest up. I did, and had a half-hour meeting with the Judge. It was obvious the Judge knew little about the country from which my visitor came, nor much about our programs. However, in those 30 minutes, the Judge asked me all the right questions: who this man was, why he was seeing him, who he knew in the region, and more. As we finished, the Judge asked me, "What questions do you want me to ask him?" and "What should I ask him to do for you and our station that we are not currently doing or that you having trouble getting them to do?" I gave the Judge several suggestions in both areas and left to escort the visitor up.

The meeting went extremely well. Our visitor was very impressed with the Judge's knowledge of the area and of our programs. Additionally, when I returned to the country, we got even better cooperation in the areas we needed. I learned a good deal about managing large organizations from watching the Judge in action.

Robert Gates (November 1991–January 1993)

There is no doubt that Bob Gates was one of the most politically savvy directors of Central Intelligence in the history of the Agency. And, he certainly earned his shot, having served at both the Agency and at the National Security Council as well. He also had the unique distinction of being the only director ever confirmed on a second nomination, having been denied his post after a first nomination.

I have heard Gates talk about his support for the Directorate of Operations in public forums. But Gates has long been a critic of the DO, which may have had something to do with his first, unsuccessful nomination hearings, when President Reagan nominated him to succeed William Casey. There can be no dispute that anyone inside the CIA who was nominated to follow Casey was headed for a firestorm in the hearings. The Iran-Contra scandal ensured that. Gates was surely burned by the operational activities of the DO, and it is unlikely he forgot it. During this eight-month-long go-around, he had to settle for the position of acting DCI until Webster stepped in.

But loyalty and persistence have their own payoff, and President Bush nominated Gates for his second try in 1991. Gates continued to take arrows in the chest from those who opposed his nomination from a number of areas. Iran/Contra haunted him again, but it was the charges that he politicized intelligence that caused the most controversy during the hearings. I cannot fairly comment on those charges, not having been in the Directorate of Intelligence. On October 18, 1991, after more than a month of torturous testimony, the Senate Select Committee for Intelligence passed his nomination by a lethargic 11–4 margin. Gates was confirmed by the full Senate, 64–33, the lowest approval percentage of any DCI in history. Gates served well, but without any particular disturbances during his tenure—the Berlin Wall went down during Webster's reign, and the Gulf War was well over by the time Gates took his post.

But Gates served his country in more positions than probably any intelligence officer in history. He certainly was the ultimate insider and probably knew more about the security system of the United Stated and how to manage it than any DCI before him or after. And no one should miss his memoirs, *From the Shadows*.[9]

James Woolsey (February 1993–January 1995)

Jim Woolsey was arguably one of the smartest DCIs ever. A graduate of Stanford and Yale and a Rhodes Scholar—he had all the intellectual credentials anyone could hope for. And he was a Washington insider par excellence. He served in the Office of the Secretary of Defense (1968–1970) and the National Security Staff (1970), and was advisor to SALT (1969–1970), general counsel to the Senate Armed Services Committee (1970–1973), and undersecretary of the navy (1977–1979). Further, he was a START and NST delegate (1983–1986), a member of numerous presidential commissions (1983–1989), and ambassador and U.S. representative to the Conventional Armed

9. Robert Gates, *From the Shadows: The Ultimate Insider's Story of Five Presidents and How They Won the Cold War* (New York: Simon & Schuster, 1996).

Forces, Europe negotiations (1989–1991). You could argue that he was well trained to become DCI.

I knew Jim Woolsey well. He was DCI when I was chief of the East Asia division. I traveled with him, and took a number of visitors up to see him in informal situations. He was a good, decent man who really enjoyed being DCI. He understood the power of his office, and he used it well and wisely. He was a joy to brief. He listened, asked great questions, and you only had to tell him something once.

During one of the trips we took, we began briefing foreign governments on issues on which Woolsey had no particular reason to be well informed. He set up a structure in which several key analysts and I would meet with him in the morning for breakfast. Prior to that, he had us submit on note cards the key points that we were going to discuss in the breakfast meeting. By the time breakfast was over, he was prepared for the day's activities. I noted that in the early phases of a trip, he would occasionally call on one of the analysts to answer a question or two, but after several stops, this was no longer necessary, as he had mastered the subject well enough to tackle things himself.

I remember well Woolsey's first day as DCI. He came into the auditorium to make his first comments to the Agency he now ran. The audience stood up, and he quickly asked everyone to sit down. Rather than use the podium, he strolled around the auditorium and informally took questions and answers. It stunned some in the audience. Some liked the new, informal approach, others did not.

And I remember early on the fuss over the fact Woolsey had declined to take a polygraph test, citing "concerns over the legal aspects of it." He finally did take the exam. I understood his reluctance, and hoped he would not take the damned infernal test. I never believed the polygraph works (ask Aldrich Ames, who passed it), and believe to this day that it is absolutely overly intrusive and insulting to our employees. Added to this, there is an unhappy history—you are bound to have a hard time if you have to take one right after one of our frequent counterintelligence flaps, when the screws get tightened. In the aftermath of the Ames case, the vigorous use of the polygraph resulted in the destruction of hundreds of officer's careers solely because the results from the damned machine were inconclusive.

Woolsey was also one of the first to really focus on the fact that, after the fall of the Berlin Wall, we were in reality no safer than we had been before the demise of communism. I recall that, at every opportunity, he would raise the specter of terrorism as the threat for the future. His line was prophetic: "America has slain a large dragon [the Soviet Union], but we live now in a jungle filled with a bewildering variety of poisonous snakes." It was, of course, all too true.

I recall well also the uproar over the actions Woolsey took in the aftermath of the Ames case. He scheduled a meeting in the CIA auditorium to announce his findings and decisions. Everyone was absolutely certain that heads were going to roll. There was dead silence when he announced that there would be letters of reprimand (eight, I believe) and a host of verbal reprimands, but that no one would lose their job. The whole community was shocked—some, I would say, were actually disappointed. But I remember his comment about why he didn't take stronger measures: "Based on the evidence, I have determined that the punishments are suitable. I realize some would prefer firings and stiffer punishment. But that is not the American way, it is not the CIA way, and it is not Jim Woolsey's way." I believe this was illustrative of the character of this DCI.

In the aftermath of his tenure as DCI, Woolsey undertook, pro bono, the case of Kurdish and Iraqi personnel who had served the Agency attempting to carry out a covert-action rebellion against Saddam Hussein. Unfortunately, in the aftermath, no one in the Agency stood up for these people to plead their case to be admitted to the United States in accordance with what was surely our tacit agreement with them. To his great credit, and despite criticism, Woolsey successfully represented them, and justice triumphed.

Jim Woolsey had one of the finest senses of humor of anyone I have ever known. He was delightful to be around. He was never pretentious about his position, and whenever we traveled with the VIP aircraft, he would abandon his private DCI's cabin early on and spend his time with the rest of us. He had a story about every situation, some of them hysterically funny, and he had a great delivery. He also knew more German drinking songs than most Germans. This came from his days at Stanford, when he was, I believe, president of the German Club.

The sad truth was that President Clinton simply neither understood, nor had any use for, intelligence. In the nearly two years he was DCI, Woolsey reportedly had only two face-to-face meetings with the president. That may have been why Woolsey decided to resign.

John Deutch (May 1995–December 1996)

John Deutch was forced by President Clinton to take the job of DCI. In my mind, that set the stage for the troubles that followed. Deutch never wanted the job; he loved being at Defense, and in fact hoped to land the job of secretary of defense. Nevertheless, he did what any good public servant would do when the president asked him the second time—he took the job.

That turned out to be unfortunate for Deutch and for the CIA. Deutch in reality had no use for the CIA. It was obvious everywhere, from his first suggestions to close most of our overseas field stations, to the fact that he brought all of his top personnel in from outside. He either felt he couldn't trust the CIA personnel, or he simply didn't believe that they were capable of advising him on anything. In either case, the result was that he stacked the upper level with people who didn't know the job of intelligence. He brought in an outsider as executive officer, moved an operations officer over to head administration, and brought an analyst in to oversee the clandestine service, the Directorate of Operations.

241

Furthermore, he brought in his own legal counsel. To those inside the CIA, the message was clear—he didn't like us.

Deutch loved the pomp and ceremony of the military. His marine aide told me once, "John loves to move battleships around, and likes motorcycle outriders and sirens and flags flying." That, of course, was not possible for a traveling DCI who himself would be the target of any terrorist who knew he was in the vicinity. I remember handling arrangements for one of his first visits. Everything was laid on well. The ambassador, the head of the local intelligence service, and the government chief of protocol and I were at the ramp when Deutch's plane landed and he deplaned. His first words, before any welcoming comments, were, "Where is everybody?" I told him our people were out doing surveillance and providing escort and safety patrol to get him safely and securely to his next stop. He didn't like the lack of a large retinue, as he would have had in his positions at Defense.

Deutch had a manner that aggravated many of the foreigners he dealt with. He was exceptionally bright, but he was impatient with those he felt were not up to his standards, and, in those cases, he could be downright rude.

I personally like Deutch. I learned from experience when he was deputy secretary of defense that John would ride roughshod over anyone who let him—and I never did. One time I led a delegation of two foreigners over to the Pentagon when he was deputy secretary for a meeting about sensitive subjects. Deutch walked in, said a few words to one of the guests, then turned suddenly to me and asked, "Who the hell are you?"

I looked directly at him and said, "I am your chief in Germany, who the hell are you?" It went very well after that.

At another time, after he became DCI, we were in a small meeting with foreigners when social talk led Deutch to declare, "I am the smartest mathematician in the United States." Unfortunately, our foreign guest chuckled a bit at that, and Deutch responded, "I am at least the smartest mathematician in the United States government."

Things were tense, when the foreign guest turned to me and said, "How about you, Floyd, what are you the best at?"

I paused a second, looked directly at him and replied, "As you should know, I am the best spy in the United States government!" Everyone laughed, and we continued on.

I was very sorry to see the troubles that plagued Deutch at the end of and following his tenure as DCI. Was I surprised? No. The evidence I have seen indicates his taking of classified information off the computer to take home started way before the CIA. I can't help but note reactions to this: first, I have heard numerous people say, "It's the same thing Wen Ho Lee did." And, of course, "Do you suppose if I had done it I would only have my clearances revoked?" It is hard not to believe a double standard was at work here.

George Tenet (July 1997–July 2004)

I believe history will judge George Tenet as one of the best directors in CIA history. He followed the mold set by Judge Webster—he came in as director at a very crucial time, and cleaned things up and restored the morale and reputation of the CIA. I think a fair assessment must wait until the aftermath of his sudden resignation settles down, however long that turns out to be. And, I believe that the assessment will have to consider what happened on 11 September 2001. (The panels investigating the intelligence failures of 9/11 have made their reports, which we need not rehash here.)

Few give credence to the notion that Tenet resigned in order to spend more time with his family. While he is indeed a devoted family man, waiting until his son's senior year in high school to resign to spend more time with him simply does not ring true to many. Nor, in my view, does the idea that Tenet chose his time to resign—just before the congressional committees put out their highly critical reports on the intelligence failures not only for 9/11 but also a litany of other supposed intelligence failures.

The most prominent failures during Tenet's tenure as DCI:

Missing the signs of India's and Pakistan's nuclear test preparations and tests in 1998.

Failure to prevent the bombings of two U.S. embassies in Africa in August 1998.

Failure to apprehend Osama bin Laden and penetrate his organization.

Failure to properly substantiate claimes that Iraq had "weapons of mass destruction" (he supposedly guaranteed the president that it was a slam dunk that Hussein had a robust WMD program).

The failure to detect and provide early warning of the 9/11 plot.

It is not within the scope of this book to address these failures one by one and in depth. All of the above are of course intelligence failures. But let's also look at the facts about the CIA at the time Tenet took over:

By 1996, the CIA in particular and the intelligence community in general had undergone *six years* of ferocious budget and personnel cuts. The Agency closed many of its overseas posts in the very locations where the terrorists operated—in the Mideast and Africa in particular. The truth was, the human intelligence apparatus that Tenet inherited was weak and inadequate.

At the same time, the CIA was languishing with terrible morale and inadequate numbers of case officers, the people who were responsible for recruiting spies. One of Tenet's first accomplishments was to drastically increase the funding to attempt to rebuild and repair the United States' human intelligence capability. Even now, seven years later, that job is not complete, so great was the damage from a decade of neglect.

Nor had the CIA's analytical capability survived the terrible cuts. As a result, at the time of the India/Pakistan nuclear detonation, no one was tasked solely with following India and Pakistan nuclear developments. At the time, only one analyst was charged with following worldwide proliferation.

Lastly, what about 9/11? Given the lack of human sources to penetrate the terrorist's organizations, the CIA and the community were left with interpreting what they could from Signals Intelligence and Overhead Imagery. DCI Tenet provided warnings to both Presidents Clinton and Bush, but barring detailed information from human sources, the entire intelligence apparatus was unable to provide the most important element of all: timing and intent to harm.

From my personal perspective, I continue to believe that 9/11 was a terrible intelligence failure. I believe the real question, however, is not "Was it an intelligence failure?" but "Why was it an intelligence failure?" I believe I have made the case in earlier chapters that the continual disembowelment of our human intelligence system, beginning with President Carter and escalated by President Clinton, must surely shoulder the preponderance of any blame assigned. And, it must also be recognized that under Tenet, the rebuilding process began well before September 11, 2001, and is on its way. Still, that effort is yet incomplete. As DCI Tenet himself told Congress, the Directorate of Operations is still at least five years away from having adequate trained personnel deployed to the field.

I knew Tenet well, and offer a few observations. He gets tremendously high marks for his involvement in the Israeli-Palestinian Peace Process. He was exceptionally proactive, and I believe without his personal involvement the process would have died long ago. Most people are not aware of the historical involvement of the CIA in the Middle East Peace Process, but Tenet knows it well, and made a major contribution to world peace by pushing the process.

He understood and embraced support to the military like no other DCI before him. I believe he understood early that the CIA was going to be forced to operate to provide the "war fighting commanders" in ways they had only done during crisis operations. With the current war against terrorism, the CIA is providing more and better support to the military than ever done before.

In discussions with many of my colleagues after Tenet announced his resignation, it was generally agreed that, although his family reasons were important, Tenet cared more about keeping the CIA and the DCI position out of the politics of the upcoming election of 2004. With the highly critical reports due to be released, he made his move in the hope that neither the intelligence community—nor the CIA in particular—would be a political football. Tenet realized resigning later could be seen as giving in to political pressure, and leaving when he did allowed the president the option of not getting a new DCI nomination into the works until after the election as well. Thus, he protected both the CIA and the DCI position. As usual, Tenet chose nation above self.

I believe this to be one of the most decent, effective, caring men to ever occupy the position as Director of Central Intelligence. He was great with Congress; he cared deeply about the job; and he was approachable. He was an exceptional DCI, and the Agency—and the country—were lucky to have him.

NINETEEN

PRESIDENTS AND INTELLIGENCE

P residents have been users and abusers of intelligence since the inception of the republic. Some have been great users, some have been indifferent, and some have had no use for intelligence—particularly human spies. But they all have had one thing in common—they had some idea of what they expect intelligence to do. Bob Gates, Director of Central Intelligence (DCI) from 1991 to 1993, may have said it best: "Presidents expect that . . . the product [of intelligence] should be able to predict coups, upheavals, riots, intentions, military moves, and the like with accuracy. . . . Presidents and their national security teams usually are ill informed about intelligence capabilities; therefore they often have unrealistic expectations of what intelligence can do for them."[1]

I'll now offer some observations about U.S. presidents and intelligence through history, and I'll confine most of my comments to those presidents who were in office during my active days with the CIA from 1967 to 2001.

None other than the father of our country, President George Washington (1789–1797) ran spy networks himself, and set the precedent for requesting contingency funds from Congress for that purpose. Washington also used ciphers and directed several covert action operations. Perhaps the best-known failed American spy, Nathan Hale, was in fact one of the first spies recruited and dispatched by Washington. The successful interception and decryption of Lord Cornwallis' dispatches precipitated Washington's final victory

1. Robert Gates, "An Opportunity Unfulfilled: the Use and Perceptions of Intelligence at the White House," *Washington Quarterly*, Winter 1989, pp. 38–39.

at Yorktown. Washington's spy adventures were reputed to have been the inspiration for James Fenimore Cooper's highly successful novel *The Spy*, which was first published in 1821.

With the precedent set, most presidents since have actively used intelligence for a variety of purposes. One of the great advocates of democracy, Thomas Jefferson (1801–1809), used covert action against the pirates of the Barbary Coast. James Madison (1809–1817) and John Tyler (1841–1845) both undertook overseas actions based on intelligence, although Madison may also be best known for one of the first intelligence failures—the failure to learn of the British approaching Washington during the War of 1812. The British thus burned the White House, giving Madison and his wife time enough only to save Gilbert Stuart's portrait of Washington and the original draft of the Declaration of Independence.

President James K. Polk (1845–1849) also dispatched secret agents on missions, but is best remembered for his eloquent defense of the contingency fund and the right of the president to protect sources and methods from an inquisitive and demanding Congress. In Polk's own words: ". . . in time of war or impending danger the situation of the country may make it necessary to employ individuals for the purpose of obtaining information or rendering other important services who could never be prevailed upon to act if they entertained the least apprehension that their names or their agency would in any contingency be divulged." That defense remains legal precedent today for the protection of U.S. intelligence agency sources and methods.

During the Civil War, in the tradition of Washington, Abraham Lincoln (1861–1865) was also his own spymaster. Lincoln recruited and ran a spy by the name of William Lloyd, a publisher of rail and steamship guides who had access to every Confederate state. Lincoln tasked and paid Lloyd personally. Unfortunately for Lloyd, no records were publicly available to substantiate this. Lloyd sued for monies due him after Lincoln's assassination, and helped to create law when the Supreme Court ruled against him in "Totten, Administrator, v. The United States" (1875), when it upheld a president's absolute right to contract and dispatch secret agents. The court ruled that Lloyd would have to seek redress from his employer—who of course was dead!

Additionally, Lincoln employed the famous Alan Pinkerton to set up spy networks in the Confederacy. Lincoln also pioneered the use of overt press to gather and analyze intelligence. An avid reader of the southern press, Lincoln made many of his decisions on the basis of press reporting from southern newspapers and other periodicals.

Both presidents, Abraham Lincoln and Jefferson Davis, actively used intelligence during the Civil War. However, with the end of the war, most later presidents were relatively passive about the use of intelligence. Presidents neglected intelligence so much during this period that, during the Spanish-American War, when the United States military discovered they had no maps of Cuba, they were reduced to getting copies from the British.

The one exception was Teddy Roosevelt (1901-1909), who benefited from good intelligence during the Spanish-American War. Enamored with clandestine operations, Roosevelt actually instigated a covert action in Panama to acquire the Canal Zone. Roosevelt immodestly claimed all the credit, stating: "I do not think that any feat of quite such far-reaching importance has been to the credit of my country in recent years; and this I can say was my own work. . . ."[2]

It wasn't until World War I boiled over that presidents again generally became active users of their own intelligence services. Woodrow Wilson (1913–1921) was on the receiving end of an intelligence coup—the Zimmerman Telegram that drove the U.S. to abandon neutrality and enter the war. And, to Wilson goes the accolade of being the developer of independent analysis when he created an independent unit called the Inquiry. This was a group of businessmen and academics whose job was to help the president develop

2. Elting E. Morrison and John Blum, eds., *Letters of Theodore Roosevelt* (Cambridge, Mass.: Harvard University Press, 1975), Vol. 6, p. 1444.

249

courses of action following the end of World War I. Indeed, it was the Inquiry that wrote most of Wilson's Fourteen Points.

The other Roosevelt, Franklin (1933–1945), was president during the worst intelligence failure in U.S. history before 9/11, the Japanese sneak attack on Pearl Harbor. Although he was intrigued with intelligence, and also reportedly ran one or two agents of his own, Roosevelt liked the fractured nature of U.S. intelligence at the time—with the army competing with the navy, and the FBI competing with both. Roosevelt had a cozy, close relationship with British intelligence operating out of New York and liked the British patrician way of doing business. Although he finally agreed to the first national U.S. intelligence apparatus, the Office of Strategic Services (OSS), Roosevelt never supported closer overall coordination of a national U.S. intelligence effort.

During Harry Truman's presidency (1945–1953), a more systematic use of intelligence finally began to take shape with the establishment of the first national intelligence service in history, the CIA, in 1947. When he assumed office, Truman was ill prepared to oversee the nation's secret operations. Incredibly, when Truman was vice president, he was denied knowledge of the Manhattan Project—the development of the atomic bomb. Truman set about to ensure that no future president-elect would be taken by surprise by either foreign events or intelligence operations conducted on behalf of the current administration. Truman instituted a procedure that became tradition and offered all presidential candidates secret intelligence briefings even before the elections. That tradition endures today, although the frequency and depth of these briefings has varied widely. All presidents-elect, however, have received substantial, in-depth intelligence briefing before taking office.

President Dwight D. "Ike" Eisenhower (1953–1961) was the first recipient of these candidate briefings when he first ran for president in 1952. Ike knew the value of intelligence from his days as Supreme Commander during World War II. Ike further knew the

250

value of technical intelligence and pushed technical collection to new heights during his two terms. The U-2 was developed and deployed with Ike's backing. Ike is also known as the first president to publicly acknowledge spying on another country, the U.S.S.R., during the Cold War. This incident was when a U-2 spy plane was shot down over Russia, which greatly embarrassed the administration when the pilot, Gary Francis Powers, was captured alive.

In fact, following Eisenhower, in several instances candidates have believed that pre-election briefings have influenced the presidential debates before the elections. Candidate Richard M. Nixon was persuaded that his opponent, John F. Kennedy, had been briefed on the planning for the Bay of Pigs and took advantage by attacking Nixon as being soft on Cuba. Historians remain divided as to whether or not Kennedy was briefed on the CIA's Cuba operations. Regardless, Nixon never really forgave the CIA.

And, the 1960 election was the first where the vice-presidential candidates received at least rudimentary briefings. All vice-presidential candidates since then have also received briefings in various forms.

But John F. Kennedy (1961–1963) was himself surprised by some of the intelligence he did *not* receive in briefings from President Eisenhower and his staff. As the specter of Vietnam arose, Kennedy complained once in private, "Dammit, Ike never mentioned Vietnam. He talked about Laos and the 'Secret War,' but he didn't say a word about Vietnam." Kennedy had a fascination with intelligence, particularly human intelligence and covert action. Kennedy was the benefactor of two of the greatest spy operations in history. The first was Colonel Oleg Penkovsky of the U.S.S.R., who spied for the United States and Great Britain and provided near-real-time intelligence to the president during the critical time of the Cuban Missile Crisis of October 1962. Additionally, Kennedy benefited from the excellent photography of the U-2 during that same crisis. Perhaps no other president has faced such a crisis—near nuclear war—and saved his nation and perhaps the world due to human and technical intelligence.

President Lyndon Johnson (1963–1969) never liked or trusted the CIA or other U.S. intelligence organizations. Johnson considered intelligence analysts who took official positions to be unhelpful to his own domestic agenda, the Great Society. When I came into the CIA in 1967, Johnson was president, and we were engaged in the escalation of what was to become the Vietnam quagmire. In CIA headquarters, it was said there were three kinds of case officers: those who had been to Vietnam, those who were in Vietnam, and those who were going to Vietnam.

It is entirely possible that Johnson's first experiences with security and intelligence—the tragic assassination of JFK—left him jaded about intelligence, analysis, and warnings. Johnson's first question to his foreign policy team was to ask if the assassination could be part of a Soviet plan to strike, followed by a full-scale missile attack.

But a more likely reason for Johnson's aversion to the Agency was that he reportedly held a grudge, believing the CIA had conspired to help Kennedy get the Democratic nomination at the 1960 convention. Further, Johnson felt the Kennedys—Jack and Bobby— had a mutual admiration with top levels of the CIA that he did not have. Johnson's uneasiness extended to his immediate relationship with the CIA director he inherited, John McCone, with whom he was never comfortable. Given that, it is not difficult to understand Johnson's ultimate rejection of any intelligence on Vietnam with which he disagreed. Further, as documented by Christopher Andrew in his excellent work, *For the President's Eyes Only*, Johnson was really only interested in what the CIA could do in the field of covert action in North Vietnam.[3]

Johnson firmly believed that the increasing military losses absorbed by the North Vietnamese would ultimately lead them to conclude that they couldn't win the war. When CIA analysis

3. Christopher Andrew, *For the President's Eyes Only—Secret Intelligence and the American Presidency from Washington to Bush* (New York: HarperCollins, 1995).

repeatedly stated that, in fact, the North Vietnamese would and could sustain such heavy losses, Johnson simply discarded the CIA analysis and relied even less on their product. In fact, during perhaps the defining moment of the Johnson administration, the Gulf of Tonkin incident in August 1964, Johnson showed no interest at all in CIA information about the incident.

History has proven that CIA assessments during the Vietnam War were accurate, and reflected the deepening quagmire in Southeast Asia. Interestingly, this was in opposition to Johnson's inclination to believe information from his favorite—J. Edgar Hoover—and the reports of growing widespread domestic opposition to the war. Ultimately this led to Johnson's decision in April 1965 to replace McCone with a Texas crony, Vice Admiral William Raborn. Bob Gates captures Johnson's views about intelligence and the CIA with one of his most revealing quotes: "Let me tell you about these intelligence guys. When I was growing up in Texas, we had a cow named Bessie. I'd go out early and milk her. I'd get her in the stanchion, seat myself, and squeeze out a pail of fresh milk. One day I'd worked hard and gotten a full pail of milk, but I wasn't paying attention, and old Bessie swung her shit-smeared tail through that bucket of milk. Now, you know, that's what these intelligence guys do. You work hard and get a good program or policy going, and they swing a shit-smeared tail through it."[4]

Johnson's crony for DCI didn't last long. In June 1966, Johnson surprised everyone, including Richard Helms, by announcing that he would be the new DCI.

History blames Johnson and his administration for the terrible events in the tragic attack on the U.S.S. *Liberty*. Although the Arab-Israeli War of 1967 ended in a sweeping Israeli victory, the attack on a U.S. naval vessel with the resultant death of 34 American sailors continues even to this day to taint the Johnson administration. And the continual denial of access to relevant files at the Johnson Library does nothing to alleviate this.

4. Gates, "An Opportunity Unfulfilled," p. 42.

The final blow to support for the war in Vietnam struck on January 31, 1968, when Tet exploded. During the early hours of the traditional lunar holiday, the Vietcong and North Vietnamese regular forces attacked more than 100 cities in South Vietnam. This ranked with Pearl Harbor in the pantheon of intelligence failures, and ultimately led to Johnson's decision not to seek re-election. On November 5, 1968, Richard Milhouse Nixon was elected President of the United States of America.

As an aside, during Johnson's run for the office in 1964, his opponent, Barry Goldwater, in addition to receiving a crushing electoral defeat by Johnson, "set a precedent by declining to receive any intelligence briefings."[5]

Interestingly, even though President Nixon (1969–1973) was peeved at the CIA because he believed that it provided information to Kennedy in the 1960 election, he did accept candidate briefings when he next ran in 1968. His opponent, Vice President Hubert Humphrey, also received the briefings. And in another twist, two other presidential candidates, Governor George Wallace of Alabama and dark-horse candidate Lester Mattox of Georgia, received the briefings.[6]

After Richard Nixon arrived in the White House, he selected Henry Kissinger as his national security advisor. Together, they made perhaps one of the most experienced foreign policy teams in U.S. history. But ironically, although Nixon was no fan of the CIA, he was enamored of the Agency's covert action capabilities and what they could do for his foreign policy, as was his predecessor.

If there was one thing that bound Nixon to his national security advisor, Henry Kissinger, it was their mutual love of secrecy and foreign policy. And, although Nixon kept Richard Helms on as his DCI, he hedged his bets by moving his former military advisor Lieutenant General Robert E. Cushman in as Deputy Director of Central Intelligence.

5. John L. Helgerson, *Getting to Know the President: CIA Briefings of Presidential Candidates, 1952–1992* (Washington, D.C.: The Center for the Study of Intelligence, Central Intelligence Agency, 1996), p. 71.
6. Ibid., p. 81.

Combined with this penchant for secrecy and action, Nixon dragged a reluctant CIA into expanding Operation Chaos, actually begun in 1967 by his predecessor. As with Johnson, Nixon was convinced that student strikes and riots, both domestic and foreign, were being fed by money from the international communist movement. He thus ordered the CIA and FBI to engage in illegal domestic surveillance on American campuses, activities for which the CIA later—and properly—was called to task. It's important, however, to note that during the academic year 1969–1970, there were 174 bombing incidents on American campuses.[7] This further fueled Nixon's conviction that subversive elements were at work.

Nixon wanted the Vietnam War to end. He had acknowledged that, following the Tet Offensive, a military victory was no longer likely. In an effort to bring negotiations about, Nixon ordered the secret invasion of Cambodia's Parrot's Beak in April 1970. News of this immediately leaked and fueled additional protests on U.S. campuses, to include the tragedy at Kent State University on May 4, 1970, when National Guardsmen shot into a crowd, killing four student demonstrators.

Nixon's foreign-policy focus turned to Chile in October 1970, when the Marxist Salvador Allende was poised to become Chile's democratically elected president. In response, Nixon ordered the CIA to take action, and ordered two simultaneous tracks of covert action: find some way to prevent Allende from being elected to office by the Chilean congress, and, more sinister, engineer a military coup. Incredibly, Nixon also ordered that the proposed military coup be kept secret from the State Department, the Pentagon, and even the U.S. Embassy in Santiago.

The attempted military coup resulted in disaster. Books have been written on this subject, but in short, even though the CIA tried to put together a coup, the CIA was unable to engineer it at such a late date. Allende was elected, and Nixon never forgave the CIA for its failure to stop Allende's election.

7. Ibid., p. 364.

Nixon made a fatal decision in his attempt to set up a covert action capability to operate right out of the White House. Given that one of their tasks was to identify leakers, the unit called itself "the Plumbers." The team included two ex-CIA operatives, E. Howard Hunt and G. Gordon Liddy. It was a farce, breaking into the office of a psychiatrist of an administration critic, Daniel Ellsberg, in hopes of getting damaging evidence. And later, this group was responsible for the Watergate episode that ultimately brought down Nixon. The Watergate burglaries—to tap the phones of the Democratic National Committee in the Watergate building—were almost comic in their ineptitude. The first attempt on May 26, 1972, was aborted. On May 27, a second attempt failed for lack of proper equipment. On May 28, the burglars were able to make entry and place the bugs, but several of the listening devices didn't work. On the morning of June 17, an attempt to enter and fix the malfunctioning bugs ended in the burglars' arrest and the beginning of the Watergate scandal. Incredibly, the scandal did not develop in time to become an issue in the 1972 presidential campaign, when Nixon swept to victory. But Nixon got his revenge on the CIA by firing DCI Richard Helms on November 20, 1972, and sending him off to be Ambassador to Iran. And, it was at this point that President Nixon was heard on tape to say, "What the hell do those clowns do out there in Langley?"

The election of 1972 also had its unique aspects. Nixon's opponent, Governor George McGovern, was scheduled to receive intelligence briefings as the Democratic candidate. Unfortunately, a scandal over McGovern's running mate, Senator Thomas Eagleton, resulted in a cancellation of the briefing, which subsequently never took place.[8]

Nixon began his second term with a great foreign policy success, the Paris Peace Accords, ending 10 years of American involvement in Vietnam. And the year began also with a new Director of Central Intelligence, James R. Schlesinger, who took the position in February 1973. Schlesinger was an arrogant, abrasive man, albeit

8. Ibid., p. 94.

one of many talents. A Washington insider, Schlesinger was a former deputy director of the Office of Management and Budget and Chairman of the Atomic Energy Commission at the time of his selection as DCI.

Schlesinger's stay as DCI lasted only five months, but, per instructions from the president, he wanted to shake up the CIA. In that he succeeded. Schlesinger forcibly fired and retired over 1,500 CIA employees, two-thirds from the elite Directorate of Operations, the spy arm of the nation. Morale at the CIA fell to rock bottom. Overseas assignments were cancelled; many employees overseas received cables advising them to return home to be fired. In my first decade of espionage, this was the lowest point I had experienced. It was devastating, and we expected worse as rumors abounded that Nixon and Schlesinger had only begun.

In retrospect, we were lucky that Schlesinger really had no interest in remaining DCI after the cuts, and that Nixon became obsessed and involved with the problem of surviving Watergate. Nixon moved Schlesinger to Defense (as a reward?) and appointed William Colby, a career professional, as the next DCI in May 1973.

But the turmoil was only beginning. On October 10, 1973, Spiro Agnew resigned the vice-presidency, and Nixon appointed Gerald R. Ford. On August 8, 1974, Nixon announced his resignation, and Ford (1974–1977) became the first non-elected President of the United States.

Although Ford had been appointed and therefore had not received presidential candidate briefings, he had had access to intelligence information during his time on the House Appropriations Committee from 1957 to 1965. This made for a smooth transition when he did begin getting regular CIA briefings.

But in addition to the task of restoring confidence in the presidency, Ford faced the task of restoring confidence in the CIA as well. And, he tackled both. But in the midst of his efforts, working with

DCI Colby, Congress decided to begin its own investigations of American intelligence. To counter this, President Ford set up his own inquiry and established the Rockefeller Commission to look into the alleged misdeeds of the CIA in January 1975. Not to be out-maneuvered, Congress countered with the Senate establishing the Senate Select Committee (the Church Committee), and the House, not to be outdone, fielding the Pike Committee, both with the mission of probing the activities of the CIA.

Fortunately, I was overseas when these hearing made prime-time TV. But their effect was immediate and enormous on the morale of our CIA employee population. Even overseas, the films of Senator Church holding up CIA-made guns for assassination and the jocular handling of this by members of the committees was dev-astating to those of us trying to recruit people to spy on behalf of the United States government. It was the Church Committee that coined the now famous comparison of the CIA to the rogue elephant. And, President Ford, one of Congress' own, continued to have to battle the intelligence committees of both houses of Congress to keep what secrets were left. Also, during this time, in December 1975 the CIA station chief in Athens, Richard Welch, was brutally gunned down by the cowards known as "November 17."

Ford's difficulties with Congress finally ended. His early efforts to restore CIA morale in 1976 were aided by the fact that the Pike Committee self-destructed in controversy when the entire com-mittee voted not to release its own report for security reasons. Additionally, the Rockefeller Commission, and even the Church Committee, found in the end that "the CIA has done its job."

As an important footnote, from 1975 to 1979 I personally recruited more high-level spies than at any other juncture in my career. The truth was that all the publicity about the CIA enhanced the belief by foreigners that the CIA could do anything.

At the Republican National Convention in August 1976, Ford barely defeated another Republican, whose criticisms of him were fatal—Ronald Reagan. And the result was that Ford lost to Jimmy Carter in November by less than two percent of the vote.

President Jimmy Carter (1977–1981), in the words of author John L. Helgerson, "distinguished himself in the eyes of CIA officials by becoming the first presidential hopeful to request intelligence briefings even before receiving his party's nomination."[9] None of us intelligence professionals will ever forget the four years under President Carter. He made being a Washington outsider into a plus in the early stages of his presidency. And, we faced in Walter Mondale, Carter's vice president, one of the most anti-CIA senior cabinet officers in history. However, I must note that, after he became ambassador to Japan, Mondale had an awakening. He had refused to deal with the CIA when he visited Japan in the mid-1970s, but when I visited Tokyo as chief of the East Asia division, Ambassador Mondale hosted a reception for me.

It was very difficult to deal with Carter's belief that HUMINT—spying by people—was distasteful, but the interception of their communications—SIGINT—or the photographing of their denied areas—IMINT—was acceptable. Carter's ultimate rejection of spying came when he refused, for the first time in history, to retain the sitting DCI, George H. W. Bush. And, although Carter eventually replaced him with a crony from the Naval Academy, Stansfield Turner, most people forget that Turner was not Carter's first choice. That honor went to ex-JFK aide Theodore Sorensen. However, Sorensen's background as a conscientious objector worked against him, and during confirmation he withdrew his nomination, clearing the way for the later nomination and confirmation of Turner.

The nomination of Turner, who, along with Carter, had no use for human spying, drove the sagging morale at the CIA even lower. The clandestine service, the DDO, was a shell of its former self, being reportedly nearly only half of its previous size when Turner took charge. In August 1976, Turner announced that the spy directorate would have to take another 820 cuts in the next two years, 147 being immediate forced retirements.[10]

I was overseas when the bombshell was announced, and the lack of sensitivity in the way this was handled was incredible. A number of officers found out they were on the list of 147 by being notified of their retirement electronically. Confidence in Turner, and Carter by extension, was lost. It didn't help that it took Carter a year and a half from Turner's confirmation to make his first visit to the CIA headquarters.

It's ironic that, with the decimation of our human intelligence collection network, it was the subsequent lack of human intelligence on Iran that let Carter down in the end during the hostage crisis. But you can't have it both ways—fire and retire hundreds of experienced, language-qualified officers, and still enhance your ability to recruit spies. By February 1979, when Ayatollah Khomeini returned in triumph, the stage was set for tragedy in Tehran.

Meanwhile, as with every recent president before him, Carter became enamored with the idea of CIA covert action capabilities helping solve a political/foreign policy problem. This took root when, on December 27, 1979, the Soviet Union invaded Afghanistan. Carter was determined to make the Soviet Union pay the price. Under a presidential covert action finding (the requirement that a president find that a covert action is essential to American foreign policy before it can be funded in Congress), in January 1980 Carter authorized the CIA to begin funneling arms to the Mujahideen guerrillas. Again, ironically, it was Carter's successor, Ronald Reagan, who got the credit for driving the Soviets out of Afghanistan via one of the most successful covert action programs ever run—begun by Carter.

But the takeover of the American Embassy in Tehran on November 4, 1979, left Carter with a problem that dominated the remainder of his term. To his credit, Carter authorized a rescue attempt for six diplomats who had managed to escape to the Canadian embassy undetected, and, through daring and good intelligence, these

10. Ibid., p. 434.

six were rescued in January 1980. Details of that escape are contained in Antonio Mendez' book, *Masters of Disguise*. That success encouraged Carter to direct a military rescue attempt to save the other 43 hostages being held in Tehran; Operation Eagle Claw was born.

The CIA and intelligence units of the U.S. military had done their jobs right. Agents and support mechanisms for the rescue were in place. April 24 was set as the date. But things went wrong from the start, and at a refueling location in the Iranian desert, eight Americans and one Iranian interpreter were killed in a mishap when helicopters and refueling aircraft collided. Combined with the earlier loss of three essential helicopters, Carter had no choice but to abort the rescue and announce its failure to the American people—and the world. Carter's presidency never recovered, and he was defeated decisively by Ronald Reagan that November.

In the 1980 campaign, candidate Reagan received but one intelligence briefing, but he became an intelligence advocate following his election. Reagan had a built-in intelligence advantage because his vice president—George H. W. Bush—was the first former Director of Central Intelligence to be elected to that position (and later, as president).

No president in history initiated as many covert action programs as did Ronald Reagan (1981–1989). Interestingly, Reagan's first exposure to intelligence and intelligence matters came after the end of his time as governor of California. President Ford appointed him to the Rockefeller Commission that was to look into the issue of alleged CIA abuses. And, during his campaign against Carter, Reagan scored big when he promised to unleash the CIA.[11] When he appointed as his DCI William J. Casey, an OSS veteran who hated communism and bureaucracy, it was inevitable that trouble was brewing in the intelligence arena.

Morale boomed as the administration got money to rebuild the spy apparatus and launched an all-out assault against communism. But with Casey sitting at the president's elbow, having successfully

11. Ibid., p. 459.

lobbied to be the first DCI in history to be a cabinet member, it was inevitable that this combination would push covert action and intelligence to its legal limits.

Central America was first on both the president's and Casey's agenda, and Nicaragua and the Sandinistas were first on that list. Reagan signed his first finding against Nicaragua, and this included defending El Salvador as one of its objectives. By the end of Reagan's first year, we were arming and training the anti-Sandinista guerrillas from a base in Honduras. The resistance group was known as the Contras.

Interestingly, President Reagan's hard line against the Soviets and Eastern Europe was more popular than the threat that he and Casey saw closer to our own borders. Congressional opposition came in the form of a proposal, the Boland Amendment, which was a structure to forbid the use of U.S. funds to overthrow the democratically elected communist Sandinista government. In December 1982 both houses of Congress adopted the amendment, thereby prohibiting the CIA from providing equipment, training, or advice toward the overthrow of the government of Nicaragua. Casey seethed. And while he seethed, Iran-Contra was born.

It was preceded by the incredible presidential approval for the CIA to begin placing mines in the harbors of Nicaragua, ostensibly to interdict arms shipments arriving there. The blunder worsened when six ships from six different nations—including one from the Soviet Union, struck the mines. It was only through good luck than none sank. A full crisis was now on hand as Congress learned the full extent of the operation and the CIA involvement. (Interestingly, one of my classmates was on the ships laying the mines. He told me that all of our maritime experts had told their superiors that this was an operation that would not stop the arrival of shipping, and would not likely remain covert.)

This was the point at which Reagan and particularly Casey felt the CIA was being too negative and not aggressive enough in taking on the communist threat, particularly in Central America. Thus it was that the direction of these covert action programs moved from the CIA to the National Security Council (NSC), then under National Security Advisor Robert "Bud" McFarlane. With Casey's eager encouragement, McFarlane had been attempting to find other sources than Congress to support the Contras. He found funding initially from Saudi Arabia. And he found the man to make the operation work, Lieutenant Colonel Oliver North, one of his assistants at the NSC.

Meanwhile, in the 1984 presidential campaign, Democratic candidate Walter Mondale received only an overview of world events from the sitting National Security Advisor Bud McFarlane. Mondale never requested any briefings from the CIA, and he lost the election to Reagan.

In Reagan's second term, North quickly became the driving force to Casey's and Reagan's desire to defeat the communists in Central America, no matter the cost. The entire operations left the control of the CIA. North assumed powers far beyond his Lt. Colonel position. And, covert operations began to intermingle. Reagan was also preoccupied with the developing problems in Lebanon, where, by the end of 1985, nine Americans had been taken hostage. Given the Iranian hostage crisis, which turned to his benefit, Reagan was determined to rescue these hostages. Thus, Iran-Contra was born.

Incredibly, Reagan authorized the covert sale, by Israel, of U.S.–made TOW missiles to Iran in an attempt to gain the release of the hostages held in Lebanon, taken and held supposedly under the direction of Iran. In short, the President of the United States of America was humiliated by a gang of thieves, approved of during the rogue operations of the NSC, with the result that only three hostages were released while Iran gained thousands of missiles and other equipment. The basic problem was simply that DCI Bill Casey, and President Reagan as well, simply could not pass by the opportunity to have an antagonistic state—Iran—pay for missiles, the proceeds from which the NSC would then divert to pay for the war against communism in Central America. The trouble was that it was all illegal and ignored intelligence community assessments.

The foolishness of this operation was best illustrated by the scandal which followed, greatly embarrassing President Reagan. Casey was spared the ignominy of this by his unfortunate and untimely stroke and subsequent death in 1987. And, his successor, Bob Gates, had to withdraw his nomination as Director of Central Intelligence in the uproar that followed. In all, it was an inglorious end to the reign of a president and a Director of Central Intelligence who had been provided the very best that the CIA could offer in intelligence and analysis.

During the 1988 election campaign, Democratic candidate Michael Dukakis agreed to and received only one intelligence briefing before the election. Dukakis' vice-presidential candidate, Senator Lloyd Bentsen, attended that one briefing.[12]

By 1989, however, Reagan's legacy had come full turn, and his vice president, George H. W. Bush, a former Director of Central Intelligence, became President of the United States (1989–1993). Earlier, when he had been offered the post of DCI, Bush, a savvy politician, had at first been concerned about being earmarked for a position that was a dead end for a politician—a no-win job designed to take him out of the political arena. Bush, however, was wise enough to accept it only on the condition that he gain direct access to the president—a condition President Ford had agreed to.

Despite the fact that Bush had been DCI, the DCI when he became president, William Webster, was never close to him. As a result, initially Bush relied on his National Security Advisor, Brent Scowcroft, and his deputy, Bob Gates. President Bush began to rely more and more on the advice of Bob Gates to deal with his most pressing problem, the Soviet Union.

12. Ibid., p. 143.

And the Soviet Union began to unravel early in Bush's presidency. By the middle of 1989, Soviet leader Gorbachev's own intelligence apparatus had begun to work against him, and Bush was well served by good, accurate CIA assessments about the staying power of Gorbachev and his likely successor, Boris Yeltsin. Bush was well prepared for the events that followed, due to his affinity for, and support of, good intelligence. Even though the CIA had not predicted the ultimate dissolution of the Soviet Union, they had warned well and early about the likelihood of revolt and trouble in the Eastern European countries. And Bob Gates gained still more influence with the president.

About the same time, an intelligence fiasco further diminished DCI Webster's standing with the administration. The CIA had attempted to plan a coup against Panamanian leader and thug Manuel Noriega. He had proven to be a real pain to the Bush administration, and Bush consequently wanted him removed. The failure of the CIA to implement a covert action there to remove Noriega led Bush to finally order military action to accomplish the goal. The United States invaded Panama on December 20, 1989, and secured the surrender of Noriega the following month. Operation Just Cause, as it was known, was the largest use of military force since the Vietnam War.

By mid-1990, the president was occupied by the Iraqi occupation of Kuwait—an event intelligence had warned was coming but which still surprised the administration diplomatically. The fact was both human and technical intelligence confirmed Hussein had no intention of invading our closet Arab ally, Saudi Arabia, thus freeing the administration to concentrate on a response to the Kuwait invasion. The administration responded with a full-fledged war in the Middle East, Operation Desert Storm, launched in January 1991. No president has ever been served better by intelligence than was President Bush during the war that followed. Human intelligence, imagery, and signals intelligence—all served to provide immediate and up-to-date information desperately needed by—and used effectively by—U.S. military commanders. This was to become the model for "support to the war-fighting commanders-in-chief," a phrase that would become the guiding principle for U.S. intelligence for the next two presidents, Bill Clinton and George W. Bush. It involved the total dedication of all intelligence resources—human intelligence, signals intelligence, imagery, and mazint (the measurement of emanations such as telemetry)—to provide all source collection and analysis directly to the battlefield commanders.

But the Bush administration was to learn a lesson—there are limits to what intelligence of all sorts can do. The first Bush administration got involved in what was known as the Great SCUD Chase.[13] Despite the best intelligence that the United States and Israel could garner, the U.S. forces never totally destroyed Hussein's primary weapon of fear, the SCUD missiles which continued to bring death and destruction throughout the First Gulf War. As we know, the second Bush administration made the same mistake in their mistaken pursuit of weapons of mass destruction during the 2002 Second Gulf War.

One thing the first Bush president did was to ensure a trusted intelligence professional held the nation's highest intelligence office—the Director of Central Intelligence. The first Bush did so when he made Bob Gates the DCI in the fall of 1991. The second Bush emulated his father and decided to leave the consummate intelligence professional, George Tenet, in the position following the election of 2000. In between, as we shall see, the two terms of the Clinton administration largely ignored both intelligence and the DCI.

The presidential campaign of 1992 had many unique aspects as regarded the candidates and intelligence briefings. President and candidate George Bush continued receiving the briefings he had been getting for 12 years. Given that he had also been the Director of Central Intelligence in 1976, he knew and understood the importance of making the intelligence briefings available to all candidates.

266   13. Ibid., p. 524.

Candidate Bill Clinton was offered and accepted intelligence briefings. In another unique growth in the process of acquainting the potential presidents and vice presidents with intelligence, for the first time the briefings of candidates Clinton and his running mate, Al Gore, included sessions with the outgoing chairmen of the two congressional intelligence committees, Senator David Boren and Representative David McCurdy.[14] The candidates were well prepared.

If there is one word to describe the Clinton (1993–2001) administration's attitude toward intelligence in its eight years, it is *neglect*. Along with the Clinton administration's obvious focus on the domestic economy—which won them the election—it was quickly clear that the administration in reality had little interest in intelligence as an adjunct to foreign policy. In one of his first appointments, Clinton ousted one of the most experienced professional intelligence officers to hold the position of Director of Central Intelligence, Bob Gates. The selection of R. James Woolsey as the new Director of Central Intelligence made sense in that he was an experienced Washington insider who knew the ways of Congress. What he did not have, however, was the ear of the president. Nor was the new president interested in the staple of intelligence for presidents, the president's daily brief (the PDB). Breaking with a long tradition, Clinton seldom saw the DCI (reportedly twice in two years), and only had the gist of the PDB briefed to him by his National Security Advisor, Sandy Berger—who had little intelligence experience.

And, what he also did not have by the end of his eight-year presidency was a robust, effective intelligence community. The CIA saw its elite clandestine service, the Directorate of Operations, decimated both in personnel and budget. It is estimated the Clinton administration diverted nearly 80 billion dollars a year away from Defense to its domestic agenda. And the CIA took massive hits from its portion of the Defense budget. Meanwhile, under directed personnel cuts, the CIA shut down a good share of its overseas operations, and our number of human spies (human intelligence or Humint) was decimated, with severe consequences to follow.

As almost all presidents do, Clinton directed a review of intelligence priorities and intelligence reform. There is nothing particularly bad about this; it is a well-established historical event. Harry Truman directed one via the Hoover Commission in 1949. Eisenhower did so with a second Hoover Commission in 1955. Nixon appointed the Packard Commission to review intelligence performance. Jimmy Carter opted for zero-based budgeting to reform intelligence. Ronald Reagan set up the Grace Commission to recommend restructuring.[15] But Clinton's emphasis was on being selective due to tight budget allowances for the foreign agenda. The administration set up a tier system to do this. Issues were divided into two sets—hard targets and transnational issues (such as Cuba, Iran, Iraq, China, North Korea, Libya, and weapons proliferation, narcotics, terrorism, and international crime) and global coverage" (everything else). Further, within these two sets was a tier system ranking things from 1 (top priority) to 4 (bottom).

In other words, the intelligence community was of necessity to ignore the bottom tier of requirements (known as Tier 4 countries), which it could not fund under the cuts it took. It was inevitable that some significant events were going to be missed, and the intelligence community would then be blamed for intelligence failures. The best example, and there were significant others, was in 1998 when the intelligence community missed predicting nuclear tests by both India and Pakistan. Meanwhile, in what was to become the Clinton administration's biggest and costliest overseas military deployment, Bosnia missed the cut as well. Simply put, resources were focused elsewhere under the Tier system.

It was apparent to the DCI, Jim Woolsey, early on that he was not going to have direct access to the president. Although he tried to make it work, finally, in frustration, Woolsey turned in his resignation after having served just less than two years. Never without a quip,

15. Bruce D. Berkowitz and Allan E. Goodman, *Best Truth: Intelligence in the Information Age* (New Haven, Yale University Press, 2000), p. 31.

Woolsey was later to joke that when a small plane crashed on the White House lawn people "thought it was me trying to get an appointment to see the president."

After considerable arm-twisting, Clinton finally secured the agreement of Deputy Secretary of Defense John Deutch to reluctantly take the job. Deutch lasted only one-and-a-half years before he resigned. The next DCI nominee, Clinton's National Security Advisor Anthony Lake, withdrew his nomination after an acrimonious series of events clearly indicated his confirmation hearings were going to be contentious. Finally, six months later, Clinton turned to Deputy Director George Tenet, a savvy professional with great contacts in Congress, who won easy confirmation in July 1997.

Clinton's lack of understanding about the cohesiveness of the intelligence community, and of the principled stands analysts and others are often called upon to take, is reflected in his desire at the end of his administration to pardon the convicted Israeli spy Jonathan Pollard. In 1985, Pollard had been arrested and convicted of spying for the Israelis and received a life sentence. Over the years, the Israeli government had lobbied hard to get Pollard pardoned, to remove the blight of their operation against the United States. With Clinton, they almost succeeded. Word reached the senior levels of the U.S intelligence community that Clinton was seriously considering a pardon of Pollard as one of his final acts. Sources claim that the DCI at that time, George Tenet, made it known to the president such an act would have serious repercussions. Rumor is that Tenet even threatened to resign should the president pardon Pollard, although I have no evidence that this was the case. Knowing Tenet, however, I would certainly not be surprised at such a principled stand.

President George W. Bush (2001–) took office in one of the most hotly disputed elections in U.S. history without a majority of the vote. But it was clear even before the election the new president was going to be very interested in intelligence. The candidate Bush made it clear he valued the personal intelligence briefings very much. Immediately after taking office, he asked the sitting DCI, George Tenet, to remain in position.

As of this writing it is too early to make any lasting observations about this president and intelligence. There have already been, however, two seminal events regarding intelligence—the tragedy of September 11, 2001, and the Second Gulf War.

In regards to the former, the president has made it clear that, while he reluctantly supported an inquiry into why intelligence failed to warn us of 9/11, he nonetheless had full faith in DCI Tenet and in the CIA. Regarding the Second Gulf War, the failure of UN and administration weapons inspectors to find Iraqi weapons of mass destruction (WMD) has been embarrassing to an administration that used those weapons' very presence as the main justification for going to war unilaterally and without provocation. Press releases as I was finishing this book in January 2004 indicated that there was yet another move afoot to blame the intelligence agencies for the failure to locate the WMD. I suspect that, as with other so-called intelligence failures, it will be found that intelligence performed its duty well, but what they found and reported was not in line with what an administration in power desired. Unfortunately, history is replete with similar examples.

For those who are interested in presidents and how they handle and use/abuse intelligence, I recommend three books:

• John Helgerson's, *Getting to Know the Presidents: CIA Briefings of Presidential Candidates: 1952–1992* is a seminal work not to be missed.

• Christopher Andrew's excellent work, *For the President's Eyes Only.*

• G. P. A. O'Toole's *Honorable Treachery.*

TWENTY

THE BAND:
AN OPERATIONAL TOOL

I couldn't possibly finish a book about my career in intelligence without expressing my respect for anyone who was with me or who has helped me over the years with the greatest operational tool ever employed, the Band. Taking a note from *The Blues Brothers*, we always had "a full tank of gas, and it was 300 miles to Chicago."

One of the most important tools any officer brings to the human intelligence side of the house is an interest in things other than just their work. Successful case officers all have one thing in common—a variety of outside interests that make them interesting people, interests that can be parlayed into allowing them to meet a large and varied community of people. In my own case, over 35 years, it was music and tennis. The music part started in my first tour.

I learned guitar and played in a small and inept band during my time at the University of Oregon. When I entered the military, I found myself in a lonely outpost on the East German border, and latched up with two musically accomplished individuals. One was an established presence in the theater at Harvard (a Hasty Pudding regular). The other was an accomplished solo guitarist and Irish vocalist of merit. As a result, in two years on the border, we put together a significant number of performances. I immensely enjoyed the experience.

After the army and a brief career in private industry, I found myself in Washington, D.C., with the CIA. The fellow from Harvard with whom I had performed in my army tour in Germany was living in Washington, so we did a number of private performances there. When I got my first overseas posting, to Asia, it wasn't long before another China hand and I hooked up and did a few gigs over the next few years.

I went on to a second Asian assignment, and got very heavily involved in music, both personally and operationally. I frequented a local bar famous for bluegrass music, and after several evenings of just enjoying the music, I was asked if I played and if I'd like to do a number or two on stage. Of course I did. I was asked to appear regularly as a guest from the audience. I enjoyed it, and I met a number of local government officials who happened to go there regularly. They in turn were thrilled to have me stop by their table on nights when I performed. It was, from the standpoint of putting me in touch with potentially useful contacts, a gold mine. And strangely, no one else in the band spoke any English, and I spoke their language only in rudimentary terms. We would do the songs as done in Nashville—every note right, every word correct, even though they didn't have a clue as to the meaning of the words. At a break, we would sit down, but we couldn't talk to each other.

In addition to the guitar, I studied banjo and really enjoyed it. And, when our ambassador organized the largest American celebration ever held in the capital city—the U.S. Bicentennial celebration—he personally approached me and asked if perhaps I could put together a small set of two or three bluegrass numbers, as typical of our country's music. I agreed, and my banjo teacher and I worked out a couple of nifty bluegrass tunes to fill in.

We were enjoying the massive event when the U.S. ambassador walked up to the podium, in front of what was estimated to be over 10,000 people jamming the area, and announced, "Now I'd like to present the featured performers," and introduced us.

Simple words can't explain how scared my partner and I were. As we stepped up to the mikes, my partner turned to me and whispered, "I'm too scared—I can't play," which scared *me* even more. After I threatened him with unspeakable horrors, we kicked off with "Will the Circle Be Unbroken," and the crowd went nuts. We followed with "Foggy Mountain Breakdown," and by now we could have committed a capital crime and had people cheering. We finished with "Dueling Banjos" and did three encores. Subsequently, I got invitations from the ambassador for months to every function he held. I met lots of important contacts.

I formed another band soon after arriving at my next assignment, and it was operationally useful as well. What a group it was! It was pure bluegrass and country. I played the banjo mostly, and the lead guitarist/vocalist was a rat-control specialist from the United Nations. The bass/mandolin player was a British geologist, and the rhythm guitarist/vocalist was a State Department political officer. It was quite an eclectic group.

We played at the U.S. ambassador's residence, gave a free concert for the local residents, sponsored by the United States Information Service (USIS), and to top it all, played by invitation at the home of the Soviet ambassador.

Upon posting to my European assignment, I quickly hooked up with a number of local military musicians. I formed and played in three bands while there. We played concerts at the local U.S. military clubs, and again performed at the ambassador's residence and gave a free public concert under USIS auspices. On top of that, we were paid rather well when doing regular gigs at the military clubs. I considered (only briefly) giving up my career in the CIA to play regularly when I discovered I would make more money as a musician than I could as a CIA spy.

Back to another Asian assignment; it was now becoming easier to form a good band. We played a number of gigs at the homes of various officials around the capital, and at the embassy. This time the band was good enough to cut a professional recording. In my final assignment, Germany, we put together perhaps the best band I have played with, AKA (intelligence jargon for "also known as"). It was a larger group than usual, and had excellent vocalists, both male and female. We did 11 concerts in Germany, including several resorts and free concerts for the public and for the American community. The band was good enough to reassemble twice back in the United States to play a couple of local gigs.

TWENTY ONE

WHAT'S WRONG AND WHAT'S RIGHT WITH THE CIA

W e need to be very critical of our massive intelligence structure. Criticism keeps it honest, and constantly reviewing how it operates keeps it effective. Taxpayers deserve this kind of scrutiny. I do think the CIA is a terrific organization, but I also think a number of very serious things must be addressed if the CIA is to remain the premier intelligence organization in the world.

We need to remember that the CIA's unique contribution to the United States government is that its sole reason for existence is spying. The CIA doesn't need to duplicate the efforts of other parts of the government. It has to do what no one else can do—spy, analyze the product, and produce all-source intelligence to policymakers.

Beginning in the 1990s we got away from this, and have yet to recover fully, although I believe we are making great strides in that direction. Affirmative action, diversity, and equality for all are admirable, and I support them and have supported them throughout my professional career. There are, however, some realities to spying that simply must be accepted:

Not all the people who spy will work for whomever we determine will be their case officers. A 22-year-old female case officer was sent out to me to handle a 60-year-old Asian asset. He did not want to deal with her, believing it beneath his status as an elder in his society.

I was told to make it work. That was, and is, stupid. Equal opportunity and diversity aside, we needed this man for the access he gave us, and we failed to deal with that fact.

You simply cannot operate in the overseas environment effectively without two things: language, and knowledge of the culture. By 1994, we refused to acknowledge this, and the overseas assignment system went bankrupt. People got assignments simply because they wanted a European or an Asian assignment to broaden their career path to promotion. After several years, we had numerous locales filled with officers that neither knew the culture of the countries to which they were assigned, nor spoke the language. A recipe for disaster followed, and we are still trying to catch up.

You can't spy from headquarters. Beginning around 1992, we closed a large number of overseas facilities to save money, with the idea that we could run these operations out of headquarters. We paid the price for this numerous times, and unfortunately, have yet to fix this problem. In Bosnia, Somalia, parts of Southeast Asia, and most of Africa, we have tried to go in on a temporary-duty basis whenever something comes up. We no longer have the contacts in depth in these regions that we historically had. You simply can't depend on a local police chief, or chief of intelligence, to be your buddy and confidant when you see him once a year. We are seeing the results of this in the difficulties we are having in getting intelligence in Afghanistan. Officers who don't speak the language, carrying bags of money, simply can't do the job required. A permanent presence would have alleviated this. And, in the crisis following September 11, 2001, we bolstered our capability at the Headquarters' Counter-terrorism Center (CTC). We indeed tripled the number of people working there, but took more officers back from overseas to do so when what we really needed was more spies on the ground.

We need to continue to give emphasis to languages. I have been assured this is being addressed, but it is clear now in the war on terrorism that we are woefully inadequate in language-capable officers. Many of us complained when we saw the CIA's language depth disappearing, but no one wanted to do what needed to be done. Salary incentives for difficult languages used to be granted, but that went by the wayside. Language capability used to be one of the essentials to secure an overseas assignment. That too went by the wayside. Simply put, it does no good to send an English-speaking-only officer to a country where those with the secrets don't speak English.

Spying takes unique individuals. Beginning in 1992, for reasons that tie into diversity and related trends, we determined that the trouble with the Directorate of Operations was its culture. And we undertook, unfortunately, a program that I call "Kill That Culture." And we did. We also damn near killed our ability to spy in the process. The evils in the system could have been addressed without ripping the guts out of the Directorate of Operations. The truth is, not everyone can spy. Live with it, and reward that small number of officers who can actually successfully recruit people to spy.

We need to recognize that perhaps a number of officers should spend their careers in only one or two countries, becoming the experts they need to be. We got so worried about the possibility that our officers would go native that it is nearly impossible to find officers who stay more than three years in any one country. We used to have numerous officers who made their entire career serving in only one geographical component. That practice fell to the broadening experience that came to be one of the precepts toward promotions.

The other problem greatly affecting our ability to run operations, recruit spies, and produce good intelligence relates to the badly conceived plan relating to a program called the Capital Working

Fund. The program began around 1995 or 1996. The idea of it was that activities had to pay for themselves and that everyone had to manage their own support budget. It has been a disaster, and has left the Agency in general, and the Directorate of Operations in particular, without the mechanisms it needs to focus on spying. Instead, our operating divisions spend the time of our operations personnel trying to get supplies, air tickets, and other necessities instead of doing what they were hired to do. The scheme, unfortunately, came from the administrative top. The result was the dismemberment of the very services we had come to rely on to support the difficult activity of spying.

In the meantime, the support mechanism was sold off. We no longer have our own airline; people thousands of miles away that never heard of spying and have no idea of the risks involved handle our health coverage; and, what was once the greatest retirement system in the world was handed over to the Office of Personnel Management. You can no longer get anyone to personally answer a telephone on any question regarding retirement pay or medical claims.

It is essential that we recognize that spying is not a quantifiable activity with a product that comes off the assembly line like a television set. There are some times we spend a huge amount of time, and yes, dollars, attempting to secure a spy in a needed location, and fail. We still have to pay for that. It is an imprecise art form that does not allow us to always look at the bottom line. It has led to us not having enough spies where we need them most.

Further, the Agency developed way too many superstructures over the past decade. Senior positions that are needed in the field have been taken for headquarters positions. And I cannot help but note this goes all the way to the ridiculous—a case officer was and is assigned to liaise with television and Hollywood. It would seem to me that he would be more productive spying in the back alleys of Algeria.

I am not in the minority feeling this way. During the year before the publication of this book, a whole series of articles were published delineating virtually the same observations. I believe in the CIA. I believe it has the greatest work force in the world, and it continues to hire and attract the very best and brightest. I believe its future is secure, and it will continue to gather and collect the best intelligence it can under the circumstances. But I believe in order for this to happen, the CIA needs to go back to the basics of spying and quit trying to look like a private business conducting its work for profit.

And, sadly and lastly, the Agency has lost its way in recognizing its people. Awards and recognition used to be significant individual affairs. Now, they are done in large groups to make it easier. Formerly, when any DO officer retired, he was given an individual ceremony, with a senior officer no lower than the associate deputy director of operations presenting the award. By way of example, I was honored with the Distinguished Career Intelligence Medal upon retiring. When I was called regarding the ceremony and received the paperwork, I discovered that I was one of many who would be getting awards that day. It was to be a massive ceremony in the CIA auditorium, where all awardees simply walk up to the stage when their name is called and walk off. In reality, I was quite disappointed by this. I had nearly 35 years of service, had risked my life for my country and the Agency, had been in the Senior Intelligence Service ranks for over a decade, and had served in many senior assignments. It seems to me that it merited at least a private meeting with one of the Agency senior officials for my family and me. We used to move heaven and earth to see that each of our people retiring had what Andy Warhol called their 15 minutes of fame. I called in and asked for my award to be mailed to me instead. I am not bitter about this, simply disappointed. We ought to do better than put an assembly line together for recognition.

So, what's right with the CIA? The answer is, a lot.

The Agency had consistent and good leadership at the top for the past nine years. The leadership began tackling the problems I mentioned above as early as 1998, and the expansion of our human intelligence system is well underway, although we cannot expect it to be a quick fix.

The Agency's analytical capability is second to none. The establishment of the Kent School of Analysis put the emphasis back on quality analytical work and the development of a professional cadre for the future.

The Agency continues to recruit the best and brightest from America's youth. It is extremely gratifying to refer numerous colleagues who are honor roll graduates to the Agency for employment consideration. It is this quality of new employees that will guarantee the continued excellence of the CIA.

The Agency continues to have the support of not only the political leadership on both sides of the aisles of Congress, but also of the American people. I continue to be amazed and gratified by the almost universal support for American intelligence I find everywhere I go and everywhere I speak in public. I am always moved when, as frequently happens, someone in an audience stands up and says, "I just want to thank you for what you did with your life." It doesn't get any better than that.

TWENTY TWO

PASEMAN'S
TEN AXIOMS OF SPYING

I spent nearly 35 years as a spy. I moved through the ranks of the Central Intelligence Agency from a GS-07 to an SIS-04, with a total of 12 promotions. Over 20 of those years I spent spying overseas. As a result, when I retired, I had more years in the spying end of the business than anyone else who was still on active duty. Reflecting on all of my years as a spy, I'd like to offer my 10 axioms of spying, which I believe are relevant to our problems in the post–9/11 world.

Axiom 1: *Not everyone is cut out to be a spy.*
Let's be careful whom we bring in to be professional human spies. If you can't bring yourself to ask someone to commit treason against his or her own government, you are not going to be a good spy.

Axiom 2: *Spies need to be experts in the craft of espionage, master a foreign language, and be an expert on one region of the world.*
We must return to the days in which an officer could spend his entire career in one area of the world without the career-broadening assignments out of area. A spy should be a person with the most knowledge of his assigned area.

Axiom 3: *You cannot force anyone to spy for you.*

The most misunderstood aspect of spying is that most people spy for ideological reasons. Some do spy for money, sex, revenge, or the thrill of it. But most spy because they believe in the cause of the nation for whom they spy.

Axiom 4: *Integrity is one of the most important traits of a good spy.* The temptations are many in the world of espionage. Officers have access to money and opportunities to do pretty much whatever they wish. It is well known in the business that under no circumstances will you operate against your own organization.

Axiom 5: *A spy must have state-of-the-art technological support.* Spy gear such as secret writing, miniature cameras, disguises, and agent communications are important. But so is access to imagery and analysis. The spy needs it all and needs the best there is.

Axiom 6: *Spies without good analysis behind them are useless.* A spy has to be told what to collect, what is important, what is already known, and so forth. You don't want your spy collecting information that's already known or that can be collected by other, less costly means.

Axiom 7: *Anybody can be a great spy, male or female, all races and creeds.* The spy business needs diversity to complete its mission in a diverse world.

Axiom 8: *Not everyone can or should become a manager.* Our system has let us down. At a certain stage, officers are promoted into the ranks of management whether or not they have demonstrated that they are management material.

Axiom 9: *Our senior management structure needs more officers*

who have actually spied overseas for a living.
We have three to four layers of top management without enough people who have actually spied overseas.

Axiom 10: *You can't do human spying from Washington, D.C.*
We need to move the increasingly large numbers of people gathering in headquarters back out to the field, where the spying is done.

TWENTY THREE

9/11

Having finished the original manuscript for this book before the terrible events of September 11, 2001, I was urged to put together some short thoughts about intelligence after the tragedy. The following are my observations:

The 9/11 tragedy was an intelligence failure.
I am amazed that there is even any debate about this. Given the Pearl Harbor nature of the attack and the terrible devastation, given the tremendous amount of money spent on intelligence by myriad organizations, and given that the creation of the behemoth intelligence apparatus was precisely to provide warnings to prevent such a disaster, how can it be judged anything other than an intelligence failure?

The flaws that allowed 9/11 to happen must be repaired.
The degradation of our intelligence capabilities, which happened over several administrations, both Democratic and Republican, is well on the way to being fixed—again. Enormous amounts of money are being spent, and relatively productively—particularly on satellite imagery and on the human intelligence side. But these fixes take time, and my main concern is whether or not the American public has the tenacity to stay with the process. Recruiting, training, and dispatching good case officers, with the language skills and other tools needed, takes years. From being recruited into the Agency to being deployed out on the street takes

somewhere around four years. And satellite development and deployment also takes considerable time and money to bring to full capability. Repairing the flaws that led to 9/11 will require a long and heavy commitment in fiscal and personnel resources, the likes of which we have not seen since the onslaught of the Cold War.

We must not only maintain our overseas presence, we must increase it with properly qualified and trained personnel.
Following the tragic events of 9/11, we indeed did build our centers (the Washington-based organizations working on terrorism, counter-intelligence, and crime), but did so at the expense of our overseas presence. Spying is still best done on the ground overseas.

A non-governmental blue-ribbon panel is needed.
Simply put, neither the intelligence apparatus nor Congress is equipped to investigate themselves. Already the partisan quarrelling in Congress has stymied the committee set up to conduct such an investigation. Better that the administration set up an independent panel of well-respected intelligence veterans, business leaders, and former members of Congress, and give them wide latitude and support to conduct this inquiry. The danger is that once all the dust from the Iraq operation settles, efforts to effect needed changes will simply go away.

There was no intelligence really indicating that Saddam Hussein had weapons of mass destruction or that he was affiliated with al Qaeda.
As this book goes to press, neither allegation has been substantiated.

The CIA should not be in the business of assassination.
It's one thing to destroy an enemy in combat; it's another thing altogether to compile lists of people and order your intelligence apparatus to kill them. *The New York Times* reported that,

"President Bush has provided written legal authority to the CIA to hunt down and kill the terrorists."[1]

I don't know if this report is true or not, and I have no difficulty with terrorists being killed during attempts to bring them to justice. But my worry is this can easily get out of control. Already we have seen innocent people killed as part of the collateral damage from several assassination attempts, particularly the November 2002 attack in which an al Qaeda leader was reportedly assassinated by use of a Hellfire missile. In that attack, five people other than the target were also killed. Who decides who is on the list? Who decides when enough is enough? Under what circumstances does this authority end? And it's important to remember that the presidential prohibition on assassinations first laid down by President Gerald R. Ford for good and compelling reasons has not been rescinded.

Most important, we must remember who we are and the principles that made the United States great. We do not want to become like our enemies.

There have been numerous articles by columnists of courage stressing this point. Perhaps Leonard Pitts Jr. said it best in a column published in March 2003: "For better or for worse, a new nation will be born here . . . we stand on the edge of a change that feels fundamental, profound, and permanent. We are a giant that is no longer inclined to watch its step. Less involved with or concerned by the world around us. We are becoming a go-it-alone nation, a don't-give-a-damn-what-anybody-else-says nation."[2]

As former DCI Jim Woolsey remarked, "We also have to remember who we are. We are creatures of Madison's Constitution and his Bill of Rights. . . ."[3]

1. James Risen and David Johnson, "Bush Has Widened Authority of CIA to Kill Terrorists," *New York Times*, December 15, 2002.
2. Leonard Pitts Jr., Hampton Roads, Virginia, *Daily Press*, March 22, 2003, p. 17.
3. Jim Woolsey, speech at the National War College, Nov. 16, 2000.

EPILOGUE

As you probably gleaned from my stories, the intelligence profession is replete with acronyms, things like HUMINT (human intelligence), IMINT (imagery), and SIGINT (signals intelligence). Mark Lowenthal has noted in his excellent work, *Intelligence: From Secrets to Policy*, that intelligence professionals, in some of their lighter moments, also refer to:

PIZZINT The intelligence Soviet officials gathered by noting the number of pizza vans carrying pizza into CIA headquarters late at night—a sure indication that a major event was underway.

LAVINT Information gathered from men's rooms.

RUMINT Rumor of any kind without any value.

DIVINT Intelligence gleaned via revelation from the Almighty.[1]

Similarly amusing—and formulated by someone with real experiences—are the six stages of any intelligence operation. These came to me from my military assistant in Germany. I have no idea of their origin, but everyone engaged in intelligence will see that the chain of events is closely linked to reality. The six stages are:

1. Enthusiasm
2. Promises of support
3. Disillusionment
4. Alarm
5. Search for someone to blame
6. Reward all the non-participants

1. Mark M. Lowenthal, *Intelligence: From Secrets to Policy* (Washington, D.C.: CQ Press, 2000), p. 71.

GLOSSARY

agent An individual, other than a staff employee, employed by an intelligence organization for the purpose of clandestine intelligence collection, counterintelligence, or covert action; a spy.

agent of influence An agent who is in a position to influence public opinion in favor of certain causes and in the interests of a given foreign nations. Such a person may be a journalist, politician, military leader, labor leader, author, scientist, or commentator. The agent of influence may be recruited under a FALSE FLAG.

asset Any agent, SAFEHOUSE, network, DEAD DROP, or other component of clandestine operations. When in reference to a person, *asset* is generally exchangeable for AGENT.

black Being free of hostile surveillance while on a clandestine mission; also refers to being in place undetected or unknown, such as flying in black.

blown To have one's cover exposed; to have an operation become public.

case officer A Central Intelligence Agency officer who recruits and runs spies.

Central Intelligence Agency The U.S. government organization responsible for coordinating all overseas intelligence operations.

Chief of Station (COS) The senior CIA officer overseas in charge of the intelligence activities in a particular country.

clandestine Secret, or done in secret.

clean To be free of hostile surveillance.

compartmentation The insulation of personnel from information that they have no reason to know (or need to know), to protect the operation/information from discovery by people unauthorized to know the information. Generally, there are various levels and channels or compartments concealed from discovery.

contact plan/instructions A schedule for agent meetings or communications with their CASE OFFICER. Contact plans contain meeting times, or broadcast times, visual or oral recognition signals, danger and safety signals, and meeting spots or dead-drop sites. They may also contain bona fides for another case officer.

counterespionage A form of counterintelligence in which operations are run to negate, confuse, deceive, subvert, monitor, or control the agents and operations of a foreign power.

counterintelligence The activity of gathering information to protect one's operations, self, and government against the espionage of others on behalf of a foreign power. Generally, all clandestine operations have a counterintelligence requirement to protect them from discovery, dependent upon the sensitivity of the information being gathered.

cover The identity and occupation used by a case officer or agent to conceal his espionage activities. It may be OFFICIAL COVER or NON-OFFICIAL COVER and is used to protect the person using it.

cover story The background legend you have developed to explain who you are and why you are where you are.

covert action One of the distinct categories of intelligence, covert action is the secret activities carried out under presidential authority, designed not to reveal the involvement of the United States. It generally involves paramilitary activities, propaganda, or political action in supplying financial and technical assistance to political parties or action groups designed to overthrow an existing political order or party, consistent with secret United States policy decisions. Even though the U.S. does not want its involvement in covert action revealed, this generally fails. The Bay of Pigs, the overthrow of Prime Minister Mohammad Mossadegh of Iran in 1953, and current activities like secret radio broadcasts into Iraq are examples of covert action.

covert communications (COVCOM) An agent's spy gear for communicating with his case officer. It may include secret writing, radio, microdot, or other means of secret communication.

cryptonym A false name used in official correspondence to hide the real identity of the agent, officer, or operation.

dead drop A concealed location used as a communications cutout between an agent and a courier, case officer, or other agent in the network.

deception Measures designed to mislead a foreign power, organization, or persons by manipulation, distortion, or falsification of evidence to induce them to react in a manner prejudicial to their interests.

defector A disaffected individual who renounces his citizenship and requests political asylum from another government. Generally, it is assumed the defector has some intelligence value regarding the country or activities of the country that he seeks to leave. Many defectors are persuaded to delay their departure in order to work in place.

denied area Intelligence jargon for countries considered hostile to the U.S. government and which have consequently mounted huge counterintelligence efforts against CIA personnel stationed on their soil. In other words, they denied us the ability to work safely in their countries. During the Cold War, this term was used for our operations against the Soviet Union and East Bloc, China, Vietnam, North Korea, and Cuba.

Deputy Chief of Station (DCOS) Second in command to the COS.

Deputy Director for Administration (DDA) One of the four CIA directorates, responsible for administrative matters.

Deputy Director for Intelligence (DDI) One of the four CIA Directorates, responsible for the production of all-source analysis for the U.S. government.

Deputy Director for Operations (DDO) One of the four chiefs of the CIA directorates, the DDO is in charge of the espionage directorate, and is the chief spymaster for the United States government.

Deputy Director for Science and Technology (DDS&T) The fourth CIA directorate, responsible for all high-tech development and work. This directorate was also reorganized in 2001.

Director of Central Intelligence (DCI) The president's personal head of the intelligence community.

disinformation Any information fabricated or distorted by one government on a non-attributable or falsely attributable basis for the purpose of influencing the actions of one or more government organizations.

double agent Also known as a controlled foreign agent; an agent who is recruited to work against his original service or community, either through coercion, disaffection, or defection.

espionage Intelligence activity directed toward the acquisition of information through clandestine means and proscribed by the laws of the country against which it is committed.

executive orders Directives issued by the president of the United States that spell out the parameters of a certain type of action.

exfiltration The removal of an agent or officer to safety.

fabricator/fabrication An agent who furnishes false information for financial gain.

false flag The use of a third country's nationality to effect the recruitment of an agent so they do not know an activity's true country of origin.

flap The political uproar over an operation that has become public.

Foreign Broadcast Information Service (FBIS) The CIA arm responsible for receiving and interpreting the overt broadcast literature coming from all over the world.

foreign intelligence Information relating to the capabilities, intentions, and activities of foreign powers, organizations, or persons.

House Permanent Select Committee on Intelligence (HPSI) The House of Representatives' intelligence oversight committee.

HUMINT Intelligence coming from a human source.

Illegal A deep-covered officer or agent in a foreign country who is usually, but not always, working independently of the local resident intelligence service. He may have a third country nationality, but the country that employs him will not acknowledge him.

IMINT Imagery intelligence, the product from photography by agents or satellites.

intelligence Both a product and a process; it can be as simple as knowledge of something. It is the product resulting from the collection and processing of information concerning actual or potential situations and conditions pertaining to foreign and domestic situations. Intelligence is generally, but not always, acquired clandestinely and is generally information the enemy wishes to keep secret and information that the original source does not wish you to have.

liaison General term applied to formal relationships established with other countries' intelligence services.

mole A literary and media term for a penetration agent infiltrated into an opposition intelligence service or other opposition government agency.

need-to-know The most basic element of security: unless someone has an official need to know classified information, they are not to receive it.

non-official cover A cover other than that of an official government organization, such as private business.

officer in residence (OIR) A CIA officer serving overtly in an official academic position for the purpose of teaching intelligence-related subjects.

overt A known public ally used as an intelligence officer.

penetration The recruitment of agents within or the infiltration of agents into a foreign organization for the purpose of collecting intelligence against that country or to influence its actions.

permanent change of station (PCS) Government terminology for movement from one official post to another.

persona non grata (PNG) The official designation that an official of a foreign country is to leave a host country, generally for reasons incompatible with their diplomatic standing; being thrown out.

President's Foreign Intelligence Advisory Board (PFIAB) An officially appointed blue-ribbon panel of experts from all walks of life that advises the president on intelligence matters.

recruitment The tradecraft process of enlisting a target individual to work for an intelligence service—in most cases against his own country. The process includes spotting, assessing, developing, and recruitment. Motivation may be ideological, financial, or other, such as revenge.

running an agent (or handling an agent) Spy terminology for the process of meeting with the recruited agent (spy). It involves all aspects of spying, such as teaching the agent how to communicate with secret writing or microdots; teaching the agent how to avoid detection; guiding the agent on what secrets to steal and how; paying the agent; how to meet safely and securely. All done under CLANDESTINE circumstances.

safehouse A sterile location, normally a house or apartment—but could be a hotel room as well—used to meet agents securely.

Senate Select Committee on Intelligence (SSCI) The U.S. Senate's intelligence oversight committee.

Senior Intelligence Service (SIS) The CIA's equivalent of the government's senior executive service—a cadre of top CIA intelligence business executives.

SIGINT Signals intelligence, the interception of communications for intelligence purposes.

sources and methods The basis for the security classification of intelligence, that is, by how and with whom you do your espionage. It refers generally to the names of agents and organizational specifics on how the intelligence is acquired.

station Designation of the official location of the CIA's main operating components overseas.

support agent An agent recruited to do support work, such as finding and living in safehouses, serving as a courier, or any of the other activities required to support a spy in place. In many cases, this support agent is a local citizen of the country in which the CIA operates.

surveillance The tradecraft of undetected observation. Surveillance can be physical, electronic, or acoustic. It may include audio or photographic observation and includes mail opening.

surveillance detection route (SDR) A detailed and pre-planned route an agent or case officer takes en route to and from a clandestine meeting or activity. It may involve countersurveillance, and may include photographic countersurveillance.

temporary duty (TDY) Official government terminology that someone is only temporarily in a location for a specific time and specific reason.

tradecraft The art, methodology, and know-how of conducting clandestine operations and intelligence collection techniques. Includes such things as dead drops, covert communications, how to recruit agents, secret writing and photography, surveillance, and surveillance detection.

turnover The official changing of an agent from one case officer to the other—i.e., turning him over to another.

walk-in Someone who has something to offer or sell to the intelligence service he is approaching: a volunteer spy.

RECOMMENDED READING

For those who may be interested in additional readings on the subject of intelligence, intelligence and foreign policy, and terrorism, I have compiled a recommended bibliography, which I have culled from hundreds of books in preparing my courses on intelligence. I have broken it down into categories that I hope are useful in selecting readings.

Intelligence: Memoirs

Clarridge, Duane R., with Digby Diehl. *A Spy for All Seasons: My Life in the CIA*. New York: Charles Scribner's Sons, 1997.

Colby, William E., and Peter Forbath. *Honorable Men: My Life in the CIA*. New York: Simon & Schuster, 1978.

Gordievsky, Oleg. *Next Stop: Execution*. London: Macmillan, 1995.

Helms, Richard, with William Hood. *A Look Over My Shoulder: A Life in the Central Intelligence Agency*. New York: Random House, 2003.

Holm, Richard L. *The American Agent: My Life in the CIA*. London: St. Ermin's Press, 2003.

Shevchenko, Arkady N. *Breaking With Moscow*. New York: Alfred A. Knopf, 1985.

Smith, Joseph B. *Portrait of a Cold Warrior: Second Thoughts of a Top CIA Agent*. New York: Ballentine Books, 1976.

Stevenson, William. *A Man Called Intrepid: The Secret War*. New York: Harcourt Brace Jovanovich, 1976.

Turner, Stansfield. *Secrecy and Democracy: The CIA in Transition*. Boston: Houghton Mifflin, 1985.

Wolf, Markus. *Man Without a Face: The Autobiography of Communism's Great Spymaster*. New York: Random House, 1997.

Wright, Peter. *Spycatcher: The Candid Autobiography of a Senior Intelligence Officer*. New York: Viking Press, 1987.

Biography

Brand, Clare. *The Man in the Mirror: A Life of Benedict Arnold*. New York: Random House, 1994.

Brown, Anthony Cave. *Treason in the Blood: H. St. John Philby, Kim Philby, and the Spy Case of the Century*. Boston: Houghton Mifflin, 1994.

Coulson, Major Thomas. *Mata Hari: Courtesan and Spy*. New York: Harper Brothers, 1930.

Dawidoff, Nicholas. *The Catcher Was A Spy: The Mysterious Life of Moe Berg*. New York: Pantheon, 1994.

Deakin, F. W., and G. R. Storry. *The Case of Richard Sorge*. New York: Harper and Row, 1966.

Grose, Peter. *Gentleman Spy: The Life of Allen Dulles*. Boston: Houghton Mifflin, 1994.

Hatch, Robert McConnell. *Major John André: A Gallant in Spy's Clothing*. Boston: Houghton Mifflin, 1984.

Hood, William. *Mole: The True Story of the First Russian Intelligence Officer Recruited by the CIA*. New York: W.W. Norton & Co., 1982.

Korn, David. *Blond Ghost: Ted Shackley and the CIA's Crusades*. New York: Simon & Schuster, 1994.

Maas, Peter. *Killer Spy: The Inside Story of the FBI's Pursuit and Capture of Aldrich Ames, America's Deadliest Spy*. New York: Warner Books, 1995.

——— . *Wild Bill Donovan: The Last Hero*. New York: Times Books, 1982.

Mangold, Tomas. *Cold Warrior: James Jesus Angleton—The CIA's Master Spy Hunter*. New York: Simon & Schuster, 1991.

Mitchell, Marcia and Thomas. *The Spy Who Seduced America: The Judith Coplon Story.* Montpelier, Vermont: Invisible Cities Press, 2002.

Persico, Joseph E. *Casey: The Lives and Secrets of William J. Casey—From the OSS to the CIA.* New York: Viking Penguin Books, 1990.

———. *Roosevelt's Secret War.* New York: Random House, 2001.

Tanenhaus, Sam. *Whittaker Chambers.* New York: Random House, 1997.

Thomas, Evan. *The Very Best Men: Four Who Dared: The Early Years of the CIA.* New York: Simon & Schuster, 1995.

Weiner, Tim, David Johnson and Neil A. Lewis. *Betrayal. The Story of Aldrich Ames—An American Spy.* New York: Random House, 1995.

General History

Ambrose, Stephen E. *Ike's Spies: Eisenhower and the Espionage Establishment.* New York: Doubleday, 1981.

Andrew, Christopher. *For the President's Eyes Only: Secret Intelligence and the American Presidency from Washington to Bush.* New York: HarperCollins, 1995.

Axelrod, Alan. *The War Between the Spies: A History of Espionage During the American Civil War.* New York: Atlantic Monthly Press, 1992.

Baer, Robert. *See No Evil: The True Story of a Ground Soldier in the CIA's War on Terrorism.* New York: Crown Publishers, 2002.

Barron, John. *Operation Solo: The FBI's Man in the Kremlin.* Washington, D.C.: Regnery Publishing, 1996.

Bearden, Milt, and James Risen. *The Main Enemy: The Inside Story of the CIA's Final Showdown with the KGB.* New York: Random House, 2003.

Bearse, Ray, and Anthony Read. *Conspirator: The Untold Story of Tyler Kent.* New York: Doubleday, 1991.

Berkowitz, Bruce D., and Allan E. Goodman. *Strategic Intelligence for American National Security*. Princeton, N.J.: Princeton University Press, 1989.

———. *Best Truth: Intelligence in the Information Age*. New Haven: Yale University Press, 2000.

Breitman, Richard. *Official Secrets: What the Nazis Planned, What the British and Americans Knew*. New York: Hill and Wang, 1998.

Breuer, William B. *Shadow Warriors: The Covert War in Korea*. New York: John Wiley & Sons, 1996.

Carter, John J. *Covert Operations as a Tool of Presidential Foreign Policy in American History from 1800 to 1920*. Lewiston, Maine: Edwin Mellen Press, 2000.

Cockburn, Andrew and Leslie. *Dangerous Liaison: The Inside Story of the U.S.–Israeli Covert Relationship*. New York: HarperCollins, 1991.

Colby, William E., with James McCargar. *Lost Victory: A Firsthand Account of America's Sixteen-Year Involvement in Vietnam*. Chicago: Contemporary Press, 1989.

Conboy, Kenneth, and James Morrison. *Feet to the Fire: CIA Covert Operations in Indonesia, 1957–58*. Annapolis: Naval Institute Press, 1999.

Crile, George. *Charlie Wilson's War: The Extraordinary Story of the Largest Covert Operation in History*. New York: Atlantic Monthly Press, 2003.

DeForrest, Orrin, and David Chanoff. *Slow Burn: The Rise and Bitter Fall of American Intelligence in Vietnam*. New York: Simon & Schuster, 1990.

Dulles, Allen. *The Craft of Intelligence*. New York: Charles Scribner's Sons, 1992.

———, ed. *Great True Spy Stories: 39 True Accounts from Greek Antiquity to the Cold War*. Secaucus, N.J.: Castle, 1968.

Dvornik, Francis. *Origins of Intelligence Services: The Ancient Near East, Persia, Greece, Rome, Byzantium, the Arab Muslim Empires, the Mongol Empire, China, Muscovy.* N.J.: Rutgers University Press, 1974.

Epstein, Edward Jay. *Deception: The Invisible War Between the KGB and the CIA.* New York: Simon & Schuster, 1989.

Felix, Christopher. *A Short Course in the Secret War.* New York: Madison Books, 1992.

Fishel, Edwin C. *The Secret War for the Union: The Untold Story of Military Intelligence in the Civil War.* Boston: Houghton Mifflin, 1996.

Frank, Richard B. *Downfall: The End of the Japanese Imperial Empire.* New York: Random House, 1999.

Gates, Robert. *From the Shadows: The Ultimate Insider's Story of Five Presidents and How They Won the Cold War.* New York: Simon & Schuster, 1996.

Gelfand, Lawrence E. *The Inquiry: American Preparations for Peace—1917–19.* New Haven: Yale University Press, 1963. Reprinted. Westport, Connecticut: Greenwood Press, 1976.

Godson, Roy, Earnest R. May, and Gary Schmitt. *U.S. Intelligence at the Crossroads: Agendas for Reform.* Washington, D.C.: Brassey's, 1995.

Gollomb, Joseph. *Spies.* New York: Macmillan, 1928.

Grant, Zalin. *Facing the Phoenix: The CIA and the Political Defeat of the United States in Vietnam.* New York: W.W. Norton, 1991.

Gup, Ted. *The Book of Honor: Covert Lives and Classified Deaths at the CIA.* New York: Doubleday, 2000.

Haswell, Jock. *Spies and Spymasters: A Concise History of Intelligence.* London: Thames and Hudson, 1977.

Herrington, Stuart A. *Stalking the Vietcong: Inside Operation Phoenix, A Personal Account.* Novato, California: Presidio Press, 1997.

Hersch, Burton. *The Old Boys: The American Elite and the Origins of the CIA.* New York: Charles Scribner's Sons, 1992.

Heuer, Richards J. Jr. *Psychology of Intelligence Analysis.* Washington D.C.: Center for the Study of Intelligence, 1999.

Holober, Frank. *Raiders of the China Coast: CIA Covert Operations During the Korean War.* Annapolis: Naval Institute Press, 1999.

Hulnick, Arthur S., and Richard R. Valcourt. *Fixing the Spy Machine.* Washington, D.C.: Praeger Publishers, 1999.

Jakub, Jay. *Spies and Saboteurs: Anglo-American Collaboration and Rivalry in Human Intelligence Collection and Special Operations, 1940–45.* New York: St. Martin's Press, 1999.

Jeffreys-Jones, Rhodri and Andrew Lownie, eds. *North American Spies. New Revisionist Essays.* Lawrence, Kansas: University of Kansas Press, 1991.

Johnson, Loch K. *America's Secret Power: The CIA in a Democratic Society.* New York: Oxford University Press, 1989.

———. *A Season of Inquiry: The Senate Intelligence Investigation.* Lexington: University of Kentucky Press, 1985.

Keegan, John. *Intelligence in War: Knowledge of the Enemy from Napoleon to Al-Qaeda.* New York: Alfred A. Knopf, 2003.

Kessler, Ronald. *Inside the CIA: Revealing the Secrets of the World's Most Powerful Spy Agency.* New York: Pocket Books, 1992.

Klehr, Harvey, and Ronald Radosh. *The Amerasia Spy Case: Prelude to McCarthyism.* Chapel Hill: University of North Carolina Press, 1996.

Knaus, John Kenneth. *Orphans of the Cold War: America and the Tibetan Struggle for Survival.* New York: Public Affairs Press, 1999.

Knott, Stephen F. *Secret and Sanctioned: Covert Operations and the American President.* New York: Oxford University Press, 1996.

Kornbluh, Peter, ed. *Bay of Pigs Declassified: The Secret CIA Report on the Invasion of Cuba.* New York: The New Press, 1998.

RECOMMENDED READING

Lamphere, Robert J. and Tom Shachtman. *The FBI–KGB War: A Special Agent's Story*. Macon, Georgia: Mercer University Press, 1986, 1995.

Laqueur, Walter. *A World of Secrets: The Uses and Limits of Intelligence*. New York: Basic Books, 1984.

Leary, William M. *Perilous Missions: Civil Air Transport and CIA Covert Operations in Asia*. Tuscaloosa: University of Alabama Press, 1984.

Lohbeck, Kurt and Dan Rather. *Holy War, Unholy Victory: Eyewitness to the CIA's Secret War in Afghanistan*. New York: Regnery Publishing, 1993.

Lowenthal, Mark M. *Intelligence: From Secrets to Policy*. Washington, D.C.: CQ Press, 1999.

Marks, John D. *The Search for the "Manchurian Candidate": The CIA and Mind Control*. New York: Times Books, 1979.

Martin, David C. *Wilderness of Mirrors*. New York: Harper, 1980.

Maurer, Alfred C. *Intelligence: Policy and Process*. Boulder, Colo.: Westview Press, 1985.

McIntosh, Elizabeth P. *Sisterhood of Spies: The Women of the OSS*. Annapolis: Naval Institute Press, 1998.

Mendez, Antonio J., with Malcolm McConnell. *The Master of Disguise: My Secret Life in the CIA*. New York: William Morrow and Company, 1999.

Miller, Nathan. *Spying for America: The Hidden History of U.S. Intelligence*. New York: Paragon House, 1989.

Moyar, Mark and Harry G. Summers. *Phoenix and the Birds of Prey: The CIA's Secret Campaign to Destroy the Viet Cong*. Annapolis: Naval Institute Press, 1997.

Moynihan, Daniel Patrick. *Secrecy: The American Experience*. New Haven: Yale University Press, 1998.

Murphy, David E., Sergei A. Kondrashev, and George Bailey. *Battleground Berlin: CIA vs. KGB in the Cold War*. New Haven, Yale University Press, 1997.

Nash, Jay Robert. *Spies: A Narrative Encyclopedia of Dirty Deeds and Double-Dealing from Biblical Times to Today.* New York: M. Evans & Co., 1997.

Oseth, John M. *Regulating U.S. Intelligence Operations: A Study of Definition of the National Interest.* Lexington, Ky.: University Press of Kentucky, 1985.

O'Toole, G. J. A. *Honorable Treachery: A History of U.S. Intelligence, Espionage, and Covert Action from the American Revolution to the CIA.* New York: Atlantic Monthly Press, 1991.

Perry, Mark. *Eclipse: The Last Days of the CIA.* New York: William Morrow & Co., 1992.

Persico, Joseph E. *Roosevelt's Secret War: FDR and World War II Espionage.* New York: Random House, 2001.

———. *Piercing The Reich: The Penetration of Nazi Germany by American Agents During World War II.* New York: The Viking Press, 1979.

Prados, John. *Presidents' Secret Wars: CIA and Pentagon Covert Operations Since World War II.* New York: William Morrow & Co., 1986.

Ranelagh, John. *The Agency: The Rise and Decline of the CIA from Wild Bill Donovan to William Casey.* New York: Simon & Schuster, 1986.

Ransom, Harry Howe. *The Intelligence Establishment.* Cambridge: Harvard University Press, 1970.

Richelson, Jeffrey T. *American Espionage and the Soviet Target.* New York: William Morrow & Co., 1987.

———. *A Century of Spies: Intelligence in the Twentieth Century.* New York: Oxford University Press, 1995.

———. *The U.S. Intelligence Community.* Cambridge, Massachusetts: Ballinger, 1985,1987, 1995.

RECOMMENDED READING

Richelson, Jeffrey, and Desmond Ball. *The Ties That Bind: Intelligence Cooperation Between the U.K./U.S.A. Countries.* Boston: Allen & Unwin, 1985.

Rotter, Andrew J., ed. *Light at the End of the Tunnel: A Vietnam War Anthology.* Wilmington, Delaware: SR Books, 1999.

Rudgers, David. *Creating the Secret State.* Lawrence, Kansas: University of Kansas Press, 2000.

Ryan, Paul B. *The Iran Rescue Mission: Why It Failed.* Annapolis: Naval Institute Press, 1985.

Schecter, Jerrod L., and Peter S. Deriabin. *The Spy Who Saved the World: How a Soviet Colonel Changed the Course of the Cold War.* New York: Charles Scribner's Sons, 1992.

Shulsky, Abram N. *Silent Warfare: Understanding the World of Intelligence.* New York: Brassey's, 1991; Second ed. rev. by Gary J. Schmitt. New York: Brassey's, 1993.

Sides, Hampton. *Ghost Soldiers: The Forgotten Epic Story of World War II's Most Dramatic Mission.* New York: Doubleday, 2001.

Steele, Robert David. *On Intelligence: Spies and Secrecy in an Open World.* Fairfax, Virginia: AFCEA International Press, 2000.

Troy, Thomas F. *Wild Bill and Intrepid.* New Haven: Yale University Press, 1996.

Tuchman, Barbara W. *The Zimmerman Telegram.* New York: Macmillan, 1958.

Turner, Stansfield. *Secrecy and Democracy: The CIA in Transition.* Boston: Houghton Mifflin, 1985.

Vandenbroucke, Lucien S. *Perilous Options: Special Operations as an Instrument of U.S. Foreign Policy.* New York: Oxford University Press, 1993.

Volkman, Ernest. *Espionage: The Greatest Spy Operations of the 20th Century.* New York: John Wiley & Sons, 1995.

———. and Blaine Baggett. *Secret Intelligence: The Inside Story of America's Espionage Empire.* New York: Doubleday, 1989.

Weber, Ralph, ed. *Spymasters: Ten CIA Officers in Their Own Words.* Wilmington, Delaware: SR Books, 1998.

Weiner, Tim. *Blank Check: The Pentagon's Black Budget.* New York: Warner Books, 1990.

West, Nigel. *Games of Intelligence: The Classified Conflict of International Espionage.* London: Weidenfeld and Nicolson, 1989.

Wise, David. *Molehunt: The Secret Search for Traitors That Shattered the CIA.* New York: Random House, 1992.

Woodward, Bob. *Veil: The Secret Wars of the CIA 1981–1987.* New York: Simon & Schuster, 1987.

Hostile Intelligence Services/Operations

Andrew, Christopher, and Oleg Gordievsky. *KGB: The Inside Story.* HarperCollins, 1990.

Andrew, Christopher, and Vasili Mitrokhin. *The Sword and the Shield: The Mitrokhin Archive and the Secret History of the KGB.* New York: Basic Books, 1999.

Barron, John. *The KGB Today: The Hidden Hand.* New York: Reader's Digest Press, 1983.

Costa, Alexandra. *Stepping Down From the Star: A Soviet Defector's Story.* New York: G.P. Putnam's Sons, 1986.

Dzhirkvelov, Ilya. *Secret Servant: My Life with the KGB & the Soviet Elite.* New York: Touchstone, 1987.

Faligot, Roger, and Remi Kauffer. *The Chinese Secret Service: Kang Sheng and the Shadow Government in Red China.* New York: William Morrow & Co., 1987.

Friedman, Thomas L. *From Beirut to Jerusalem.* New York: Farrar, Straus, Giroux, 1989; Second revised ed., 1995.

Golitsyn, Anatoliy. *New Lies for Old: The Communist Strategy for Deception and Disinformation.* New York: Dodd, Mead & Co., 1984.

RECOMMENDED READING

Hohe, Heinz, and Hermann Zolling. *The General Was a Spy: The Truth About General Gehlen, 20th Century Superspy, Who Served Hitler, the CIA, and West Germany.* New York: Coward, McCann & Geoghean, 1972.

Kalugin, Oleg. *The First Directorate: My 32 Years in Intelligence and Espionage Against the West.* New York: St. Martin's Press, 1994.

Kessler, Ronald. *Moscow Station: How the KGB Penetrated the Moscow Station.* New York: Charles Scribner's Sons, 1989.

———. *The Spy in the Russian Club.* New York: Charles Scribner's Sons, 1990.

Koehler, John O. *STASI: The Untold Story of the East German Secret Police.* Boulder, Colo.: Westview Press, 1999.

Kuzichkin, Vladimir. *Inside the KGB: My Life in Soviet Espionage.* New York: Pantheon Books, 1990.

Levchencko, Stanislav. *On the Wrong Side: My Life in the KGB.* McLean, Virginia: Pergamon-Brassey's, 1988.

Melman, Yossi, and Dan Raviv. *Every Spy a Prince: The Complete History of Israel's Intelligence Community.* Boston: Houghton Mifflin, 1990.

Newton, Verne W. *The Cambridge Spies: The Untold Story of Maclean, Philby, and Burgess in America.* New York: Madison Books, 1991.

Ostrovsky, Victor, and Claire Hoy. *By Way of Deception: The Making and Unmaking of a Mossad Officer.* New York: St. Martin's Press, 1990.

Richelson, Jeffrey T. *Foreign Intelligence Organizations.* Cambridge: Ballinger Publications, 1988.

Thomas, Gordon. *Gideon's Spies.* New York: St. Martin's Press, 1999.

Toohey, Brian, and William Pinwill. *Oyster: The Story of the Australian Secret Intelligence Service.* Melbourne: William Heinemann, 1989.

Trento, Joseph J. *The Secret History of the CIA*. Roseville, California: Prima Publishing Forum, 2001.

Weinstein, Allen, and Alexander Vassiliev. *The Haunted Wood: Soviet Espionage in America—the Stalin Era*. New York: Random House, 1999.

Renegades, Traitors, and Defectors

Agee, Philip. *Inside the Company: CIA Diary*. New York: Stonehill Publishing, 1975.

———. *On the Run*. Secaucus, N.J.: Lyle Stuart, 1987.

Barron, John. *Breaking the Ring: The Bizarre Case of the Walker Family Spy Ring*. New York: Houghton Mifflin, 1987.

Blitzer, Wolf. *Territory of Lies: The Exclusive Story of Jonathan Jay Pollard: The American Who Spied on His Country for Israel and How He Was Betrayed*. New York: Harper and Row, 1989.

Earley, Pete. *Family of Spies: Inside the Walker Spy Ring*. New York: Bantam Books, 1988.

———. *Confessions of a Spy: The Real Story of Aldrich Ames*. New York: G.P. Putnam's Sons, 1997.

Havill, Adrian. *The Spy Who Stayed Out in the Cold: The Secret Life of FBI Double Agent Robert Hanssen*. New York: St. Martin's Press, 2001.

Kessler, Ronald. *Escape from the CIA: How the CIA Won and Lost the Most Important KGB Spy Ever to Defect to the U.S.* New York: Pocket Books, 1991.

Lindsey, Robert. *The Falcon and the Snowman*. New York: Simon & Schuster, 1979.

Maas, Peter. *Manhunt: The Incredible Pursuit of a CIA Agent Turned Terrorist*. London: Harrap, 1986.

———. *Killer Spy: The Inside Story of the FBI's Pursuit and Capture of Aldrich Ames, America's Deadliest Spy*. New York: Warner Books, 1995.

Marchetti, Victor, and John D. Marks. *The CIA and the Cult of Intelligence.* London: Jonathan Cape, 1974.

Shannon, Elaine, and Ann Blackman. *They Spy Next Door: The Extraordinary Secret Life of Robert Philip Hanssen, the Most Damaging FBI Agent in U.S. History.* Boston: Little, Brown and Company, 2002.

Snepp, Frank. *Decent Interval: An Insider's Account of Saigon's Indecent End.* New York: Random House, 1977.

———. *Irreparable Harm: A Firsthand Account of How One Agent Took on the CIA in an Epic Battle over Free Speech.* New York: Random House, 1999.

Stockwell, John. *In Search of Enemies: A CIA Story.* New York: W.W. Norton & Co., 1978.

Straight, Michael. *After Long Silence.* New York: W.W. Norton & Co., 1983.

Wise, David. *The Bureau and the Mole: The Unmasking of Robert Philip Hanssen, the Most Dangerous Double Agent in FBI History.* New York: Atlantic Monthly Press, 2002.

———. *Cassidy's Run: The Secret Spy War over Nerve Gas.* New York: Random House, 2000.

———. *Nightmover: How Aldrich Ames Sold the CIA to the KGB for $4.6 Million.* New York: HarperCollins, 1995.

———. *The Spy Who Got Away: The Inside Story of Edward Lee Howard, the CIA Agent Who Betrayed His Country's Secrets and Escaped to Moscow.* New York: Random House, 1988.

Technical Intelligence Collection

Alvarez, David. *Secret Messages: Codebreaking and American Diplomacy, 1930–1945.* Lawrence: University of Kansas Press, 2000.

Bamford, James. *The Puzzle Palace: A Report on America's Most Secret Agency.* Boston: Houghton Mifflin, 1982.

———. *Body of Secrets: Anatomy of the Ultra-Secret National Security Agency.* New York: Doubleday, 2001.

Brugioni, Dino A. *Eyeball to Eyeball: The Cuban Missile Crisis.* New York: Random House, 1993.

Budiansky, Stephen. *Battle of Wits: The Complete Story of Codebreaking in World War II.* New York: The Free Press, 2000.

Burleson, Clyde W. *The Jennifer Project.* Englewood Cliffs, N.J.: Prentice Hall, 1977, 1997.

Burrows, William. *Deep Black: Space Espionage and National Security.* New York: Random House, 1986.

Day, Dwayne A., ed., with John M. Logsdon and Brian Latell. *Eye in the Sky: The Story of the Corona Spy Satellites.* Washington, D.C.: Smithsonian Institution Press, 1998.

Ennes, James M. Jr. *Assault on the Liberty: The True Story of the Israeli Attack on an American Intelligence Ship.* New York: Random House, 1979.

Haynes, John Earl, and Harvey Klehr. *Venona: Decoding Soviet Espionage in America.* Hartford: Yale University Press, 1999.

Kahn, David. *The Codebreakers: The Story of Secret Writing.* New York: Macmillan, 1967.

Lewin, Ronald. *Ultra Goes to War.* New York, McGraw-Hill Book Company, 1978.

Marks, Leo. *Between Silk and Cyanide. A Codemaker's War 1941–45.* New York: The Free Press, 1998.

Singh, Simon. *The Code Book: The Evolution of Secrecy from Mary, Queen of Scots, to Quantum Cryptography.* New York: Doubleday, 1999.

Sontag, Sherry, and Christopher Drew. *Blind Man's Bluff: the Untold Story of American Submarine Espionage.* New York: Public Affairs, 1998.

Van Der Rhoer, Edward. *Deadly Magic.* New York: Charles Scribner's Sons, 1978.

Weber, Ralph. *United States Diplomatic Codes and Ciphers 1775–1938.* Chicago: Precedent Publishing, 1979.

West, Nigel. *Venona: The Greatest Secret of the Cold War.* London: HarperCollins, 1999.

Yardley, Herbert O. *The American Black Chamber.* Indianapolis: Bobbs-Merrill, 1931.

Intelligence and Foreign Policy

Bagby, Wesley M. *America's International Relations Since World War I.* New York: Oxford University Press, 2001.

Berkowitz, Bruce D., and Allen E. Goodman. *Best Truth: Intelligence in the Information Age.* New Haven: Yale University Press, 2000.

Brugioni, Dino A. *Eyeball to Eyeball: The Cuban Missile Crisis.* New York: Random House, 1993.

Clutterbuck, Richard L. *International Crisis and Conflict.* New York: St. Martin's Press, 1993.

De Groot, Gerard J. *The First World War.* New York: Palgrave, 2001.

Dragnich, Alex N. *Serbs and Croats: The Struggle in Yugoslavia.* New York: Harcourt Brace Jovanovich, 1992.

Freedman, Lawrence. *Kennedy's Wars—Berlin, Cuba, Laos, and Vietnam.* New York: Oxford University Press, 2001.

Gillon, Steven M., and Cathy D. Matson. *The American Experiment: A History of the United States.* New York: Houghton Mifflin, 2001.

Holt, Pat M. *Secret Intelligence and Public Policy,* Washington, D.C.: CQ Press, 1995.

Isaacson, Walter, and Evan Thomas. *The Wise Men: Six Friends and the World They Made:* Acheson, Bohlen, Harriman, Kennan, Lovett, McCloy. New York: Simon & Schuster, 1986.

Jones, Howard. *Crucible of Power: A History of American Foreign Relations from 1897.* Wilmington, Del.: SR Books, 2001.

Kennedy, David M., Elizabeth Cohen, and Thomas A. Bailey. *The American Pageant.* New York: Houghton Mifflin, 2001.

Knott, Stephen F. *Secret and Sanctioned: Covert Operations and the American President.* New York: Oxford University Press, 1996.

Madaras, Larry, and James M. SoRelle. *Taking Sides: Clashing Views on Controversial Issues in American History, Vol. II: Reconstruction to the Present.* Ninth Ed. Guilford, Connecticut: McGraw-Hill/Dushkin, 2001.

Malcolm, Noel. *Bosnia: A Short History.* New York: New York University Press, 1994.

Miller, Nathan. *Spying for America: The Hidden History of U.S. Intelligence.* New York: Paragon House, 1989.

Neustadt, Richard. *Presidential Power and the Modern Presidents.* New York: Free Press, 1990.

Owen, David. *Balkan Odyssey.* New York: Harcourt Brace & Company, 1995.

Persico, Joseph E. *Roosevelt's Secret War: FDR and World War II Espionage.* New York: Random House, 2001.

Prados, John. *Presidents' Secret Wars: CIA and Pentagon Covert Operations Since World War II.* New York: William Morrow & Co., 1992.

Rieff, David. *Slaughterhouse: Bosnia and the Failure of the West.* New York: Simon & Schuster, 1995.

Robinson, P. Stuart. *The Politics of International Crisis Escalation: Decision-Making Under Pressure.* St. Martin's Press, 1996.

Schecter, Jerrod L. and Peter S. Deriabin. *The Spy Who Saved the World: How a Soviet Colonel Change the Course of the Cold War.* New York: Charles Scribner's Sons, 1992.

Sheehan, Neil. *A Bright Shining Lie: John Paul Vann and America in Vietnam.* New York: Random House, 1988.

Singer, P. W. *Corporate Warriors: The Rise of the Privatized Military Industry.* Ithaca, N.Y.: Cornell University Press, 2003.

Snepp, Frank. *Decent Interval: An Insider's Account of Saigon's Indecent End.* New York: Random House, 1977.

Strong, Robert A. *Decisions and Dilemmas: Case Studies in Presidential Foreign Policy Making.* New Jersey: Prentice-Hall, 1992.

Thomas, Gordon, and Max Morgan-Witts. *Voyage of the Damned.* Second ed. Osceola, Wisconsin: Motorbooks International, 1994.

Wood, E. Thomas, and Stanislaw M. Jankowski. *Karski: How One Man Tried to Stop the Holocaust.* New York: John Wiley & Sons, Inc., 1994.

Terrorism

Abu-Sharif, Bassam, and Uzi Mahnaimi. *Tried by Fire: The Searing True Story of Two Men at the Heart of the Struggle Between the Arabs and the Jews.* London: Little, Brown, 1995.

Anonymous. *Imperial Hubris: Why the West Is Losing the War on Terrorism.* Washington, D.C.: Brassey's, 2004.

Ansari, Masud. *International Terrorism: Its Causes and How to Control It.* Washington, D.C.: Mas Press, 1988.

Baer, Robert. *See No Evil: The True Story of a Ground Soldier in the CIA's War on Terrorism.* New York: Crown Publishing Group, 2002.

Ballance, Edgar O. *Terrorism in the 1980s.* New York: Sterling Publishing, 1988.

Becker, Jillian. *Hitler's Children: The Story of the Baader-Meinhof Terrorist Gang.* Philadelphia: Lippincott, 1977.

Clarridge, Duane. *A Spy for All Seasons: My Life in the CIA.* New York: Charles Scribner's Sons, 1997.

Cleveland, William L. *A History of the Modern Middle East.* 2nd ed. Boulder, Colo.: Westview Press, 2000.

Combs, Cindy C. *Terrorism In The Twenty-first Century.* Upper Saddle River, N.J.: Prentice Hall, 1997.

Dobson, Christopher, and Ronald Payne. *Terrorists: Their Weapons, Leaders, and Tactics.* New York: Facts on File, 1982.

————. *Counterattack: The West's Battle Against the Terrorists.* New York: Facts on File, 1982.

Follain, John. *The Jackal: The Complete Story of the Legendary Terrorist, Carlos the Jackal.* New York: Arcade Publishing, 1998.

Gowers, Andrew, and Tony Walker. *Behind The Myth: Yasser Arafat and the Palestinian Revolution.* New York: Olive Branch Press, 1992.

Hoffman, Bruce. *Inside Terrorism.* New York: Columbia University Press, 1999.

Hoy, Claire, and Victor Ostrovsky. *By Way Of Deception: A Devastating Insider's Portrait Of The Mossad.* New York: St. Martin's Press, 1990.

Hyams, Edward. *Terrorists and Terrorism.* New York: St. Martin's Press, 1974.

James, Daniel, ed. *The Complete Bolivian Diaries of Ché Guevara: And Other Captured Documents.* New York: Cooper Square Press, 2000.

Juergensmeyer, Mark. *Terror in the Mind of God: the Global Rise of Religious Violence.* Berkeley: University of California Press, 2001.

Litwak, Robert. *Rogue States and U.S. Foreign Policy: Containment after the Cold War.* Baltimore: Johns Hopkins University Press, 2000.

Marenches, Alexandre de, and David A. Andelman. *The Fourth World War: Diplomacy and Espionage in the Age of Terrorism.* New York: Morrow, 1992.

Meade, Robert C. Jr. *Red Brigades: The Story of Italian Terrorism.* New York: St. Martin's Press, 1990.

Melman, Yossi. *The Master Terrorist: The True Story Behind Abu Nidal.* New York: Adama Books, 1986.

Miller, Judith, Stephen Engelberg, and William Broad. *Germs: Biological Weapons and America's Secret War.* New York: Simon & Schuster, 2001.

Norval, Morgan. *Triumph of Disorder: Islamic Fundamentalism, the New Face of War.* New York: Sligo Press, 1999.

Phillips, David. *Skyjack: The Story of Air Piracy.* London: Harrap, 1973.

Pillar, Paul. *Terrorism and U.S. Foreign Policy.* Washington, D.C.: Brookings Institution Press, 2001.

Reeve, Simon. *The New Jackals: Ramzi Yousef, Osama Bin Laden, and the Future of Terrorism.* Boston: Northeastern University Press, 1999.

Reich, Walter, ed. *Origins of Terror: Psychology, Ideology, Theologies, States of Mind.* Washington, D.C.: Woodrow Wilson Center Press, 1998.

Tante, Raymond. *Rogue Regimes: Terrorism and Proliferation.* Palgrave Press, 1999.

Testrake, John. *Triumph Over Terror on Flight 847: A Story of Raw Courage that Shocked America and Changed Its Attitude on Terrorism.* Old Tappan, N.J.: Fleming H. Revell Company, 1987.

Turner, Stansfield. *Terrorism and Democracy.* Boston: Houghton Mifflin, 1991.